AMERICAN LₐFRANCE 700 & 800 SERIES 1953 THROUGH 1958

PHOTO ARCHIVE

Iconografix Inc. exists to preserve history through the publication of notable photographic archives and the list of titles under the Iconografix imprint is constantly growing. Transportation enthusiasts should be on the Iconografix mailing list and are invited to write and ask for a catalog, free of charge.

Authors and editors in the field of transportation history are invited to contact the Editorial Department at Iconografix, Inc., PO Box 446, Hudson, WI 54016. We require a minimum of 120 photographs per subject. We prefer subjects narrow in focus, e.g., a specific model, railroad, or racing venue. Photographs must be of high-quality, suited to large format reproduction.

AMERICAN LaFRANCE 700 & 800 SERIES 1953 THROUGH 1958
PHOTO ARCHIVE

Lawrence E. Phillips

Iconografix
Photo Archive Series

Iconografix
PO Box 446
Hudson, Wisconsin 54016 USA

Iconografix books are offered at a discount when sold in quantity for promotional use. Businesses or organizations seeking details should write to the Marketing Department, Iconografix, at the above address.

Library of Congress Card Number: 98-75267

ISBN 1-882256-91-3

99 00 01 02 03 04 05 5 4 3 2 1

Printed in the United States of America

Cover and book design by Shawn Glidden

PREFACE

The histories of machines and mechanical gadgets are contained in the books, journals, correspondence, and personal papers stored in libraries and archives throughout the world. Written in tens of languages, covering thousands of subjects, the stories are recorded in millions of words.

Words are powerful. Yet, the impact of a single image, a photograph or an illustration, often relates more than dozens of pages of text. Fortunately, many of the libraries and archives that house the words also preserve the images.

In the *Photo Archive Series,* Iconografix reproduces photographs and illustrations selected from public and private collections. The images are chosen to tell a story—to capture the character of their subject. Reproduced as found, they are accompanied by the captions made available by the archive.

The Iconografix *Photo Archive Series* is dedicated to young and old alike, the enthusiast, the collector and anyone who, like us, is fascinated by "things" mechanical.

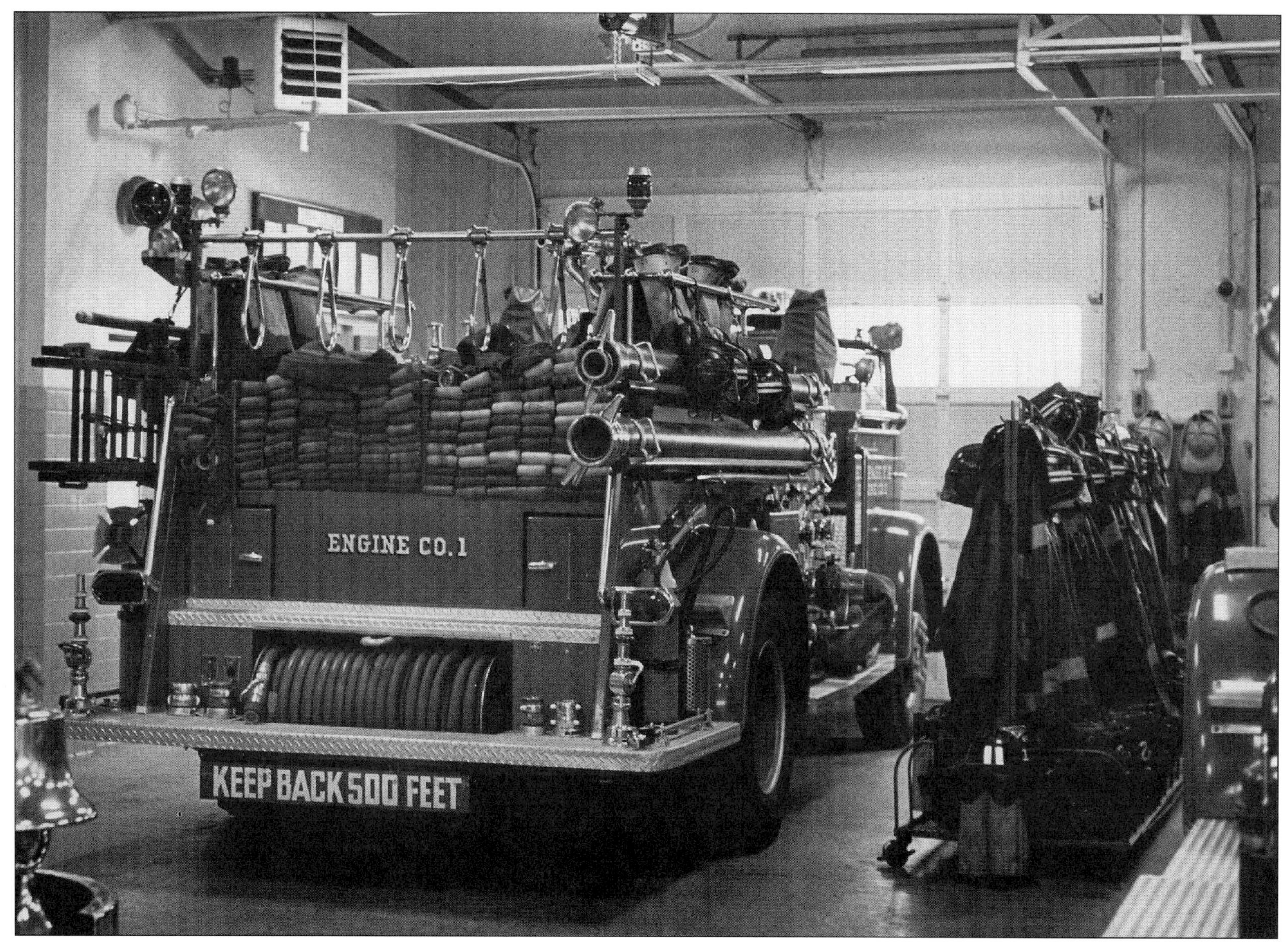

Waiting for the bell: The American LaFrance 700 Series of Fire Apparatus served in firehouses all across the country and proved their worth like no other style of fire apparatus had ever done before – anywhere or anytime.

INTRODUCTION

By 1953, the American LaFrance 700 Series of fire apparatus had proved itself in literally every state of the union, with many major cities becoming very satisfied American LaFrance 700 Series customers.

The 'daring', innovative, cab-ahead-of-the-motor design had caught on and had many other fire apparatus manufacturers looking at and even starting to copy the design.

First introduced in 1945 (with actual fire department delivery beginning in 1947), the American LaFrance 700 Series of fire apparatus continued in production until mid to late 1956.

American LaFrance was purchased by the Sterling Precision Company in 1955. The introduction of the 800 Series to follow the 700 Series was, according to *The Phoenix* (The Publication of American LaFrance History written by American LaFrance Historian John M. Peckham), mandated by them (Sterling).

An interesting note 'uncovered' during the research for this book revealed that once the go-ahead was given for the production of the 800 Series, only the pumpers received the 800 Series designation. Any custom quads, service aerials, TDA aerials and rescue trucks to come out of Elmira, NY during mid to late 1956 through mid 1958 still received the 700 Series designation.

So, while 700 Series, 800 Series and 900 Series pumpers were produced and recorded, all other American LaFrance custom fire apparatus jumped from the 700 Series right to the 900 Series...even though some of 'late' rigs had the 700 Series body style with 900 Series accessories (headlights, turn signals, mirrors, etc.).

Peckham wrote, in the March, 1998 issue of *The Phoenix*:

> The following article, *HISTORY OF THE 900 SERIES DEVEL-OPMENT OF AMERICAN LA FRANCE APPARATUS*, which has never been published (and does not have an author noted on the manuscript), was apparently written by Hubert Walker, a Vice President of American LaFrance for many years.

Peckham continued with: It was interesting to note that Walker was one of those adamantly opposed to making the 700 Series a full-width cab apparatus. [Editor's note - while the 800 Series, 900 Series and 1000 Series still weren't a full-width cab type design, the Century Series would be in the rear portion; eliminating the outside front fenders for additional interior jump-seat space]. The original designer of the 700 Series, John Grybos, however, had put forth the full-width cab design in his original ideas for the 700 Series.

In this (*Phoenix*) article, Walker now praises the widening of the cab for the 900 Series. So much for his hindsight!

While this piece is not dated, it was obviously done well into the production era of the 900/1000 Series (1959 - 1972) and probably written in the 1960s.

It should be noted that the cheapening of the 800 Series was mandated by the Sterling Precision Company which had bought American LaFrance in 1955.

Here, then, appearing for the first time in *any* book, is the first half of that article, as published by Peckham in *The Phoenix*. The second half of *The Phoenix* article, dealing with the American LaFrance 900 Series, will be printed, in its entirety, in my next book, *AMERICAN LA FRANCE 900 SERIES PHOTO ARCHIVE*, to be published by Iconografix in the fall of 1999. Walker's article began:

> The announcement of the new 900 Series design of fire apparatus in April, 1958, marked a reversal in design and manufacturing trend that had persisted for the preceding three years (mid-1956 through mid-1958). To understand the design changes made to produce the 900 Series, a review of the 800 Series shortcomings will be important.

> When the 800 Series was announced and first exhibited during the International Association of Fire Chiefs (IAFC) Conference at Miami, Florida in November of 1956, it received a very cool and adverse reception.

The 800 Series was developed by engineering and factory personnel as a joint cost reduction effort. And the final product looked it!

The product was not only cheap in appearance, but the workmanship was of poor quality. As an example, more than one caught fire before it could be delivered, due to defective wiring.

Some of the complaints were as follows: (1) 'Broken back' appearance. The cab sides (open seat) and body sides were several inches higher than the engine hood; (2) The water tank was mounted so high in the body it was possible to see across the vehicle above the chassis frame, at the rear wheel wells; (3) Compartment doors were flat stock, hard to latch, leaked water as they were not weather proof, and had a habit of coming open to spill the contents on the highway when the vehicle was in motion; (4) Cab too narrow. There was insufficient seating space for a fireman wearing protective clothing; (5) Driver's seat adjustment of inadequate range and difficult to operate; (6) Forward visibility for driver obstructed. Top of windshield was too low, cutting off vision for taller men; (7) Glove compartment of fiberboard. On open seat (open cab) models, water caused the fiberboard to separate and become useless; (8) Center of gravity on pumpers was too high, causing the vehicle to roll badly on turns, making steering control very difficult; (9) Radio compartment required mounting the radio in a vertical position, and it was not weatherproof. There were universal complaints from Fire Departments on this design of compartment; and, (10) Pump discharge gates were difficult to operate. There were many broken handles.

Sales were declining rapidly with the 800 Series and so after only a little over one year of factory production of the 800 Series, it was necessary to start the development and design of the 900 Series. The 900 Series would incorporate those changes that ten years of fire service experience (through both the extremely successful 700 Series and disappointing 800 Series) had shown to be essential to a quality product for fire service use.

The cab-ahead-of-engine design had proved its practical advantages for both fire service performance and manufacturing. Also, the design had been copied and offered by all the other fire apparatus builders. A great tribute to American LaFrance leadership!

And to regain that leadership, almost lost through the 800 Series, the 900 Series once again established American LaFrance leadership that addressed changes to every single one (and more) of the complaints listed previously.

American LaFrance might have been 'down' for a bit, but they certainly weren't 'out'... not by a long shot. They knew the weak points of the 800 Series and hit the ground running with the 900 Series. Then, they continued their leadership with the highly successful 1000 Series and Century Series after that.

As with my first book, I hope you thoroughly enjoy the historical photographs contained herein. The photographic selection choice was once again difficult, and there is still additional, sufficient and important information (and photographs) to warrant future books on the American LaFrance 700 and 800 Series of Fire Apparatus. Look for those books to be published by Iconografix in the years to come.

My next book by Iconografix will deal with the American LaFrance 900 Series of fire apparatus through its entire life span - 1958 through 1970. It will fully illustrate the design changes, features and components that brought American LaFrance 'back' to the forefront of American motorized fire apparatus. It will also include detailed and seldom seen information and sales literature about the 'Aero-Chief', American LaFrance's 'first mobile aerial platform specifically designed and built for the fire service.'

Needless to say, and after reading this, if any of you have your own American LaFrance photographs, photographic collections or information which you feel we may be able to use for this on-going series of books, please do not hesitate to contact me in care of Iconografix at 1-715-381-9755. All material will be carefully evaluated, and full credit will be given for all submissions used.

Larry Phillips
March, 1999

Acknowledgments

This editor continues his heartfelt gratitude to John M. Peckham of East Arlington, Vermont, publisher and editor of *The Phoenix* (the journal of the American LaFrance Phoenix Society). John once again spent countless hours checking and verifying the information contained not only within these pages, but my first book as well. John has also pledged his support for my future ICONOGRAFIX books on American LaFrance Fire Apparatus. His help and willingness to share his own wealth of American LaFrance knowledge and information is greatly appreciated.

The photographs appearing in this book and the technical information accompanying those photographs came from the collections of Bill Craven, American LaFrance Sales Engineer & Illustrator (retired), Fort Wayne, IN; Jack Lerch, Honorary Chief of Department, FDNY, New York City, NY; John Toomey, FDNY and Fire Apparatus Photographer, Howard Beach, NY; Jack DeRosset, Fire Apparatus Specialist and Photographer, Green Brook, NJ; Chuck Madderom, Fire Apparatus Photographer, Redondo Beach, CA; Bob Schierle, 'Commissioner', Westfield, NJ; Jack Gerhart, Fire Motor Operator, Washington, D.C. Fire Department (retired), and Fire Apparatus Historian, Shippensburg, PA; Walt McCall, Fire Apparatus Historian, Photographer and Author, Windsor, Ontario, Canada; James Giovanniello, Firefighter, Squad 270, FDNY and Ex-Captain, Ladder 3, Bethpage Fire Department, Bethpage, NY; Francis DeBobes, Ex-Chief and Commissioner, Bethpage Fire Department, Bethpage, NY; Michael Croan, Ex-Chief and District Secretary, Bethpage Fire Department, Bethpage, NY; Don Feipel, Fire Apparatus Photographer and Commissioner, Mokena Fire Department, Mokena, IL; Mark Berg, Fire Apparatus Historian and past Newsletter Editor, Fire Instructors of Minnesota (FIAM), Bovey, MN; Larry Zotti, Historian, Granite City Fire Department, Granite City, IL; Richard Adelman, Chief of Training (retired), Memphis Fire Department, Memphis, TN, John Schmidt, Fire Apparatus Photographer, Author and Firefighter (retired), Mt. Lebanon Fire Department, Mt. Lebanon, PA and the author.

Bibliography

American Fire Engines Since 1900, Walter M. P. McCall, Crestline Publishing, 1976.

Fire Apparatus Journal, January–February, 1998, pp. 18–19.

First Water, American LaFrance, Inc., 1972.

The American City magazine, May 1965, p. 20.

The Phoenix, The Journal of American LaFrance History, March 1998, pp. 4–5.

Wheels of the Bravest, John A. Calderone and Jack Lerch, Fire Apparatus Journal Publications, 1984.

Yesterday...And Today, American LaFrance, Division of "Automatic" Sprinkler Corporation of America, 1968.

Yesterday...And Today, American LaFrance, Division of ATO, Inc., 1970.

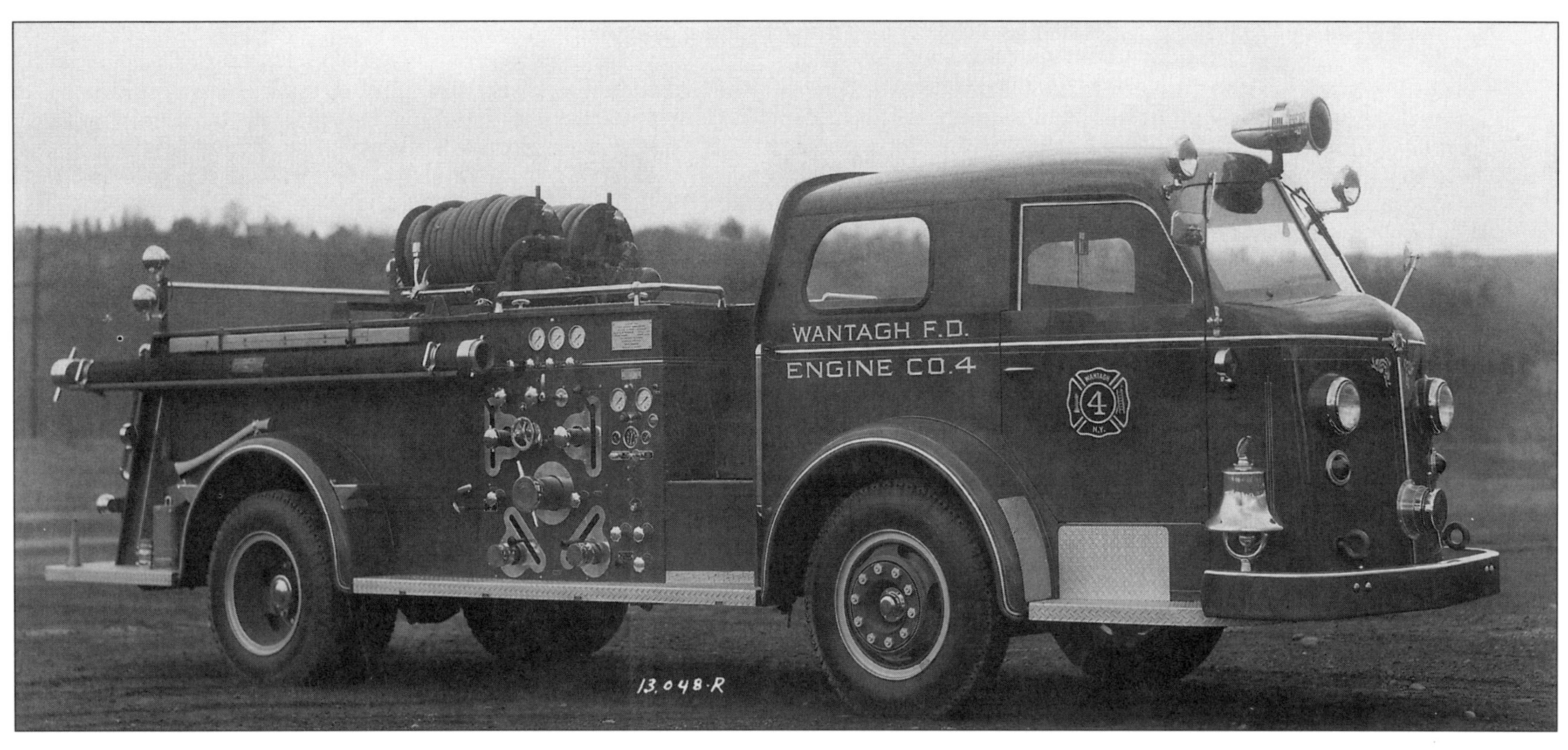

Wantagh, NY - 01/19/53; 01/20/53; Model 775-PJC; Serial #'s L-4702 through L-4704 - Wantagh's 700 Series Pumpers each featured two high-pressure booster reels and a front-mounted suction inlet.

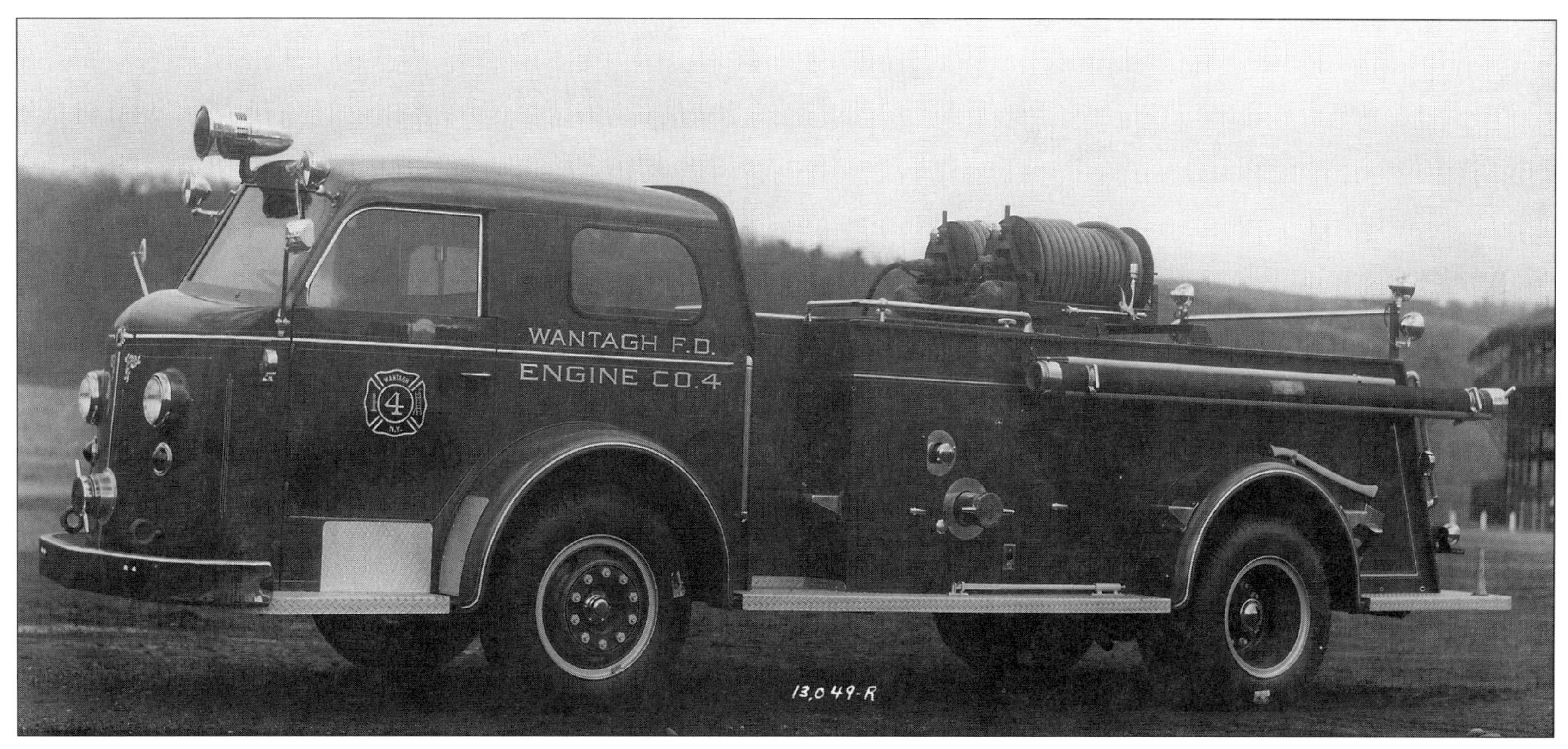

Wantagh, NY - 01/19/53; 01/20/53;Model 775-PJC; Serial #'s L-4702 through L-4704 - There were no ground ladders on Wantagh's 700 Series Pumpers; just a single piece of hard suction hose on each side.

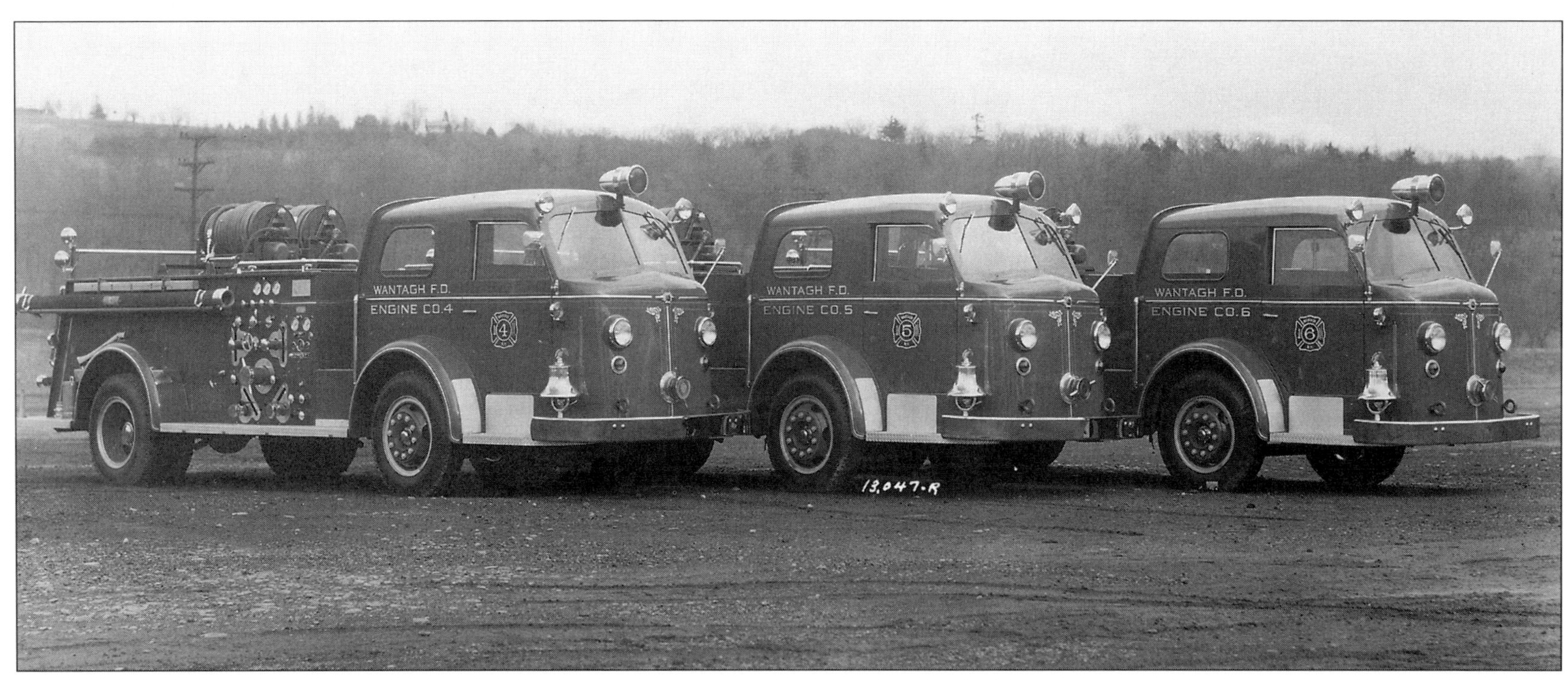

Wantagh, NY - 01/19/53; 01/20/53; Model 775-PJC: Serial #'s L-4702 through L-4704 – Although these rigs are long gone, the respective Engine Companies (4, 5 & 6) remain active today in the Wantagh Fire Department.

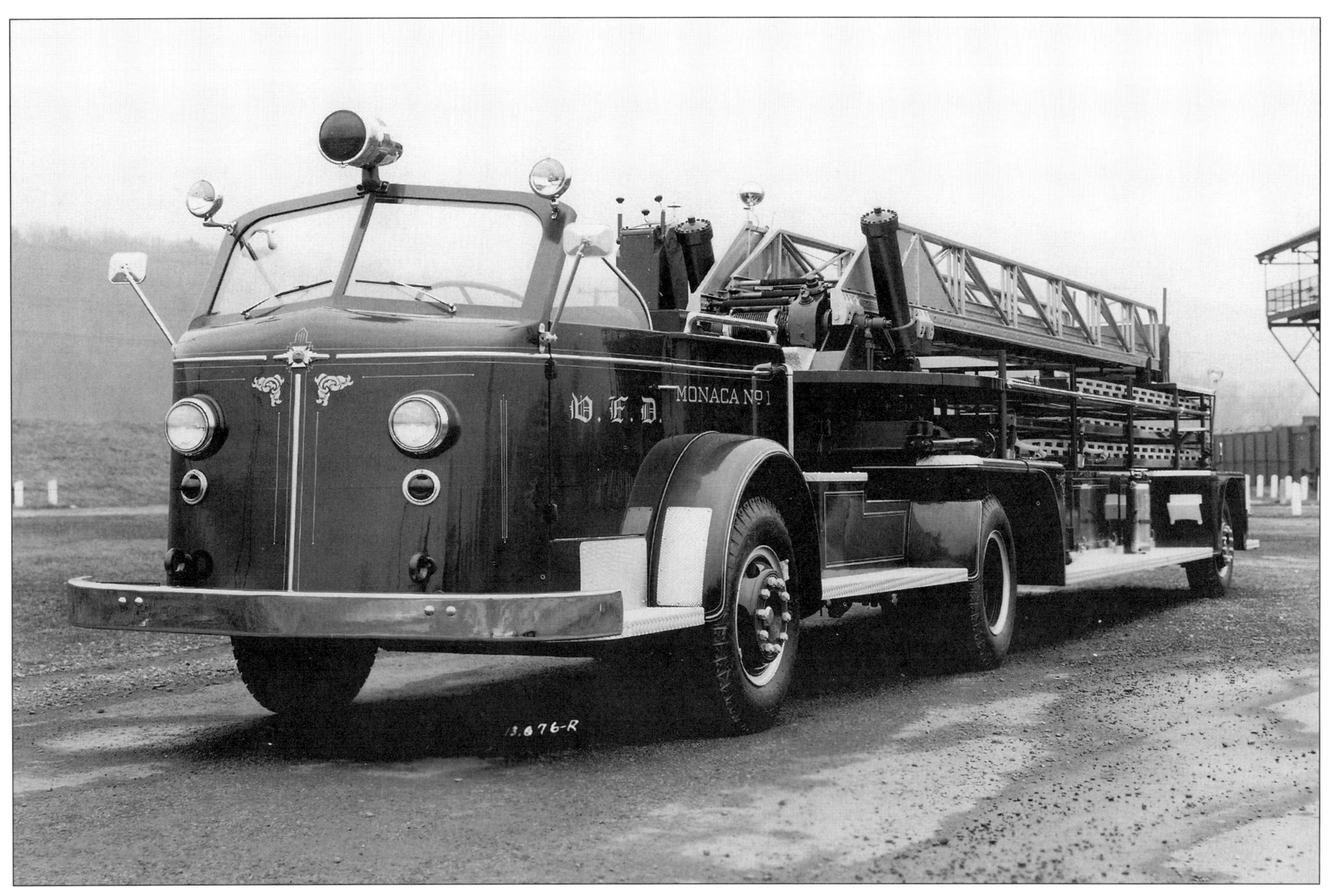

Monaca, PA - 01/20/53; Model 7-85-TJO; Serial # L-4707 - Monaca's Truck Co. #1 carried a full complement of wooden ground ladders beneath the aerial ladder on the trailer.

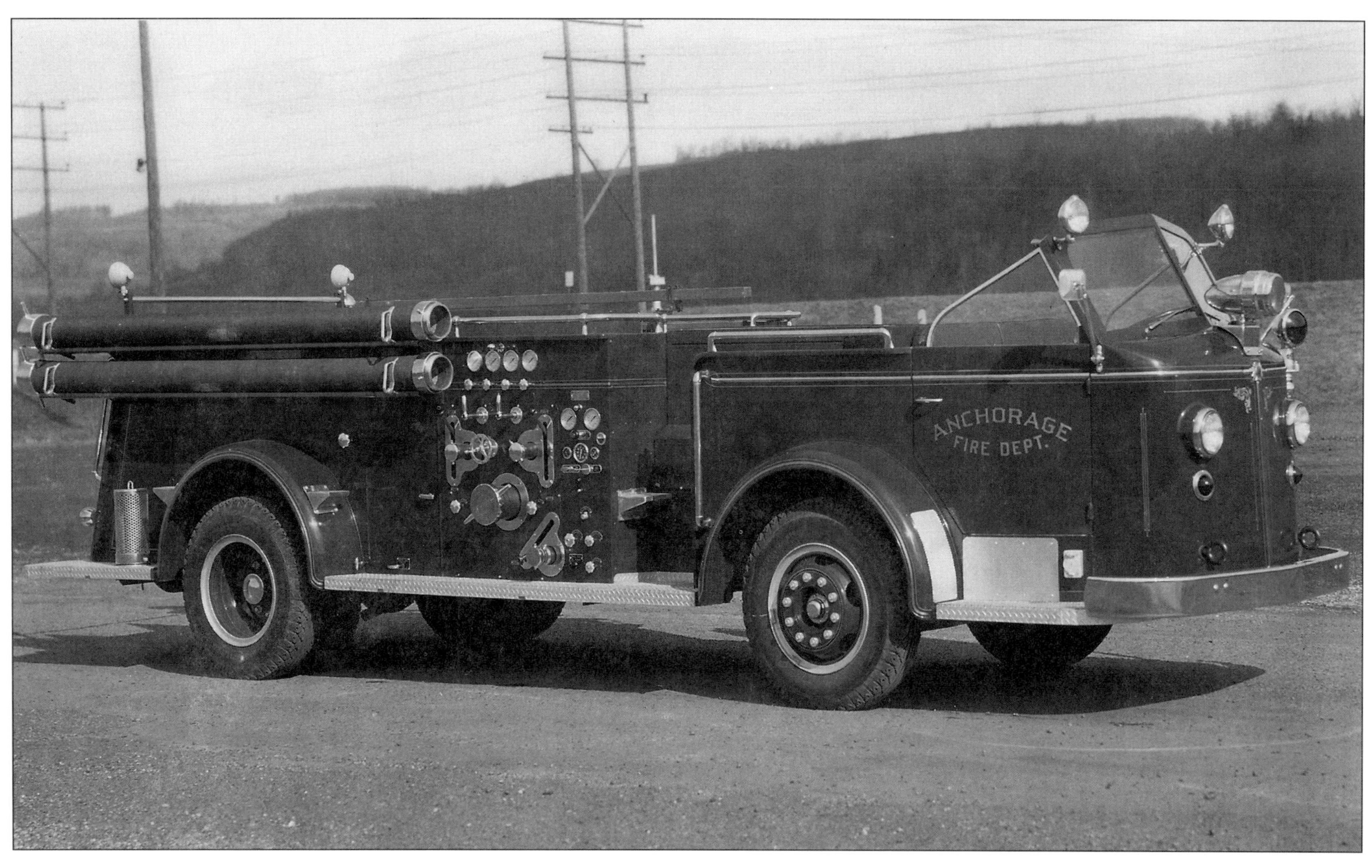

Anchorage, AK - 02/25/53; Model 710-PJO; Serial # L-4731 - Delivered by boat direct to Anchorage, this pumper had a hinged cover over a battery charger inlet beneath the forward section of each front door.

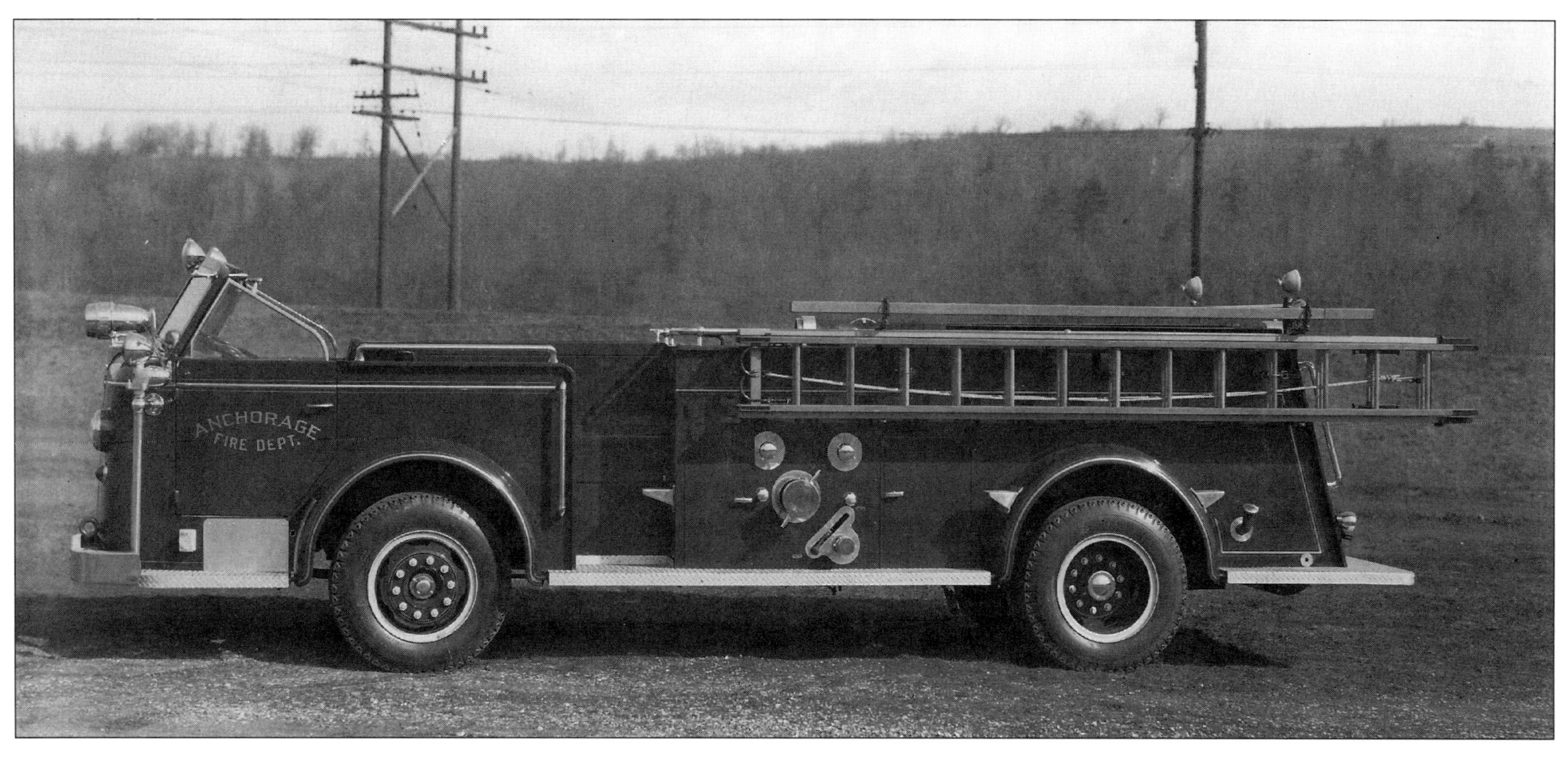

Anchorage, AK - 02/25/53; Model 710-PJO; Serial # L-4731 - The Anchorage pumper also had a Mars Figure 8 Light mounted on a stanchion just ahead of the driver's door.

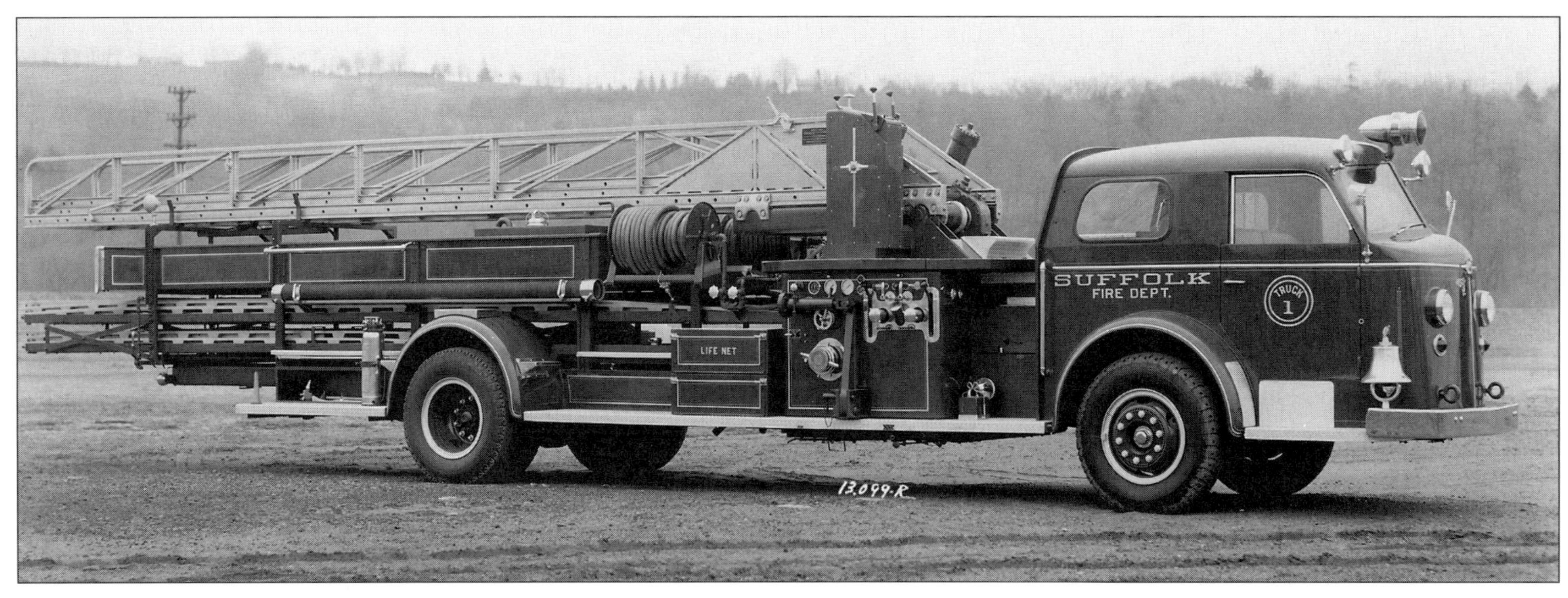

Suffolk, VA - 02/12/53; Model 710-QJC-85; Serial # L-4711 - Equipped with a 1,000 GPM pump, this ladder truck also featured twin booster reels.

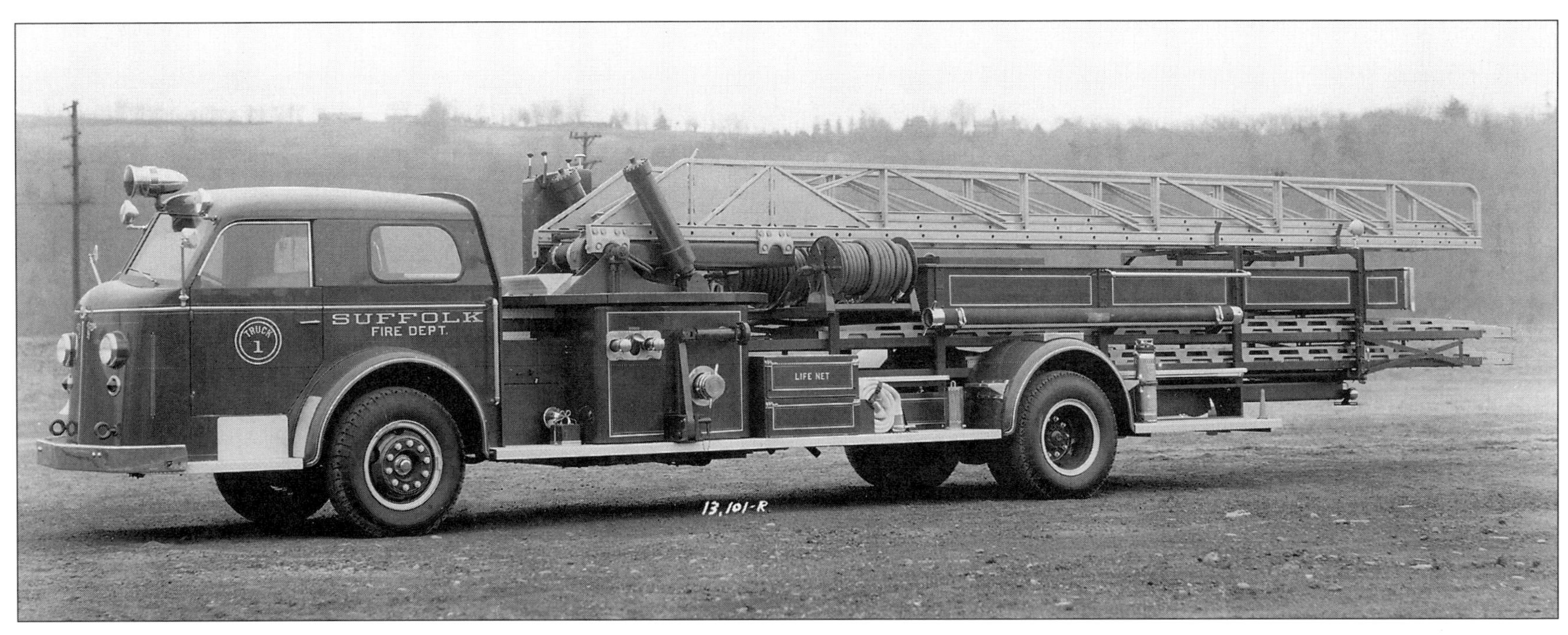

Suffolk, VA - 02/12/53; Model 710-QJC-85; Serial # L-4711 – This ladder truck was also ready for drafting with two pieces of hard suction hose and a drafting strainer located just ahead of the rear fender.

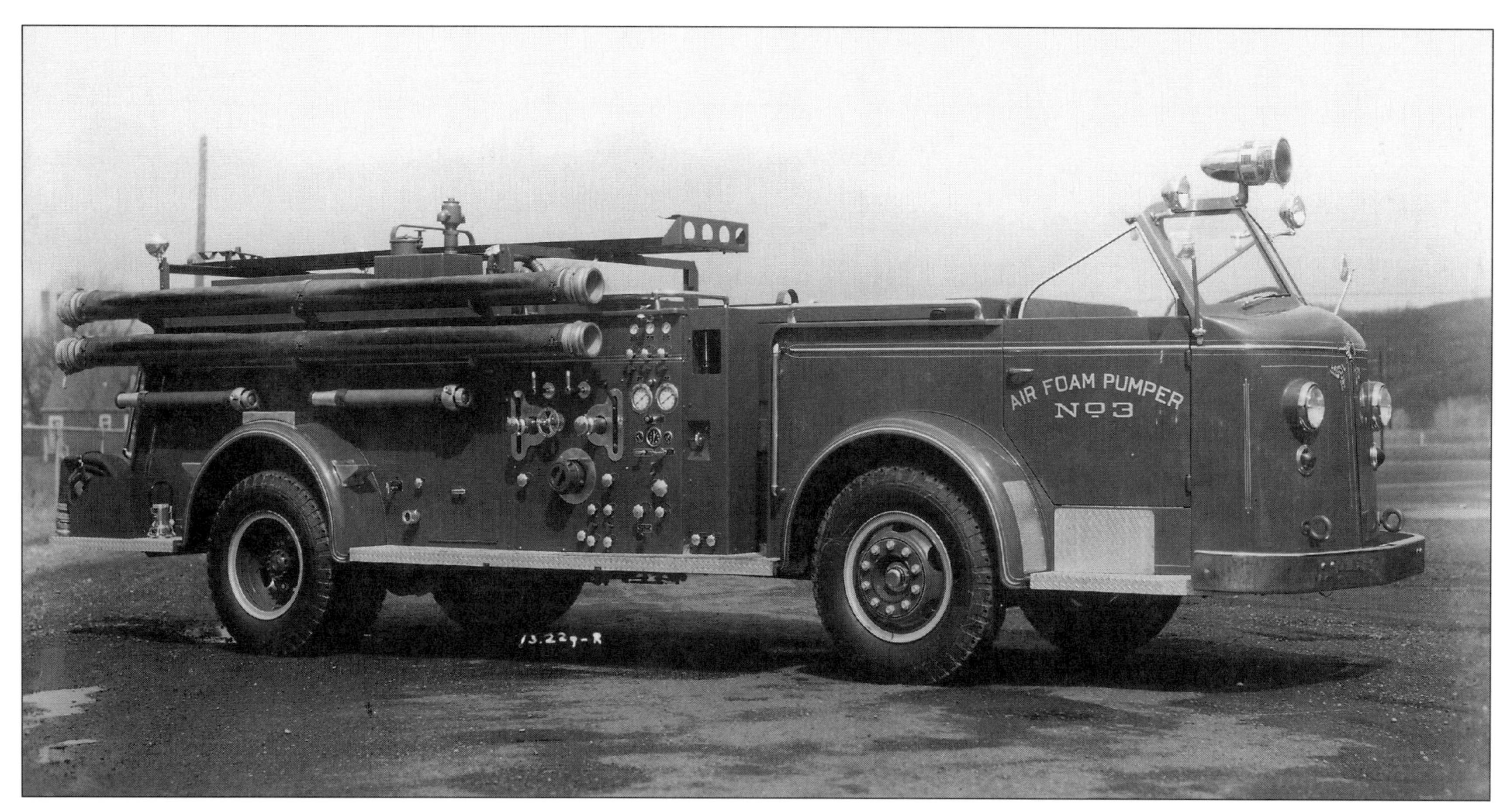

Aruba, Venezuela - Esso Standard Oil Co. - 03/28/53, 03/30/53; Model 775-PJO-FOAM; Serial #'s L-4760, L-4761 - Especially designed to mix and apply both high expansion and protein foam, this pumper was equipped with all the latest foam appliances of the day. The over-the-hosebed rack was used to carry long-handled foam applicating nozzles.

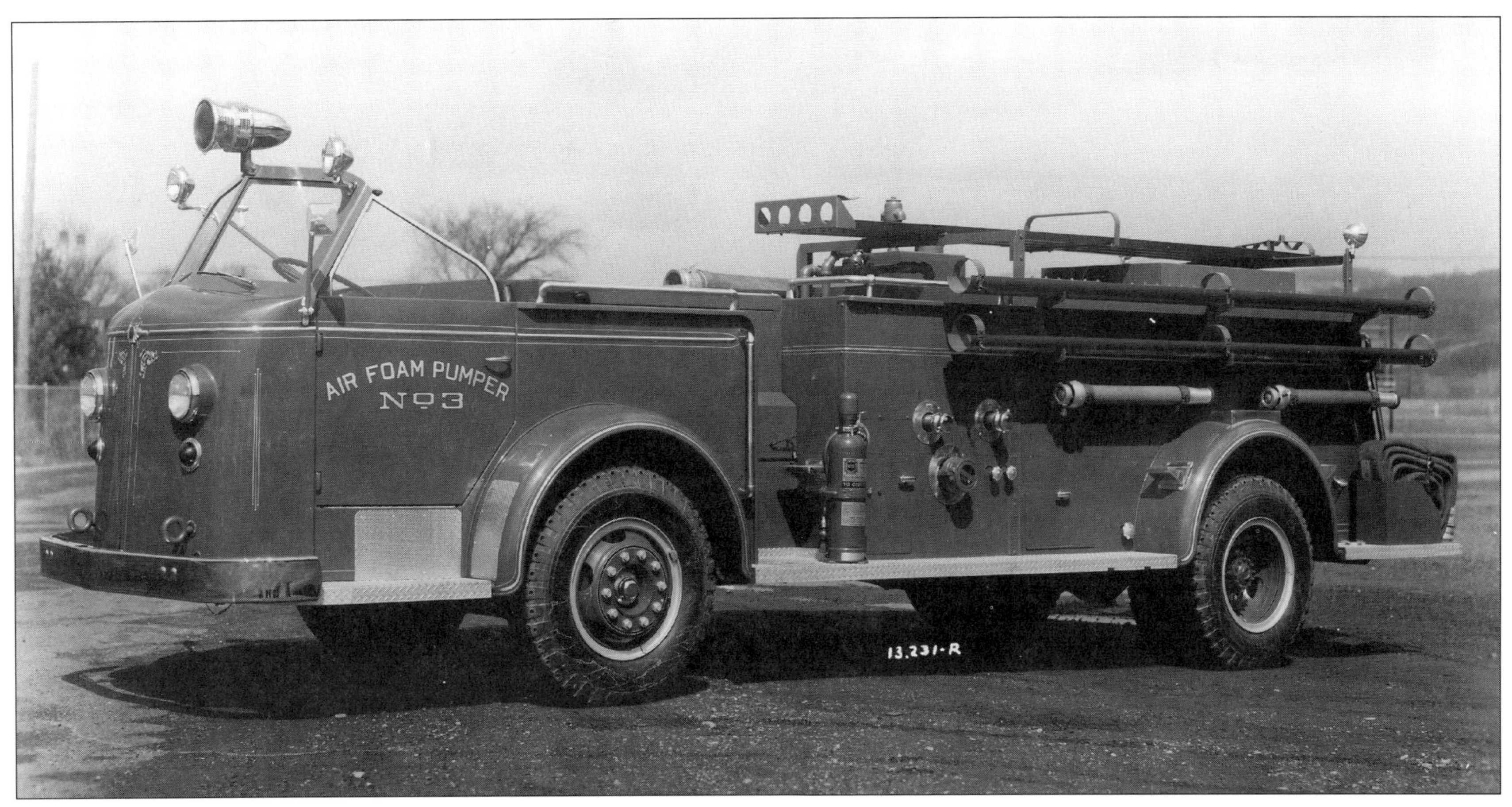

Aruba, Venezuela - Esso Standard Oil Co. - 03/28/53, 03/30/53; Model 775-PJO-FOAM; Serial #'s L-4760, L-4761 - There were no ground ladders carried on this pumper. It was equipped, however, with soft suction hose on each side of the rear tailboard for a quick hydrant hook-up.

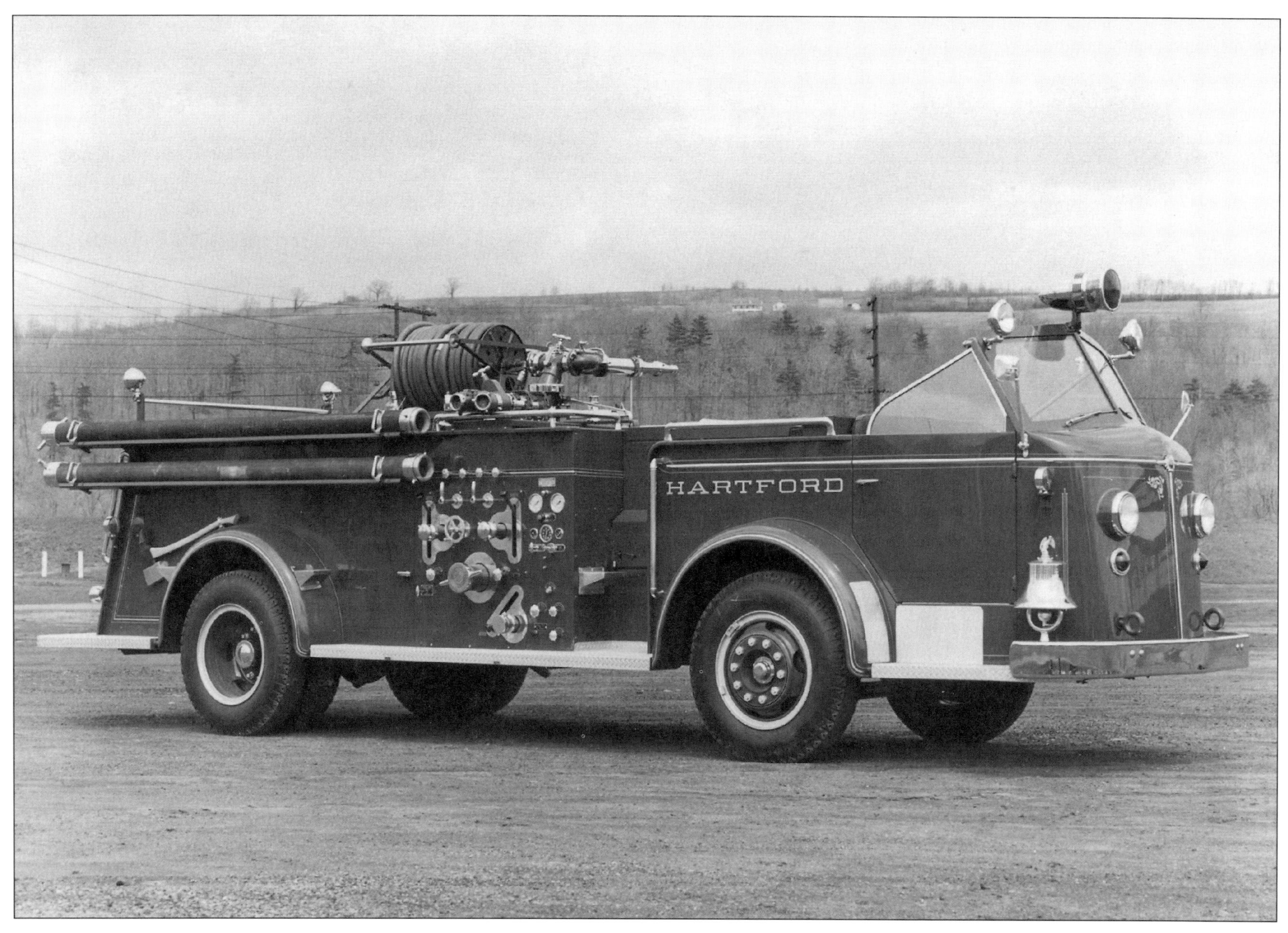

Hartford, CT - 04/21/53; Model 775-PJO; Serial #'s L-4783, L-4784 - Hartford's 700 Series Pumpers were equipped with high, over the pump panel booster reels and portable deluge guns which could be operated both from, and away from the pumper, if necessary.

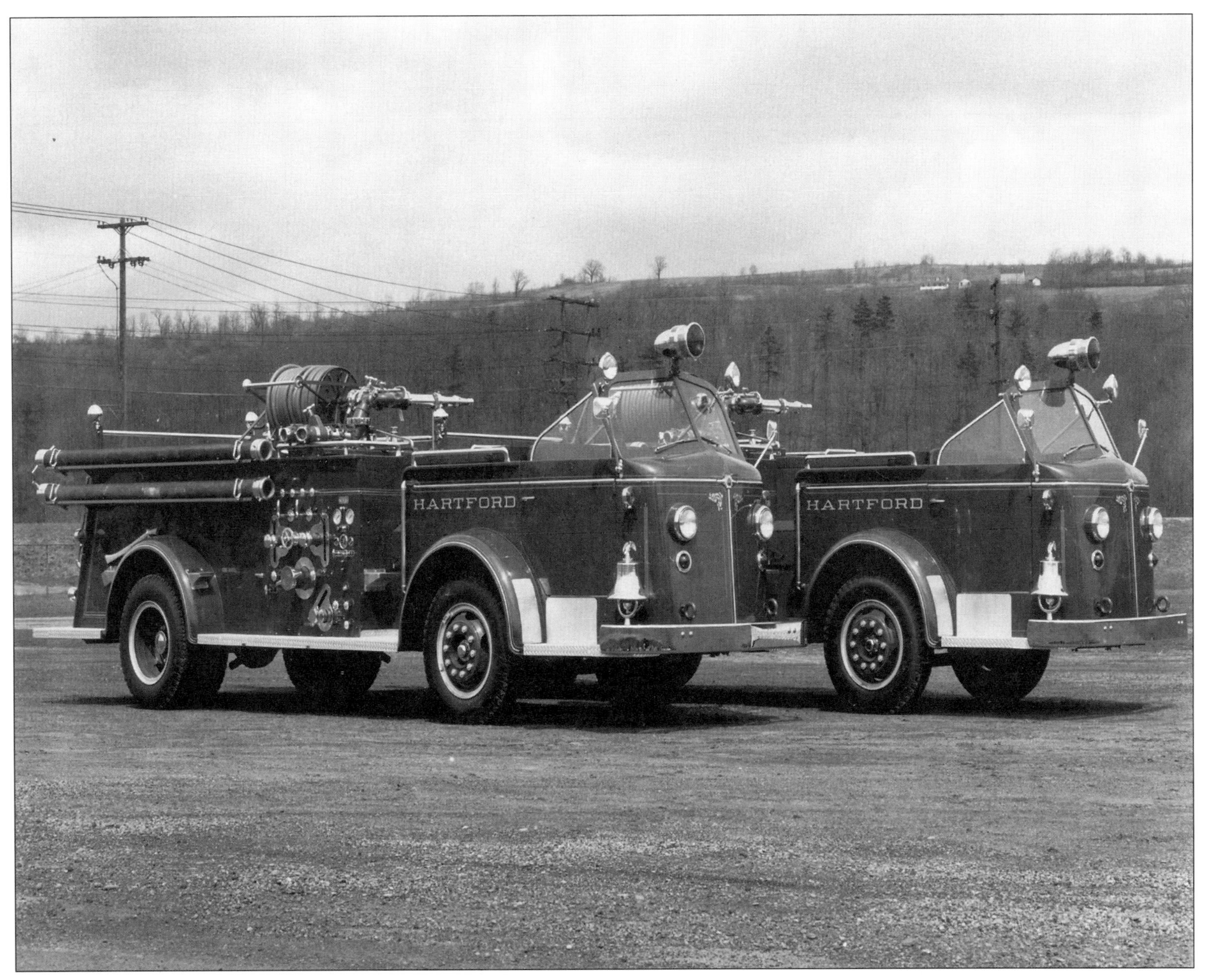

Hartford, CT - 04/21/53; Model 775-PJO; Serial #'s L-4783, L-4784 - Shown here are both of Hartford's 1953 700 Series pumpers prior to leaving Elmira.

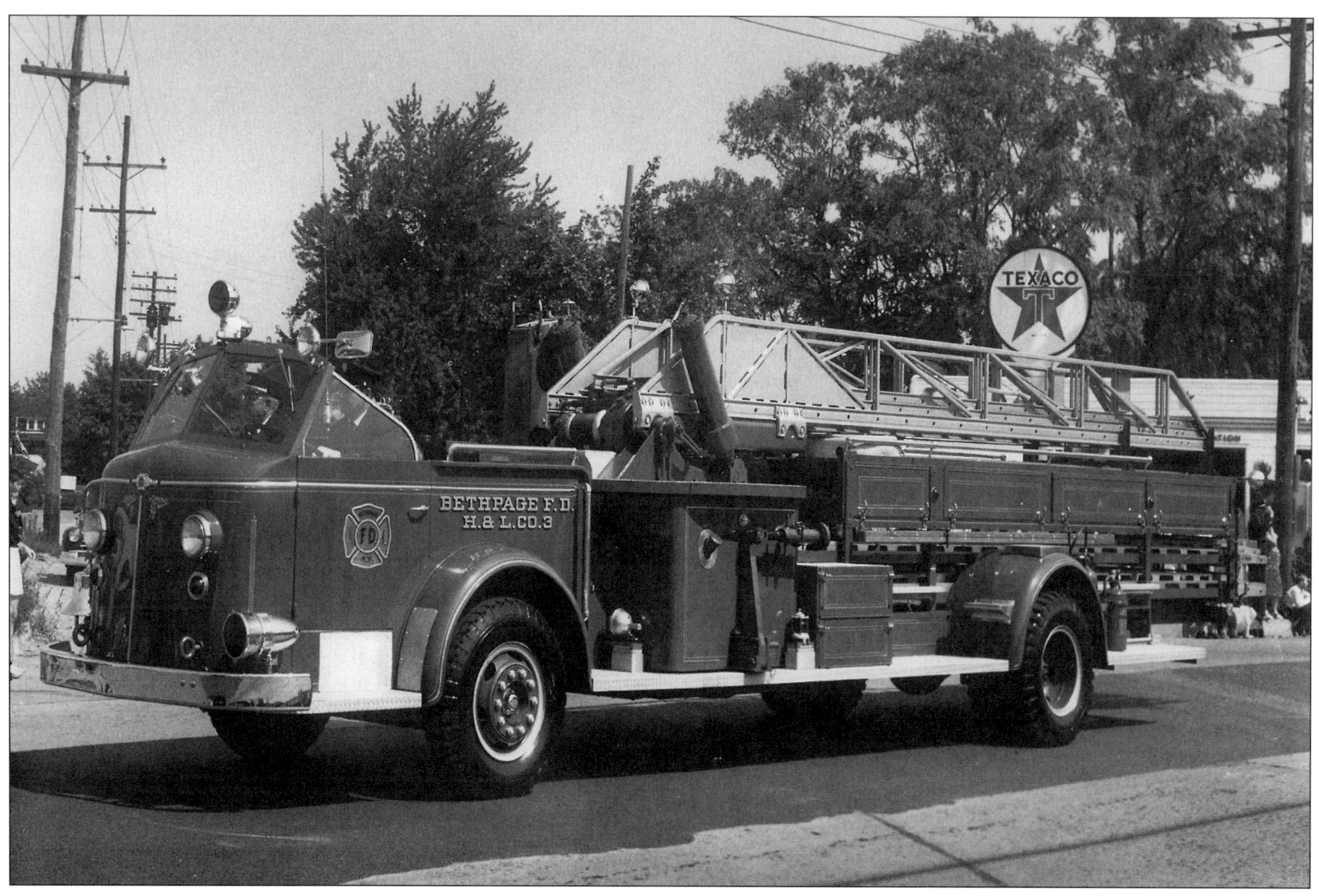

Bethpage, NY - 05/26/53; Model 7-65-AJO; Serial # L-4790 - This was the first custom American LaFrance purchased by Bethpage - at a price of $30,843.00. The 65' aerial ladder was just the right size for the town when purchased back in 1953. Of major importance here are the rear-view mirrors. Note the new location, mounted on each side of the top of the windshield frame. This would be the standard location for them (unless otherwise specified) from now on.

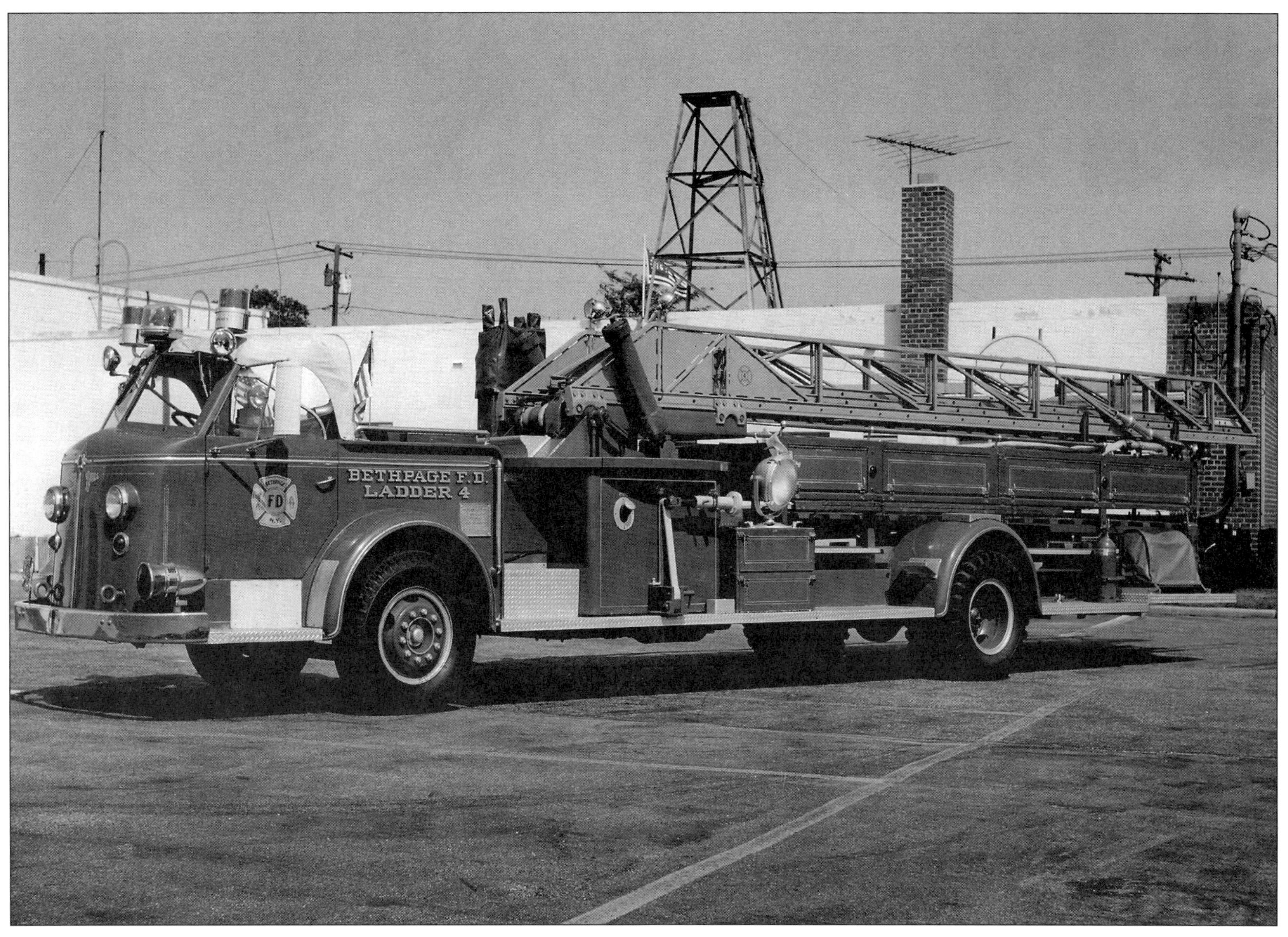

Bethpage, NY - 05/26/53; Model 7-65-AJO; Serial # L-4790 - After spending its initial assignment at Ladder Co. #3 and being replaced by a 1969 Maxim TDA, the rig went back to Elmira in 1972 for a diesel motor and a 75' aerial. Its new home was Station 4, which then became Engine & Ladder Co. #4.

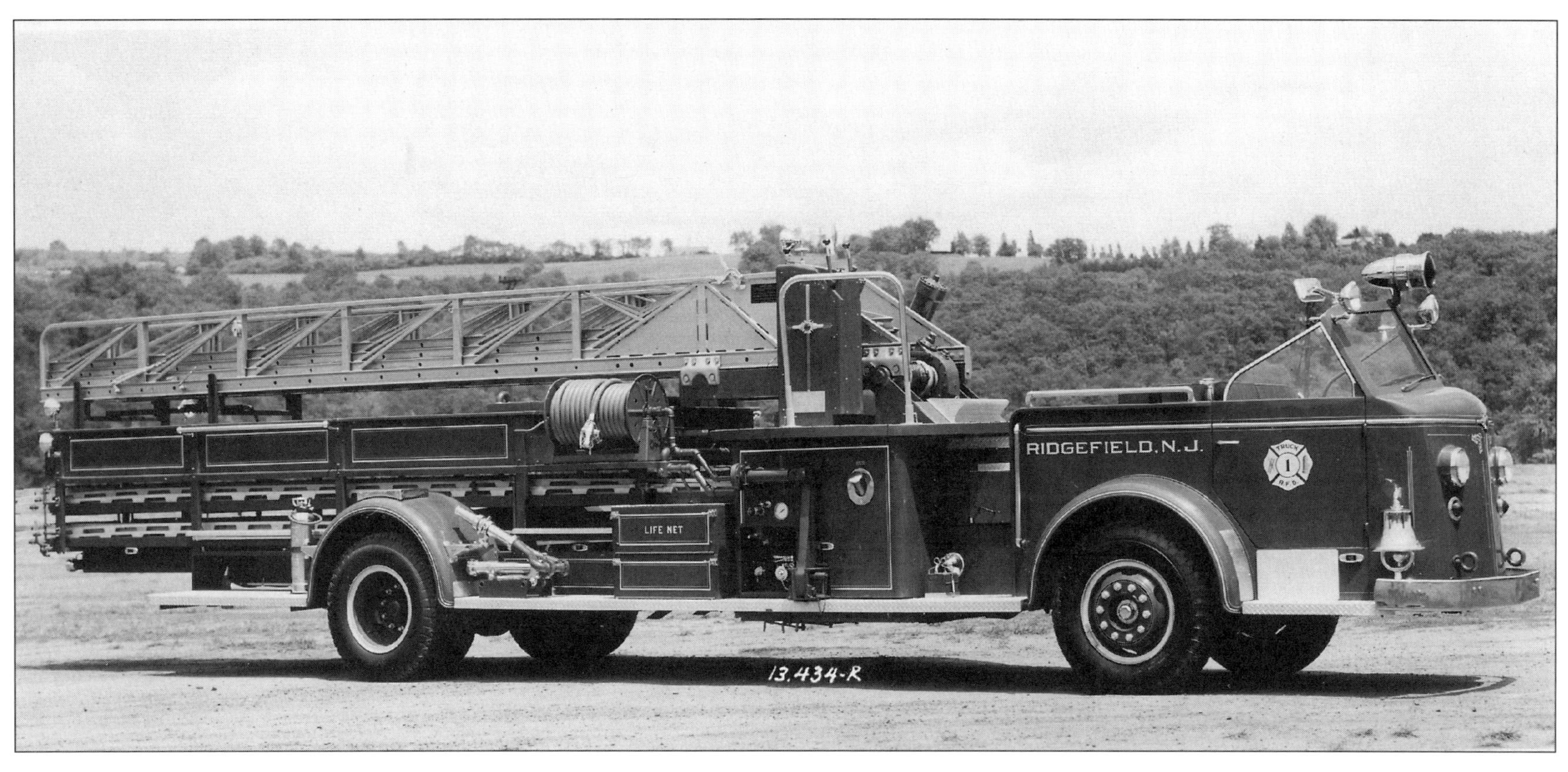

Ridgefield, NJ - 06/16/53; Model 7-85-AEO-I; Serial # 9331 - Ridgefield's ladder truck was equipped with a small booster pump and water tank, and had a 2 1/2" auxiliary inlet located just to the left of the outrigger. It also had an optional 'safety rail' opposite the operator's pedestal.

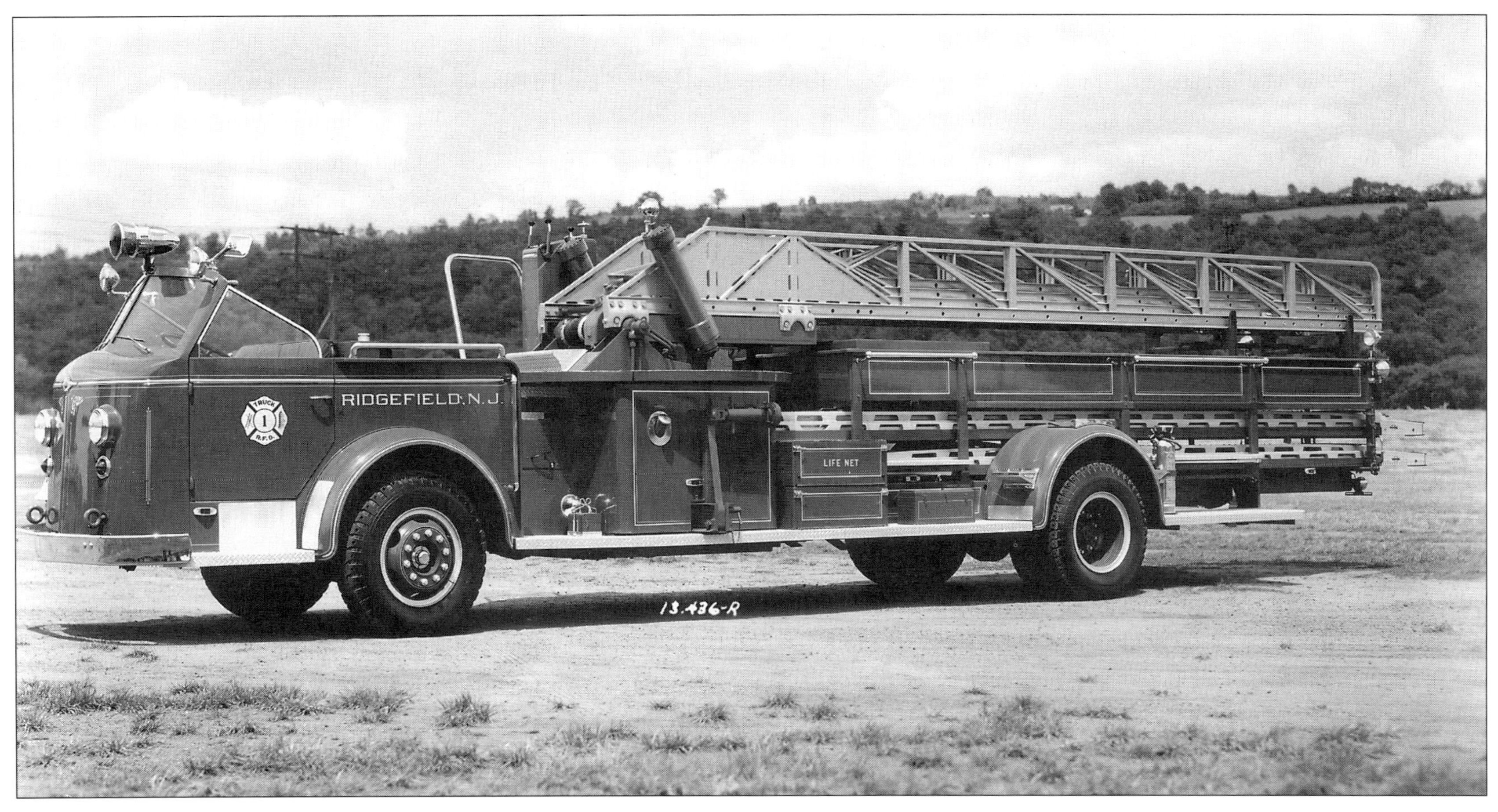

Ridgefield, NJ - 06/16/53; Model 7-85-AEO-I; Serial # 9331 - If you couldn't see the opposite side of this rig, the only indication of any water on board would be the top of the water tank, visible on this side just below the bed section of the aerial ladder.

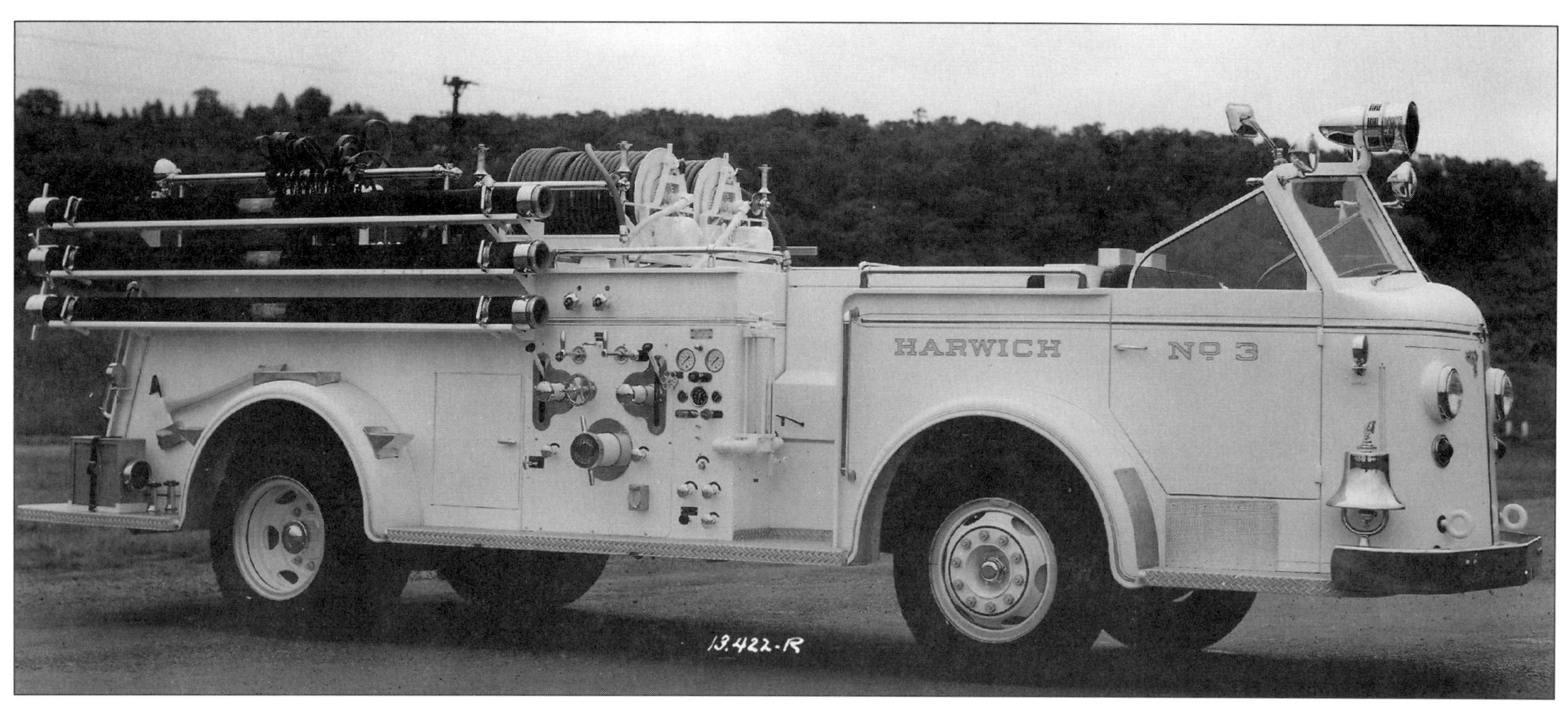

Harwich, MA - 06/15/53; Model 775-PJO; Serial # L-4809 - Take a look inside the jump seat area. The clear canister on the side wall (piped in and out at the bottom) is a Wet Water Cartridge Chamber. The cartridge was inserted at the top: then, the product was mixed with water prior to the (mixed) solution entering the pump.

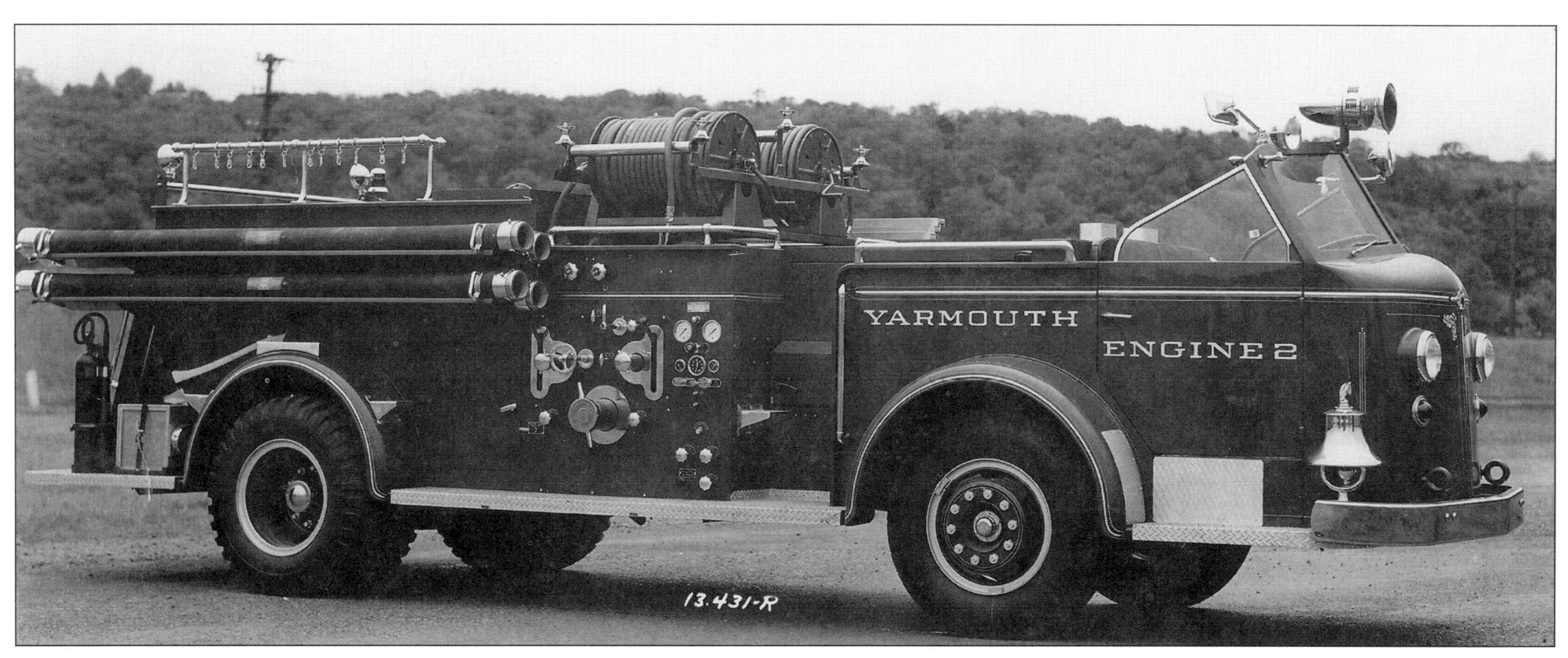

Yarmouth, MA - 06/15/53; Model 775-PJO; Serial # L-4810 - Four sections of hard suction hose are carried in two groups of two above the rear wheel fender. This rig was also equipped with a high pressure booster pump.

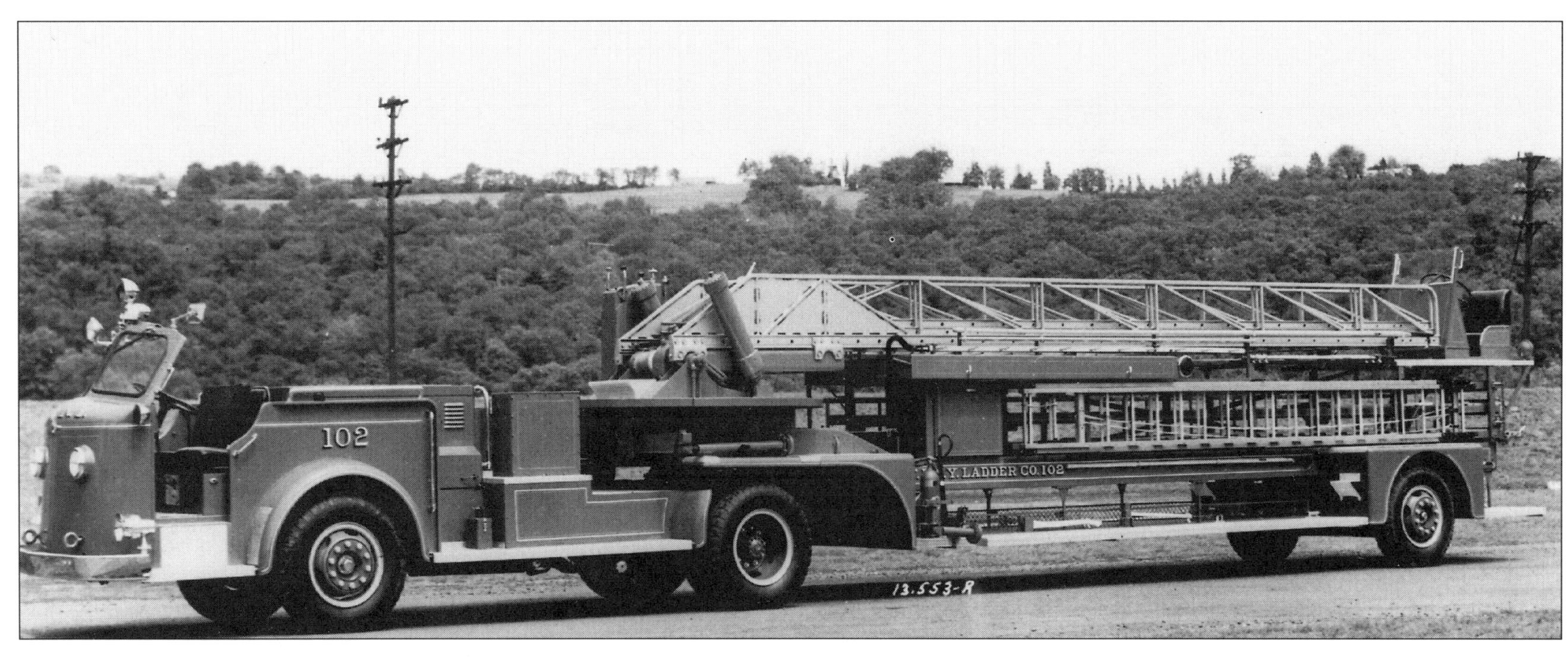

New York City, NY - 08/06/53 through 11/10/53; Model 7-85-TLO; Serial #'s N-1 through N-21 - FDNY's second purchase of American LaFrance steel aerials included a quantity of twenty one pieces. All were delivered without cab doors on the tractor.

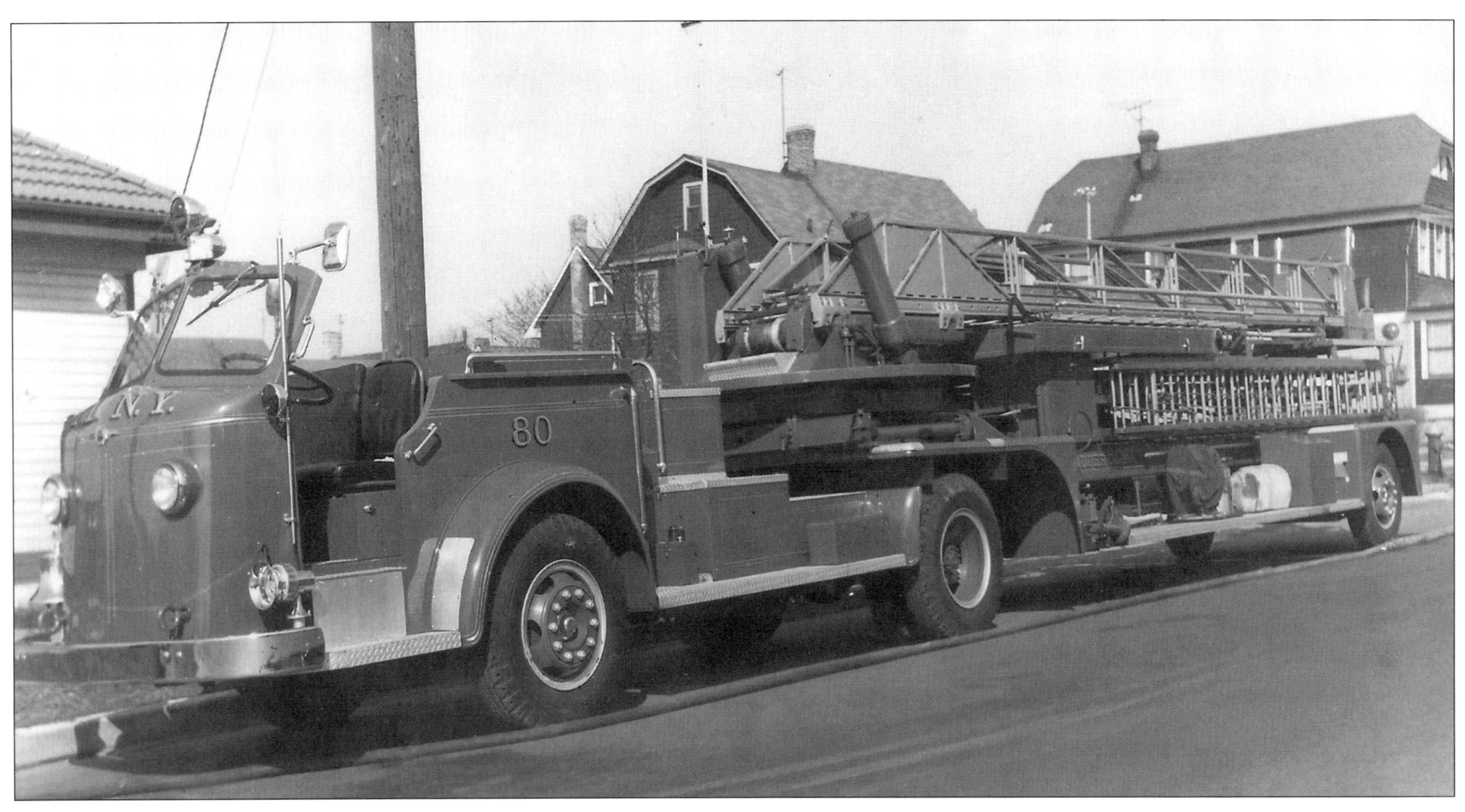

New York City, NY - 08/06/53 through 11/10/53; Model 7-85-TLO; Serial #'s N-1 through N-21 - Initial unit assignments for the trucks included FDNY Truck Company(s) 2; 5; 9; 12; 17; 19; 22; 25; 28; 38; 43; 80; 102; 109; 111; 122; 126; 129; 131; 154; and 156.

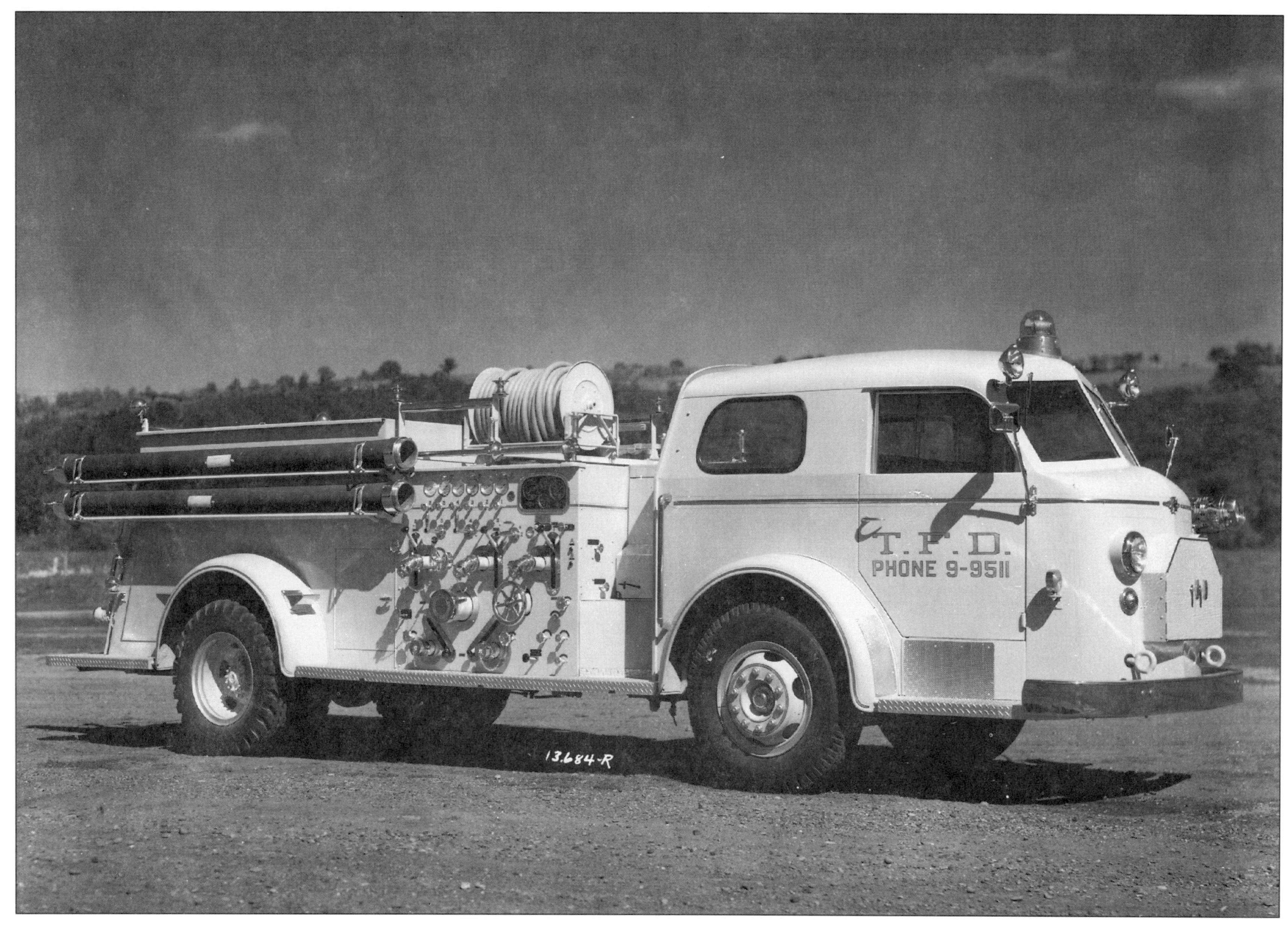

Topeka, KS - 09/23/53; Model 712-PEC; Serial #'s 9339 through 9341 - Although rated at 1,250 GPM, this pumper had six 2 1/2" discharges all equipped with individual pressure gauges. The chrome gate valve (wheel) controlled the front intake.

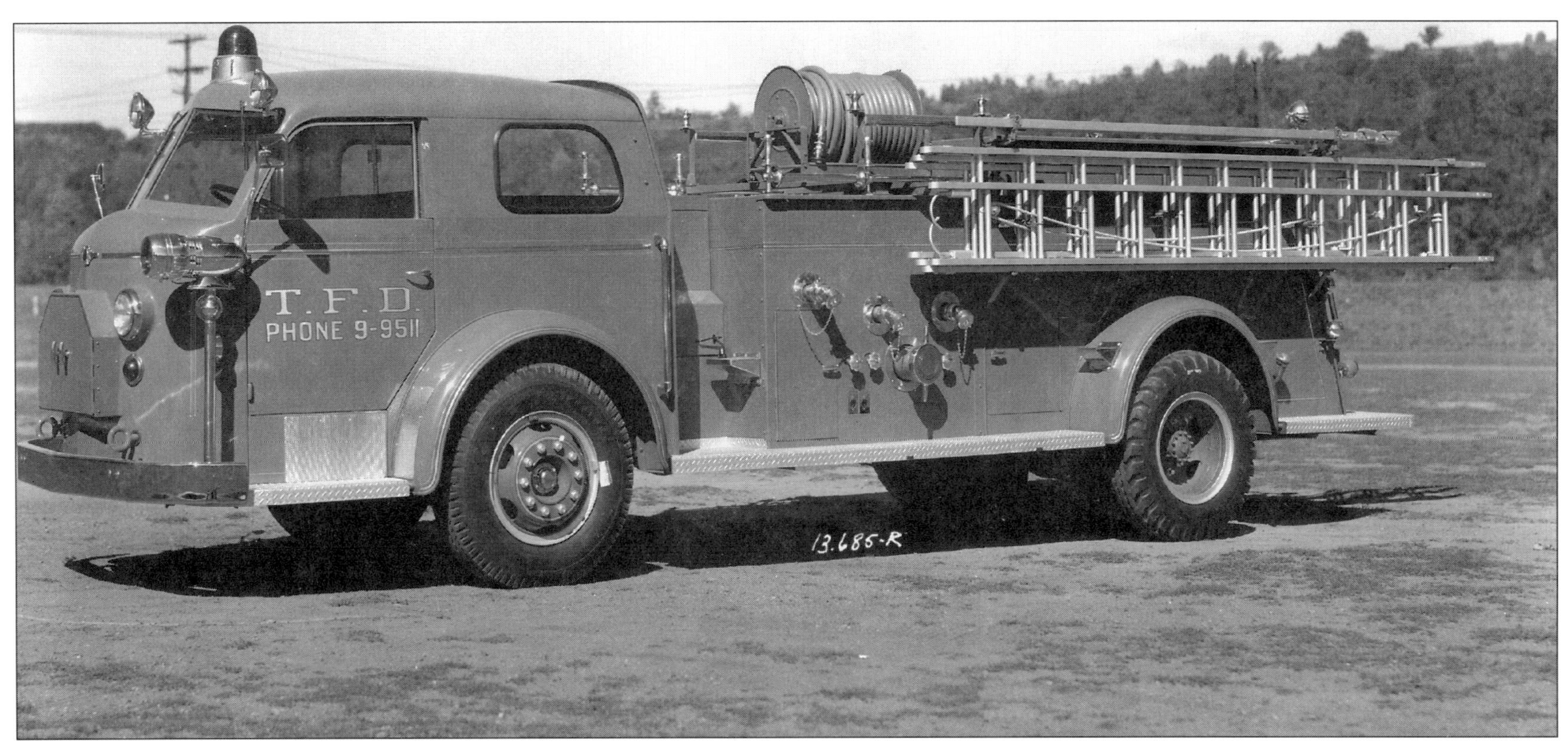

Topeka, KS - 09-23-53; Model 712-PEC; Serial #'s 9339 through 9341 - It was recorded that the Topeka FD specified front mounted cabinet carried 20' of 4 1/2" pre-connected soft suction hose. Three 2 1/2" discharges can be seen on this side with the siren mounted on a stanchion ahead of the cab door step.

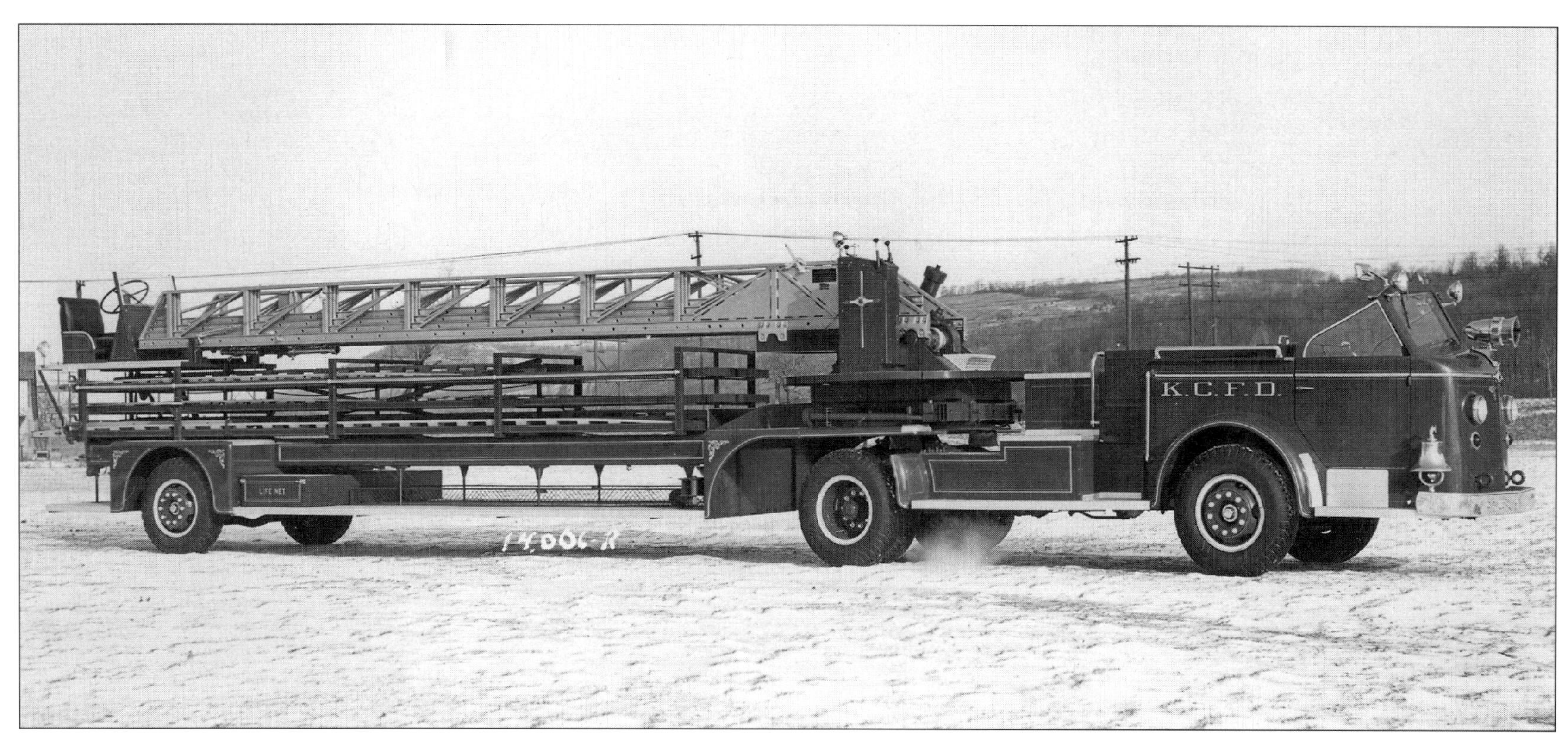

Kansas City, MO - 01/13/54; Model 7-100-TEO; Serial # 9344 - Kansas City ordered an additional TDA to the same specifications as the one delivered in June of 1952. The KCMO FD Shops would later mount the typical truck company equipment on it.

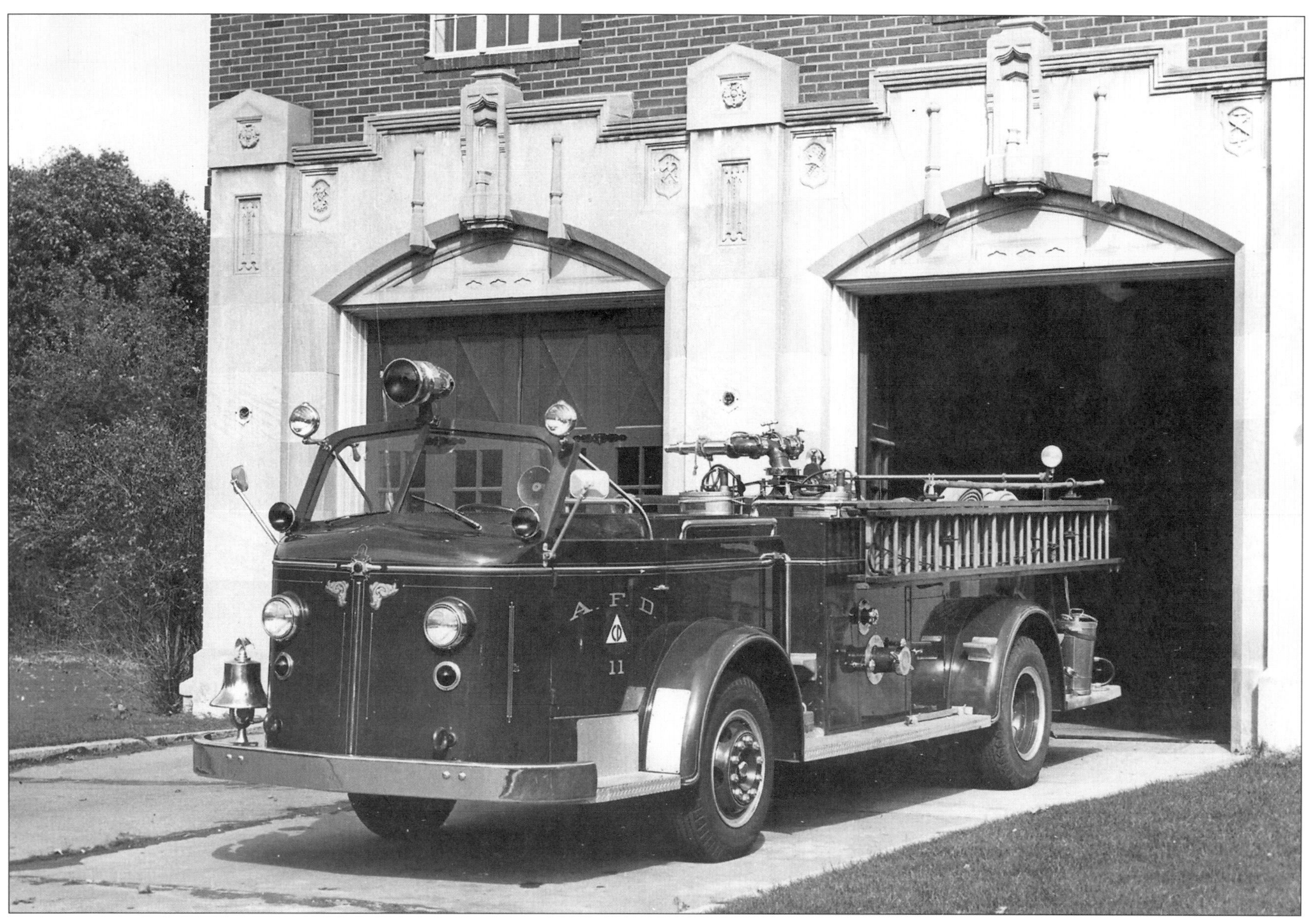

Albany, NY - 03/18/54; Model 775-PGO; Serial # L-4764 - Albany received federal funds through the (then) United States Civilian Defense Program to purchase four pumpers. L-4764 was the last one delivered, and was assigned to Engine Company #11.

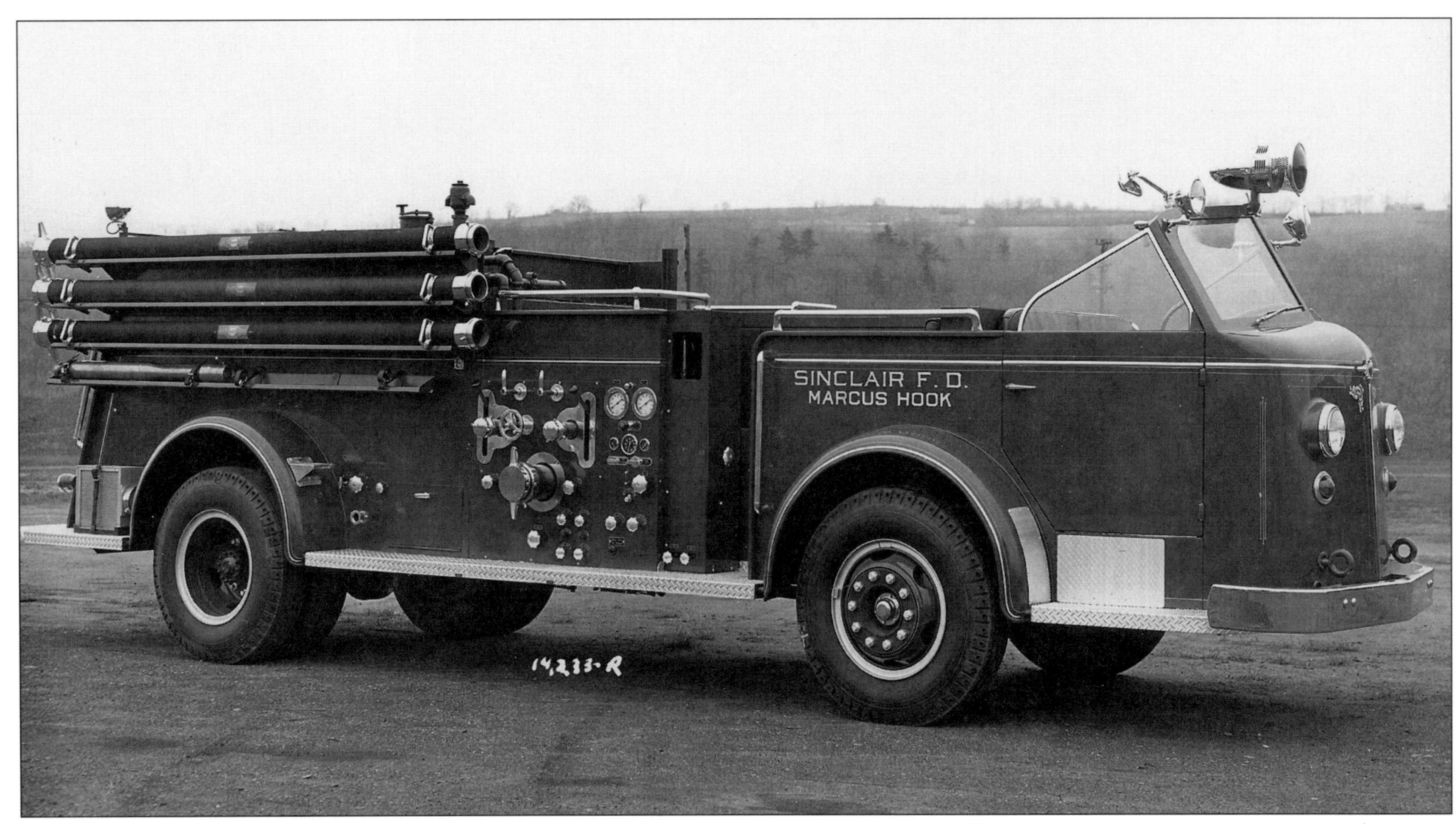

Marcus Hook, PA - 04/29/54; Model 710-PJO-AF; Serial # L-4978 - Purchased for the Sinclair Refinery at Marcus Hook, this pumper was equipped with an on-board foam system. The 'standard' size equipment cabinet normally located just to the left of the pump panel was made smaller to accommodate a special foam line connection just ahead of the rear fender.

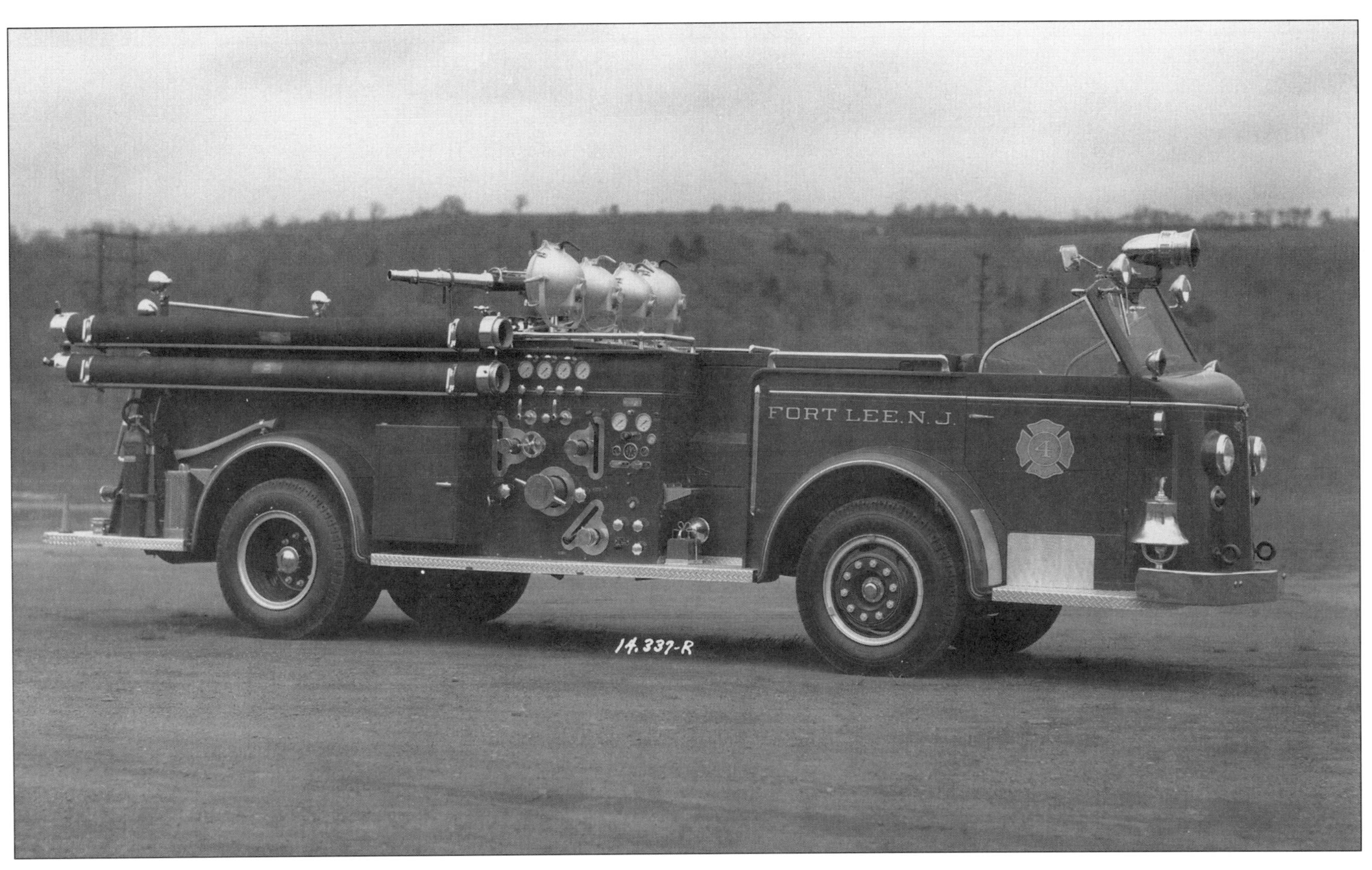

Fort Lee, NJ - 05/12/54; Model L-710-PJO; Serial # L-5021 - Located just across the George Washington Bridge from Manhattan, Fort Lee's 700 Series Pumper carried four portable floodlights above the pump panel.

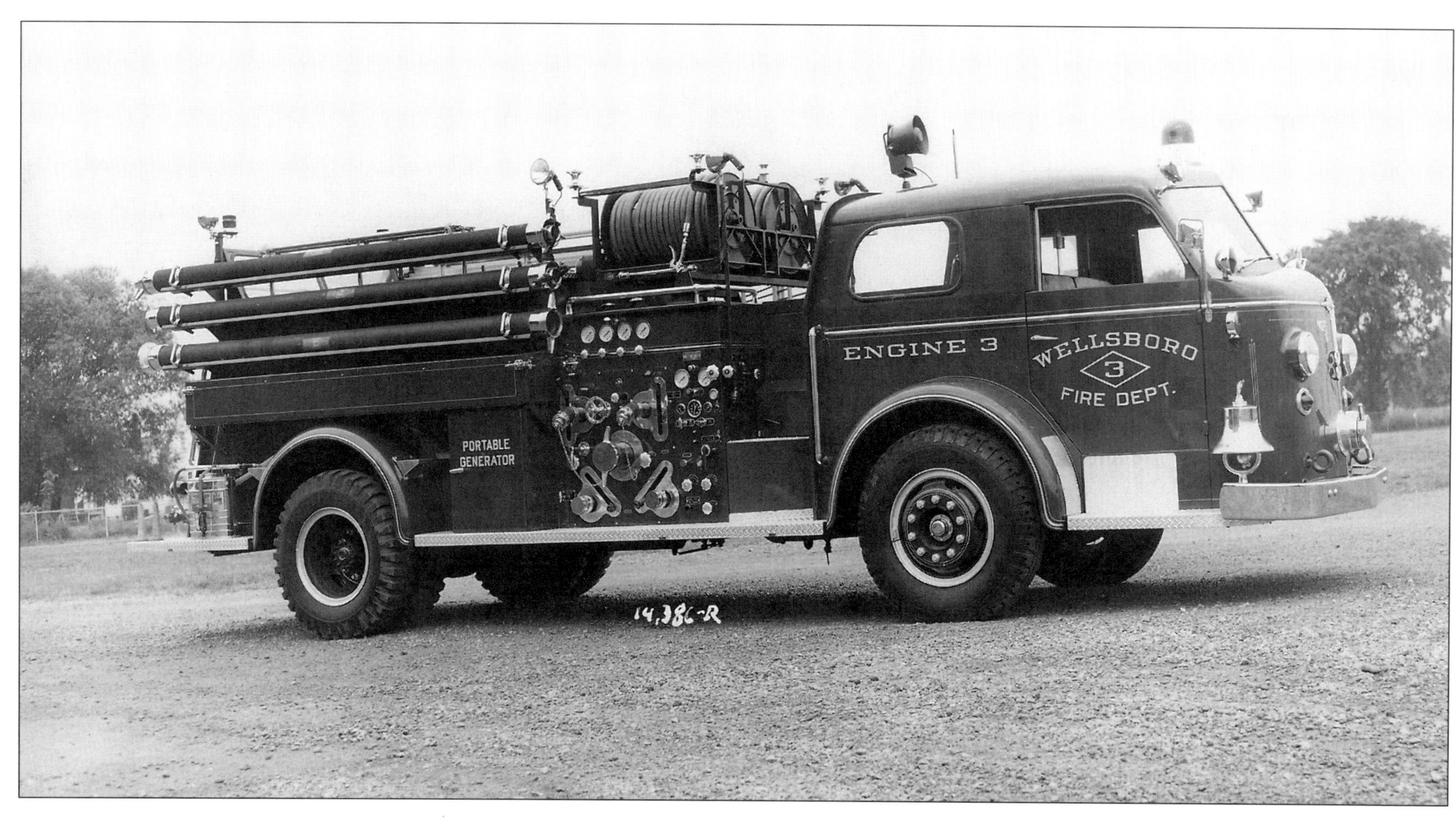

Wellsboro, PA - 06/25/54; Model 775-PJC; Serial # L-5035 - You might call this a "700 Loaded For Bear." It had, as non-standard equipment, a portable generator; high pressure booster system; five sections of hard suction hose carried on three trays; a special compartment beneath the hard suction for a pre-connected attack line; a rear windshield; extra spot lights, and a front intake.

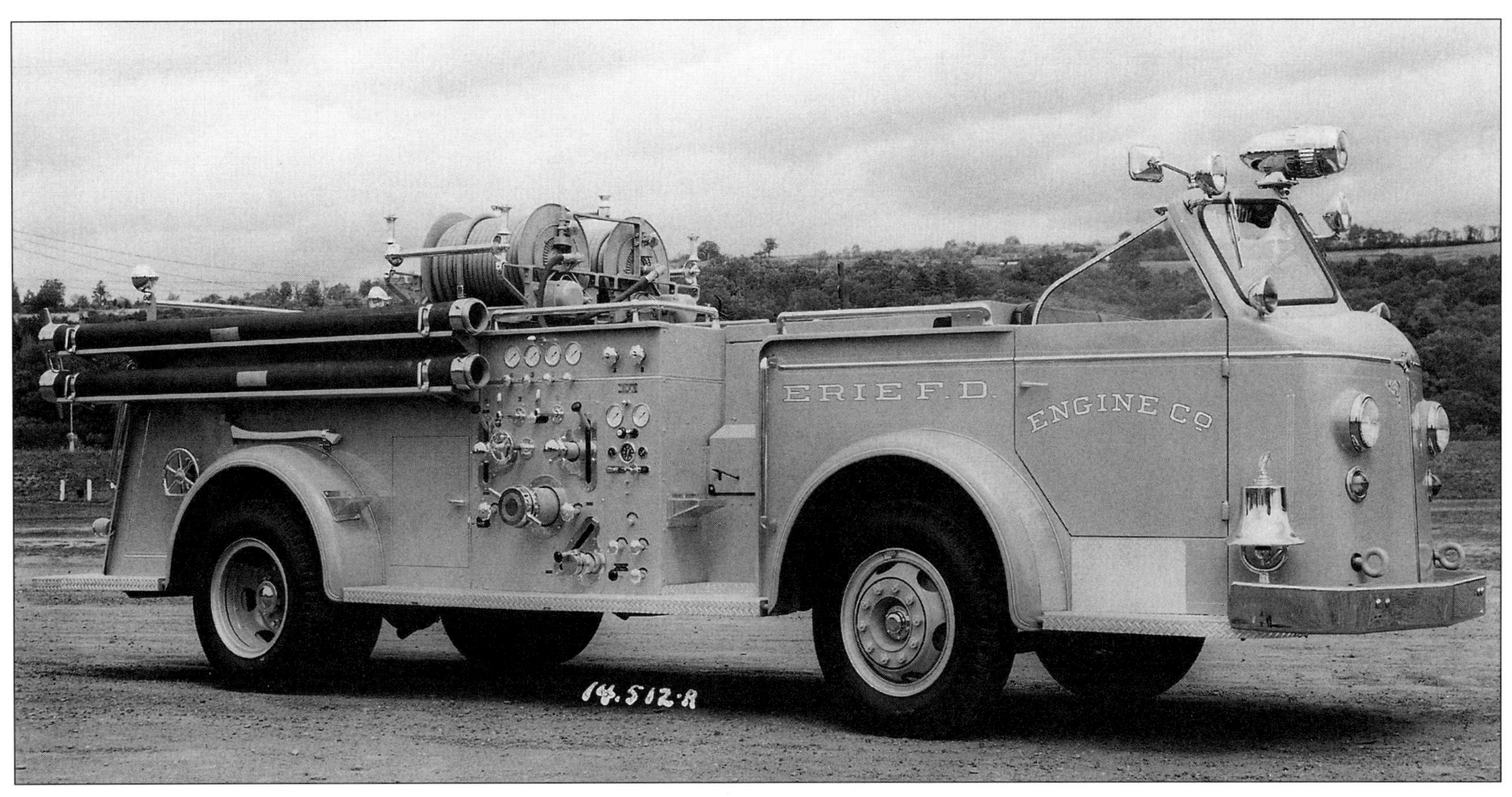

Erie, PA - 08/19/54; Model 710-PJO; Serial # L-5089 - Erie's pumper featured twin motorized booster reels, individual discharge pressure gauges and a gated rear hydrant suction. Of major importance here is the rubber grommet around each windshield section. This would become a standard feature from this point on.

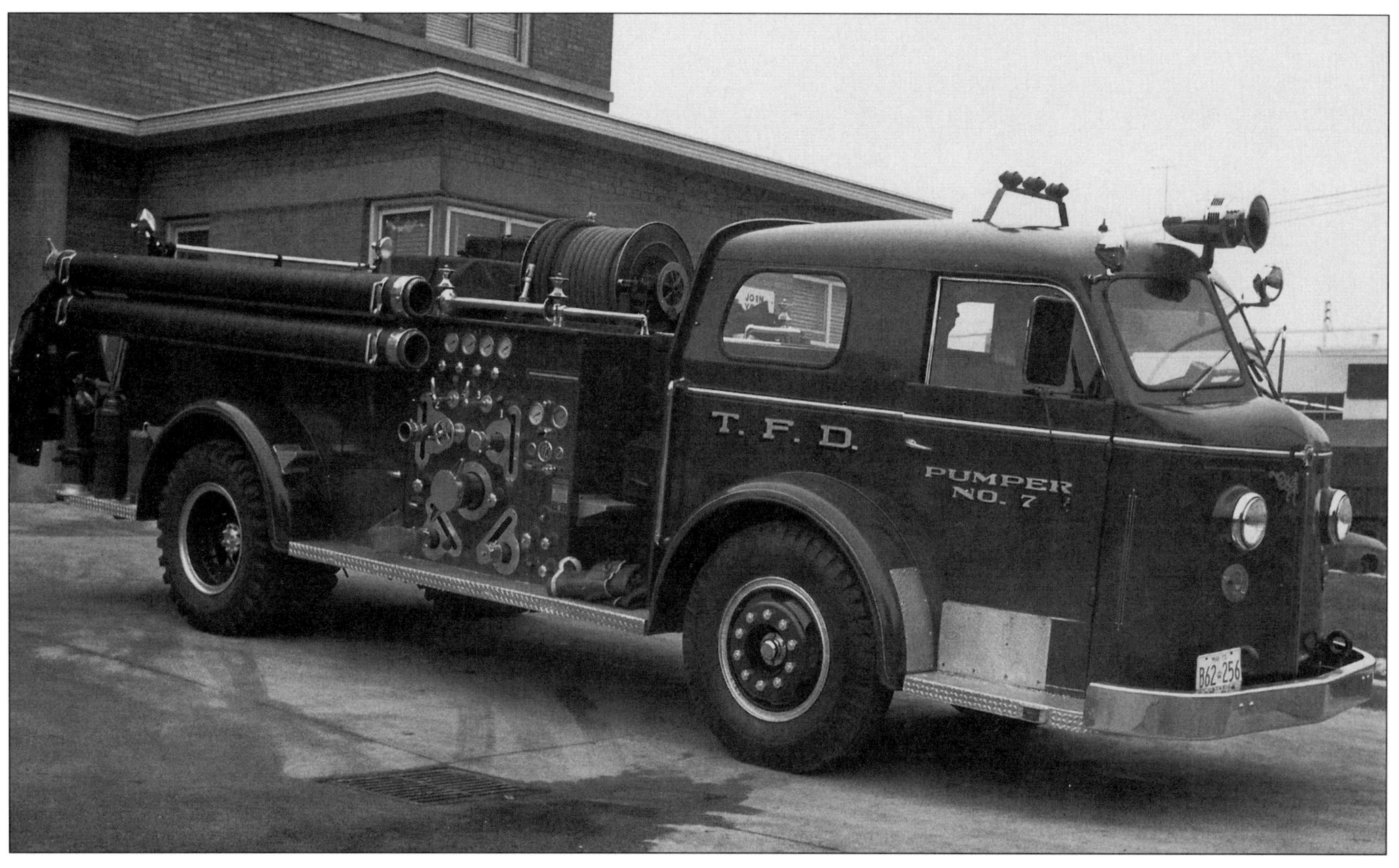

Toronto, Ontario, Canada - 09/10/54, 10/12/54, 10/20/54; Model 710-PJC; Serial #'s L-5057 through L-5059 - Toronto had a short section of 2 1/2" hose preconnected to one of the auxiliary intakes for a quick hydrant hook-up. Toronto also had three double red-faced lights installed on top of the cab roof.

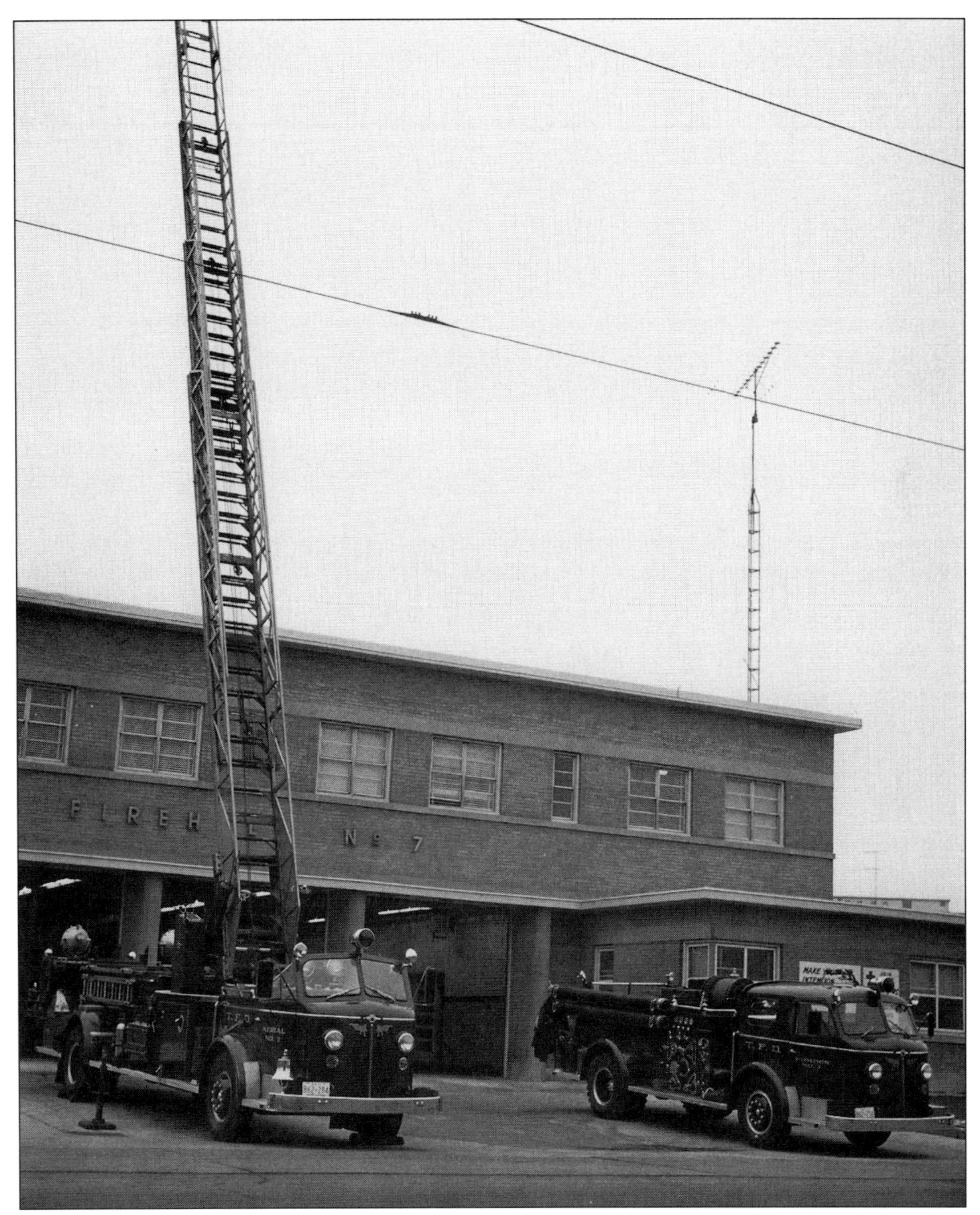

Toronto, Ontario, Canada - 09/30/54; Model 7-100-AEO; Serial # 9363 - T.F.D. Ladder # 7 is shown here with its ladder raised in front of its 'Fire Hall', as they are referred to in Canada.

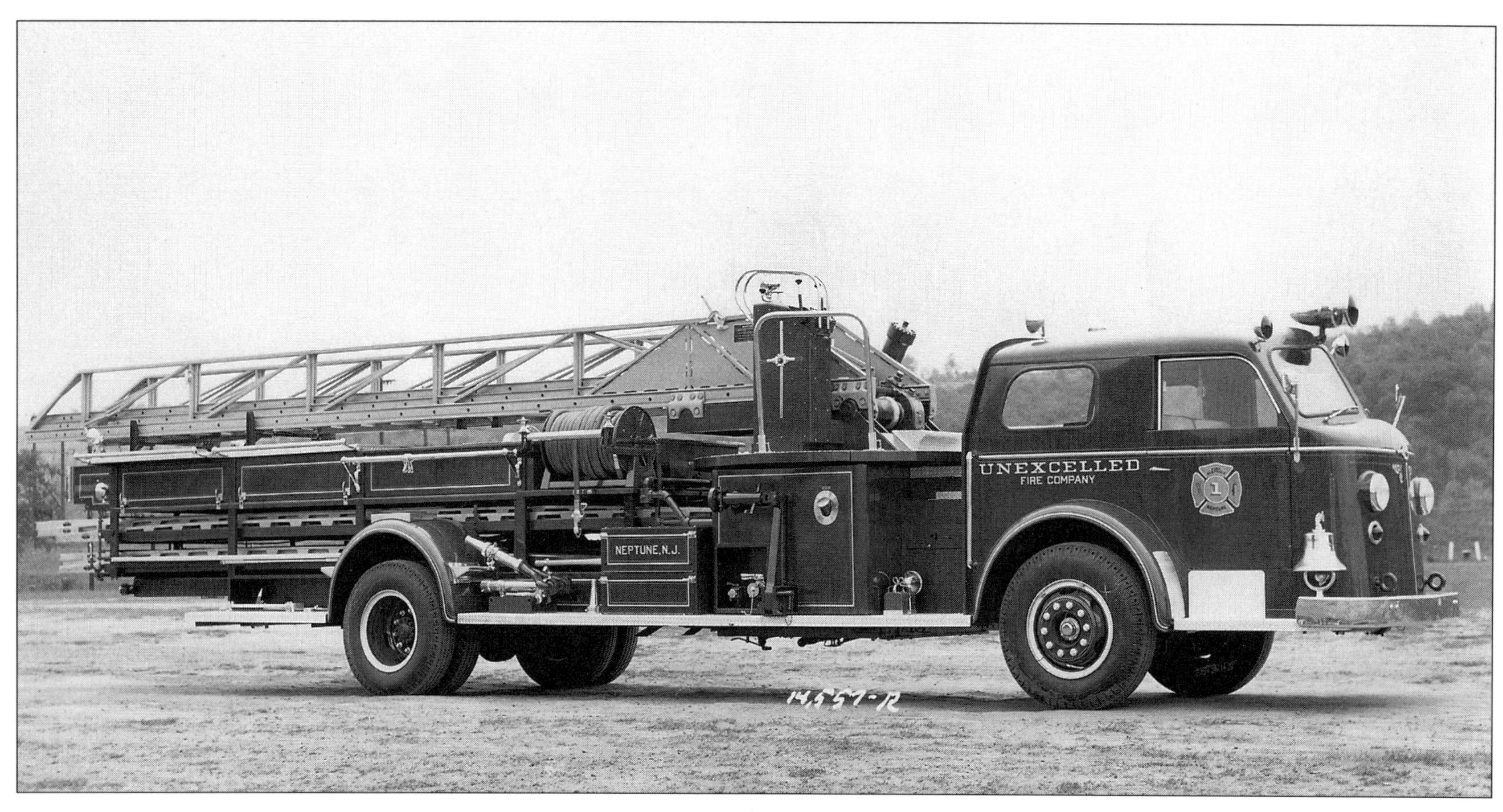

Neptune, NJ - 09/13/54; Model 7-75-AJC; Serial # L-5082 - Used in American LaFrance advertising, this 700 Series ladder truck featured a turntable "safety bar" and chrome protective rails above the control pedestal. The rig also had a small booster pump and a 150 gallon water tank. Note the red flashing lights mounted in place of where the spot lights would normally be. The spot lights were relocated over each jump seat cavity due to this specified requirement.

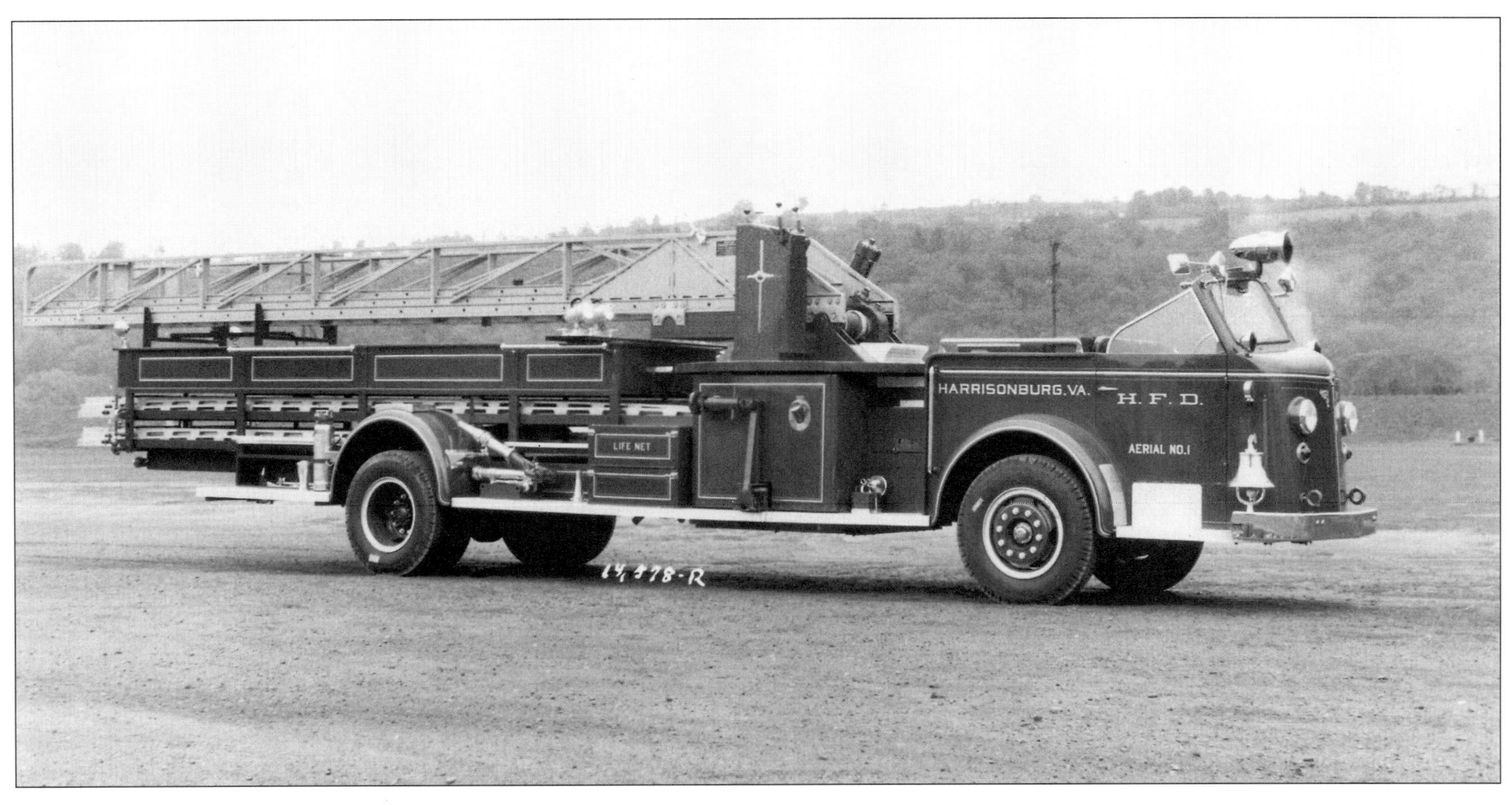

Harrisonburg, VA - 09/16/54; Model 7-85-AJO; Serial # L-5099 - Harrisonburg's aerial came equipped with factory mounted turn signals and a special mount above and to the rear of the turntable for some portable hand-lights.

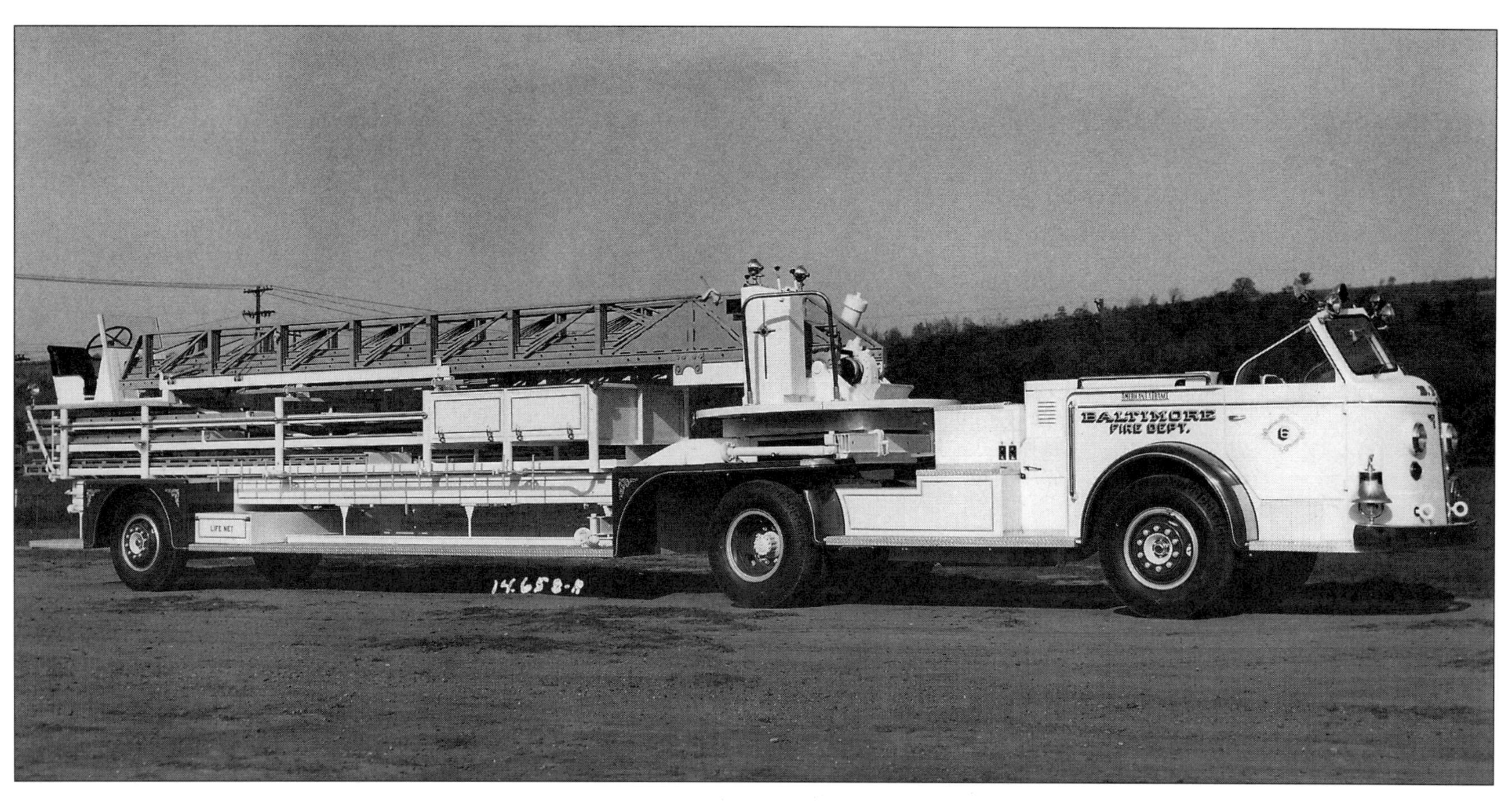

Baltimore, MD - 10/25/54; Model 7-100-TLO; Serial #'s N-22, N-23 - Baltimore received two of these TDA's in 1954 and another in May of 1955 (N-31).

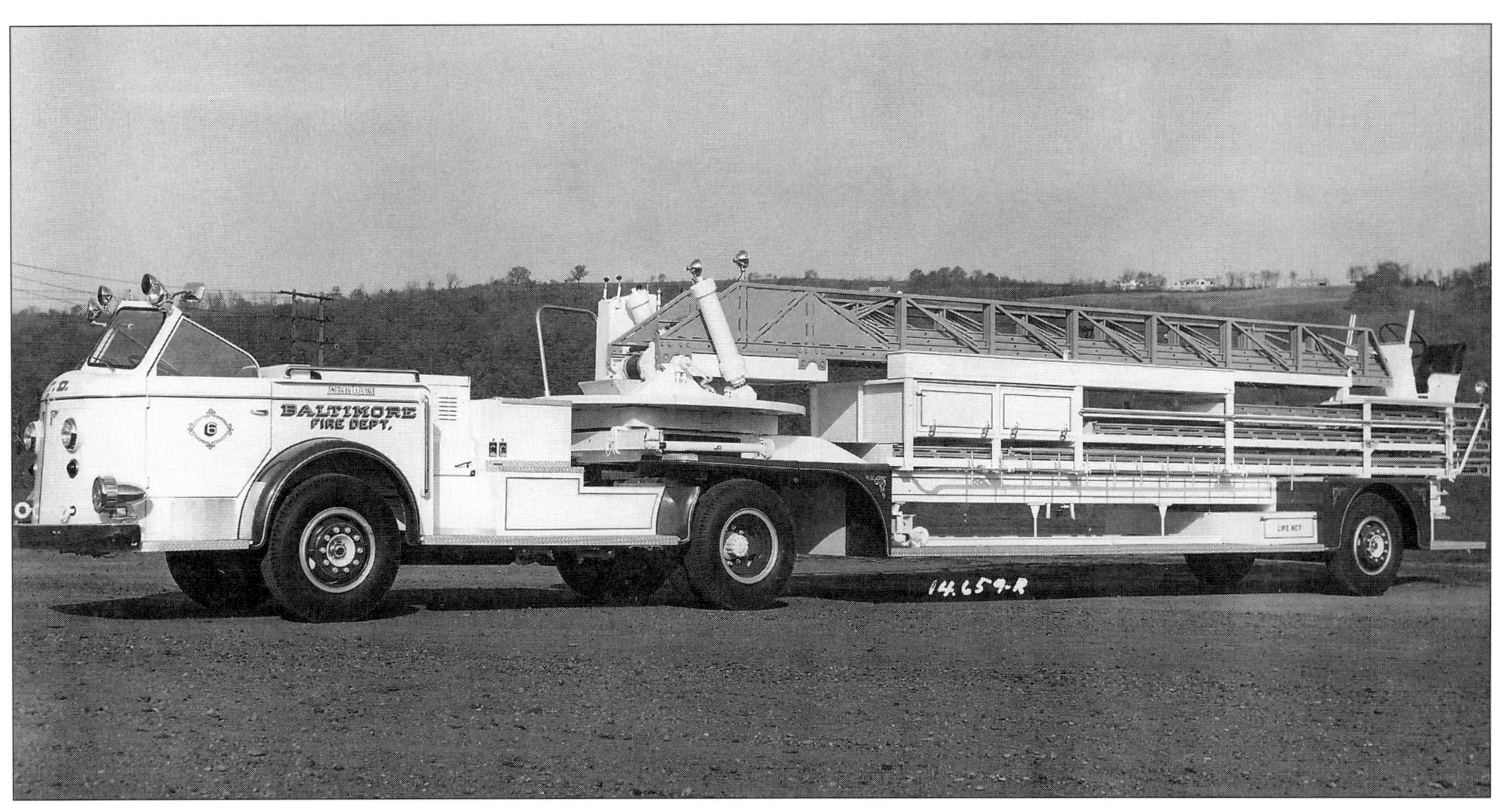

Baltimore, MD - 10/25/54; Model 7-100-TLO; Serial #'s N-22, N-23 - Baltimore's TDA's were painted a very striking white and accented with red fenders. Note an early Federal 'Q' Siren ahead of the front step. The model 'Q' has been going strong for almost 50 years!

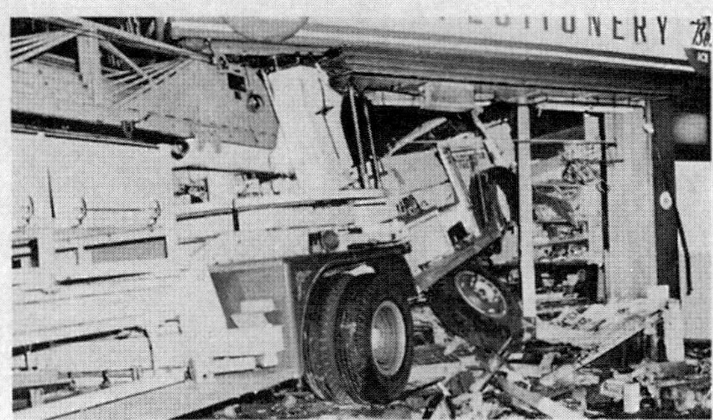

This American LaFrance ladder truck was smashed almost beyond recognition as a result of a collision with another fire engine.

Prescription for a wrecked ladder truck

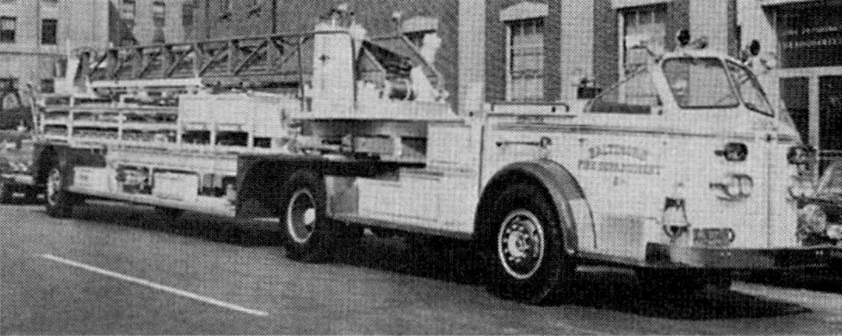

Now it's back on duty after restoration.

The Baltimore Fire Department has transformed a mangled piece of metal that once resembled a ladder truck into a vital piece of fire-fighting equipment. It happened this way.

At the height of a severe thunder and hail storm, an alarm sounded from a street box in the south central area of Baltimore. Engine Company No. 2 and Truck Company No. 6, along with other units, left their quarters enroute to the fire. They never reached the fire scene.

The storm's intensity had increased to brutal proportions. At a weather-obscured intersection, the two units collided with devastating impact. The engine came to rest a half block away. The truck careened into a store at the intersection. In seconds, seven firemen and two citizens lay strewn about the wreckage. One citizen died. The building had to be torn down due to structural weaknesses resulting from the accident.

Superintendent of Maintenance George J. W. Merle and his assistant, Charles R. Warfield, made a detailed survey of damage to the truck. After consulting with Chief John J. Killen, they concluded that the trailer and ladder warranted repairs. Also, cost estimates justified reconstructing rather than replacing the tractor. The Board of Fire Commissioners approved the recommendations and allocated $16,000 for the project.

Temporary relocation of the Fire Department Repair Shop while a new shop was being built delayed the reconstruction work ten months.

Repair-shop personnel stripped the tractor of its cab, equipment and components. This included the removal of the engine, transmission, front-end steering assemblies, fuel system, power train and various structural members. Then they straightened and re-aligned the badly twisted frame.

One repair crew replaced all auxiliary engine components and re-installed the engine. They added a new front axle and steering assembly as well as basic structural members.

Meanwhile, another crew concentrated its efforts on restoring the ladder. These men repaired the hydraulic raising and control system. Then they tested each to insure against any system failure.

The tractor steadily took shape. Soon a new outer "skin" and engine hatch were installed. Finally, the new cab went into place.

Next, the myriad of brake lines, linkage systems and other equipment was installed, adjusted and tested. Shortly thereafter, the men rejoined the tractor and trailer. Both were completely repainted and decorated. As a last step, fire-fighting appliances and ground ladders were added. The truck was ready to return to active fire-fighting service.

JOHN T. O'MAILEY, *Executive Secretary*
Fire Department
Baltimore, Md.

For more data, circle No. 280 on reply card ⟶

Baltimore, MD - 10/25/54; Model 7-100-TLO; Serial #'s N-22, N-23 - The May, 1965 issue of *The American City* Magazine carried a full-page article about the collision of two pieces of Baltimore fire apparatus while responding to a box alarm on July 24, 1962. Unfortunately, BFD's Truck Company # 6, shown in the previous two delivery photographs, was one of the rigs involved in the incident.

44

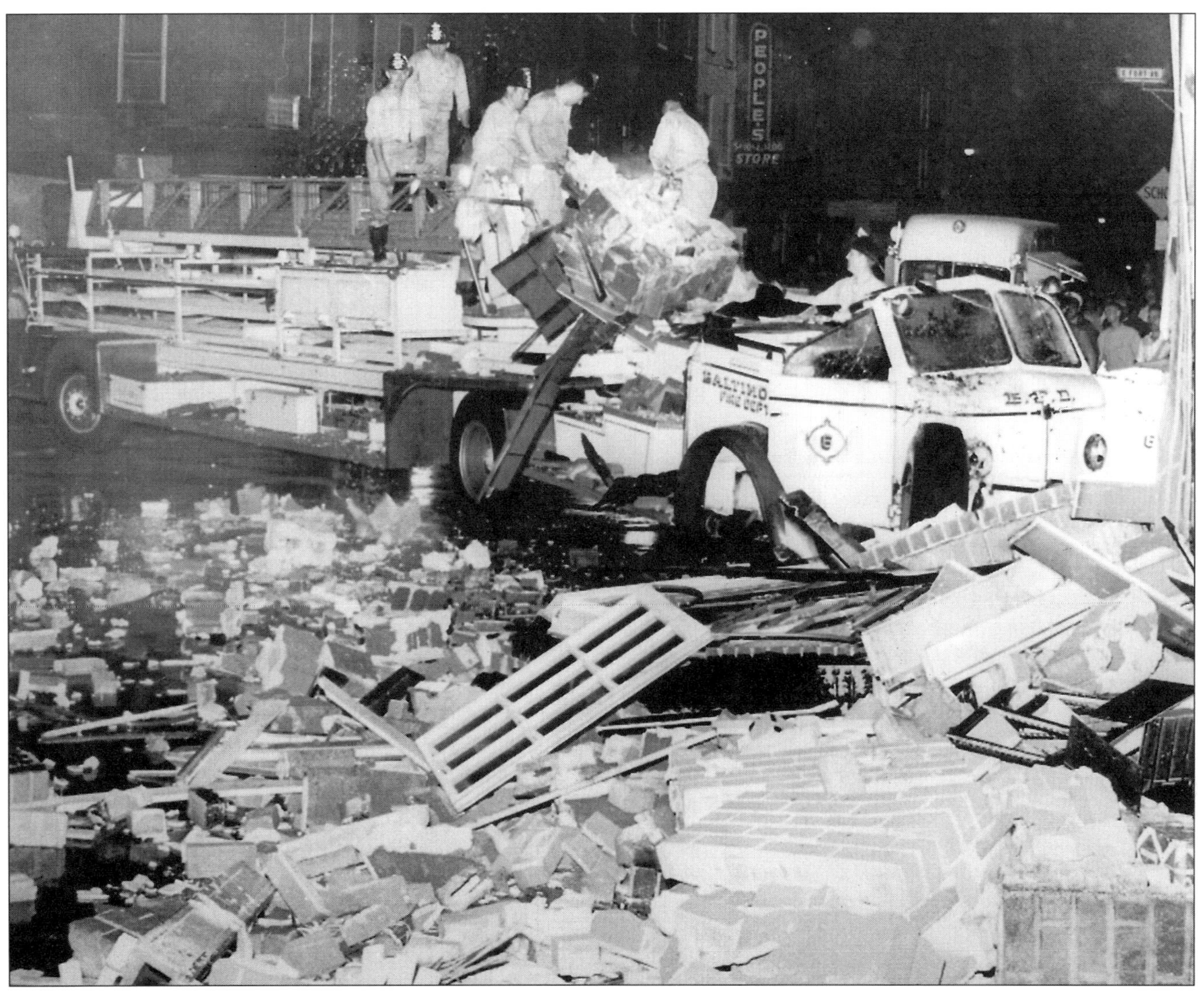

Baltimore, MD - 10/25/54; Model 7-100-TLO; Serial #'s N-22, N-23 - Nine firefighters were injured in the collision of BFD's Truck Company #6 and Engine Company #2. After colliding, Truck #6 careened into a stationery store, killing it's 62-year old owner; Engine #2 came to rest a half block away. The accident was blamed on the "brutal intensity of a storm's weather-obscured intersection." Truck #6 is shown here after being pulled back out into the street from the front of the store.

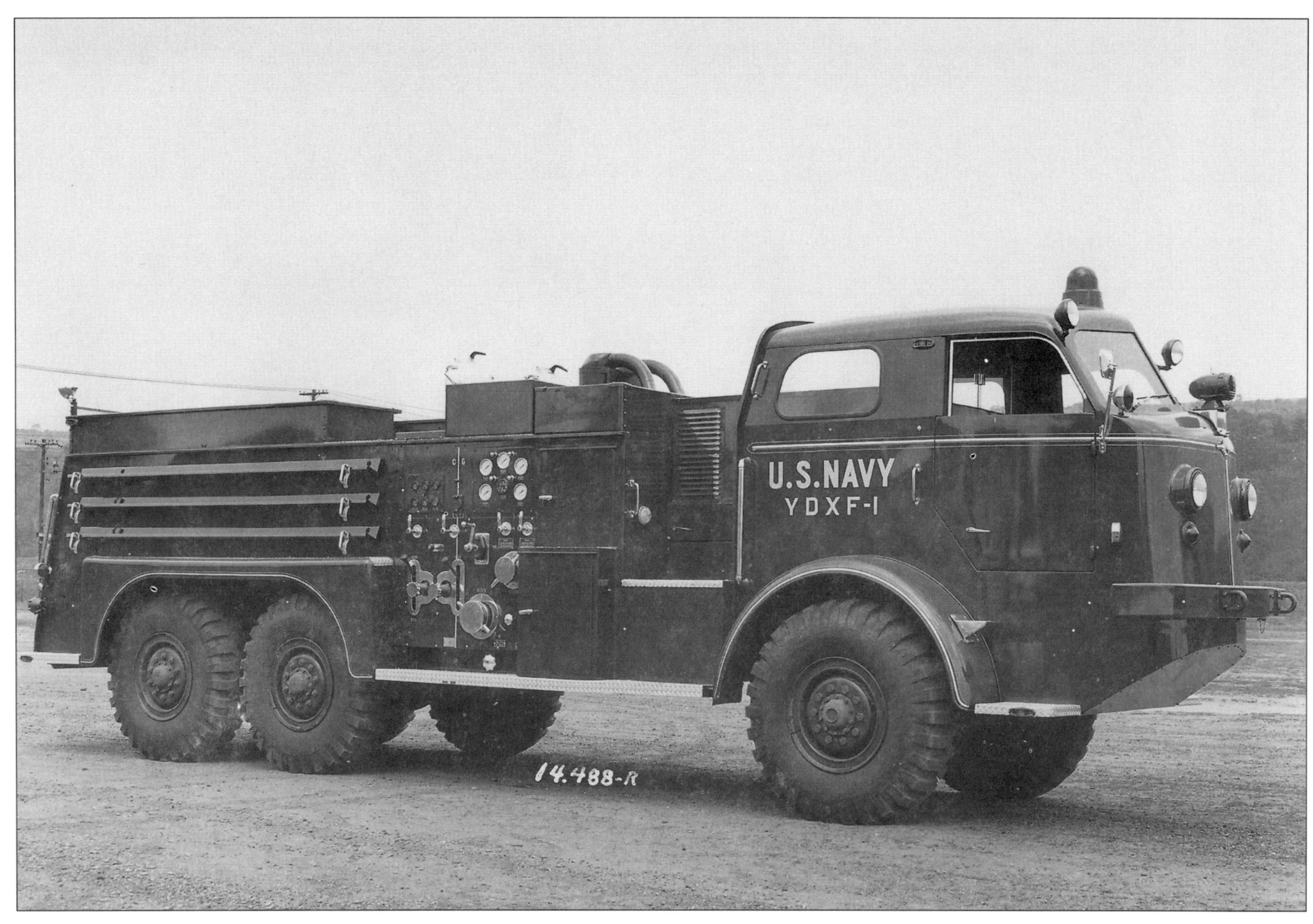

United States Navy Yards & Docks - 11/02/54, 06/27/55 (2), 07/29/55; Model YDXF-1; Serial #'s N-27 through N-30 - The basic 700 Series body style is unmistakable, but that's where it ends. American LaFrance classified this as an "Air Foam Truck," and was one of four built. Features included full 6 X 6 drive capabilities, a special pump piping configuration due to the drive mechanism, and a built in pump/foam proportioner.

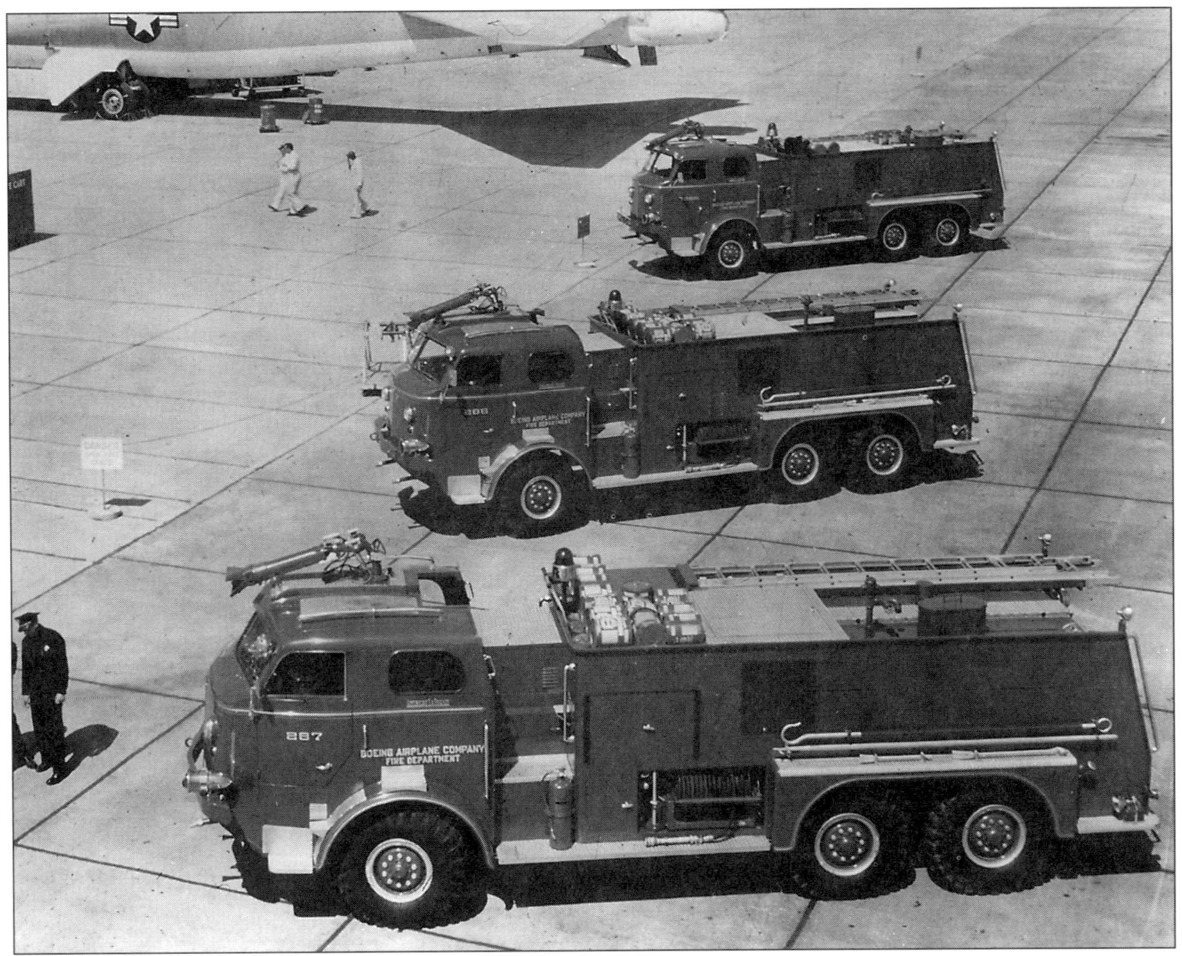

Seattle, WA - Boeing Aircraft Company - 11/16/54, 06/10/55, 06/29/55; Model 1000 GPM Crash Truck; Serial #'s N-24 through N-26 - In the mid-1950's, Boeing was knee-deep in the production of the B-52 Bomber (one can be seen in the upper left hand corner of the photograph), and their larger scale commercial aircraft as well. These 700 Series CFR units were built to handle emergency situations which could arise related to Boeing's aircraft production or test flights. These big units featured 750 GPM pumps, 1000 gallon water tanks, carried 125 gallons of foam, and weighed in at over 36,000 pounds fully loaded. According to Crash Fire Rescue authority, Mark A. Redman, Bristol, CT, these pieces were "affectionately dubbed The Boeing Queens."

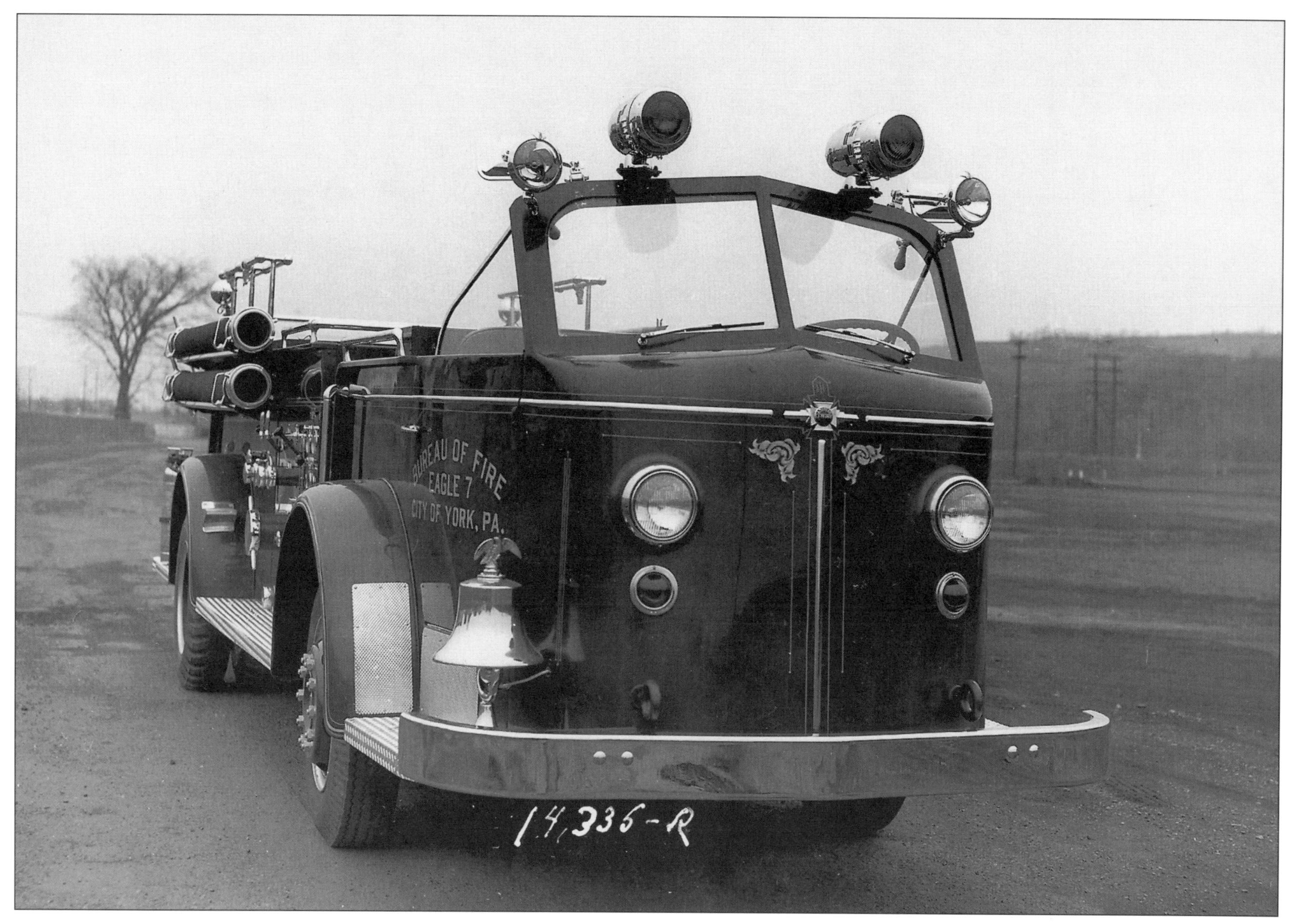

York, PA - 12/14/54; Model 710-PJO; Serial # L-5155 - Today's NFPA (National Fire Protection Association) Standards for Motorized Fire Apparatus deal with soundproofing, etc, for the cab of the apparatus. Both NFPA and OSHA would have a field day with the double siren location/open cab configuration of this 700 Series Pumper. No doubt the sirens cleared the traffic, and the ear drums of the cab occupants as well.

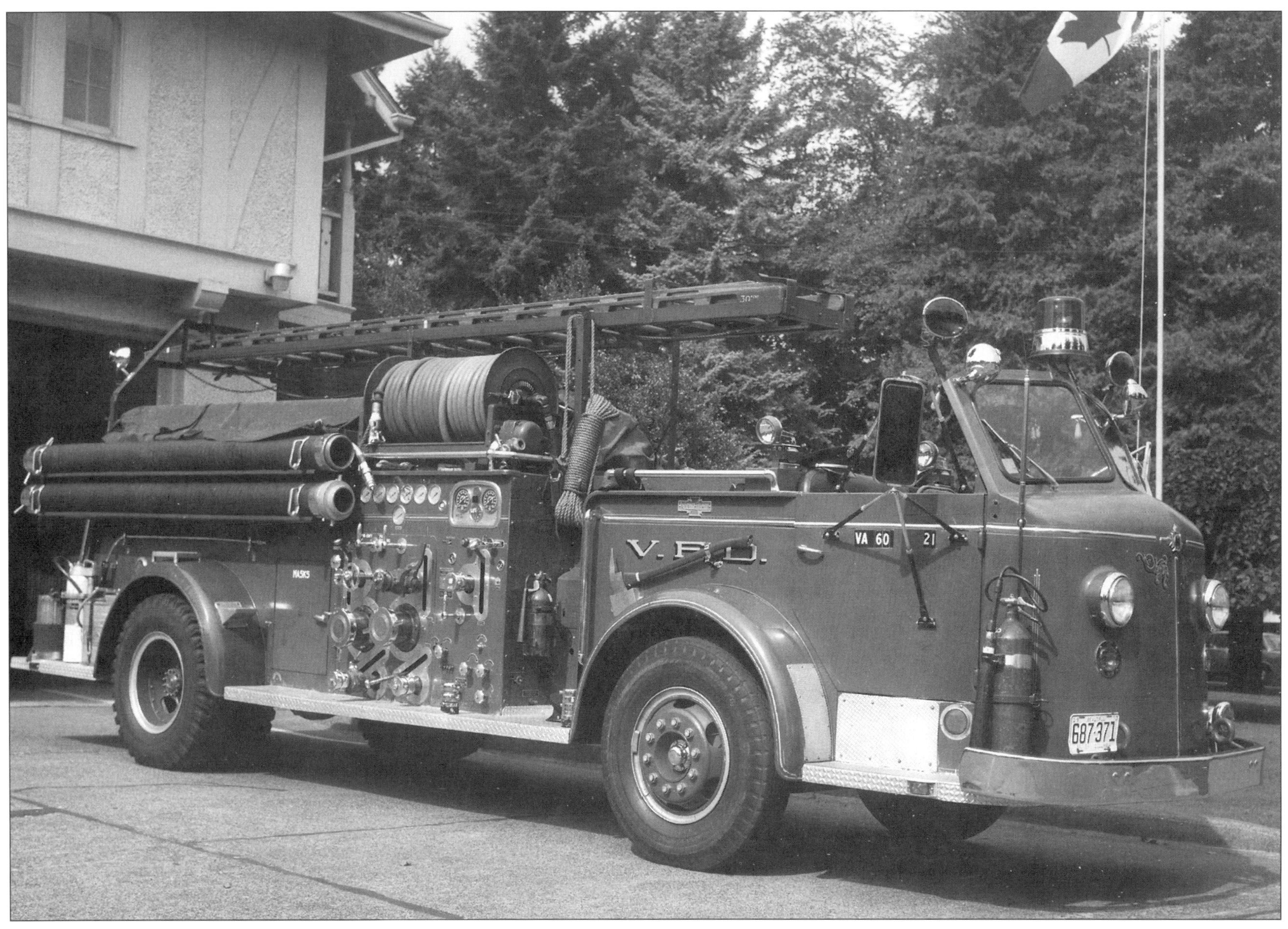

Vancouver, British Columbia, Canada - 12/20/54, 01/12/55, 01/19/55; Model 715-PEO; Serial #'s 9366 through 9368 - Called "Dominion" Pumpers by American LaFrance, these units sported overhead ladder racks, extra hose capacity booster reels, and dual master pump suction inlets.

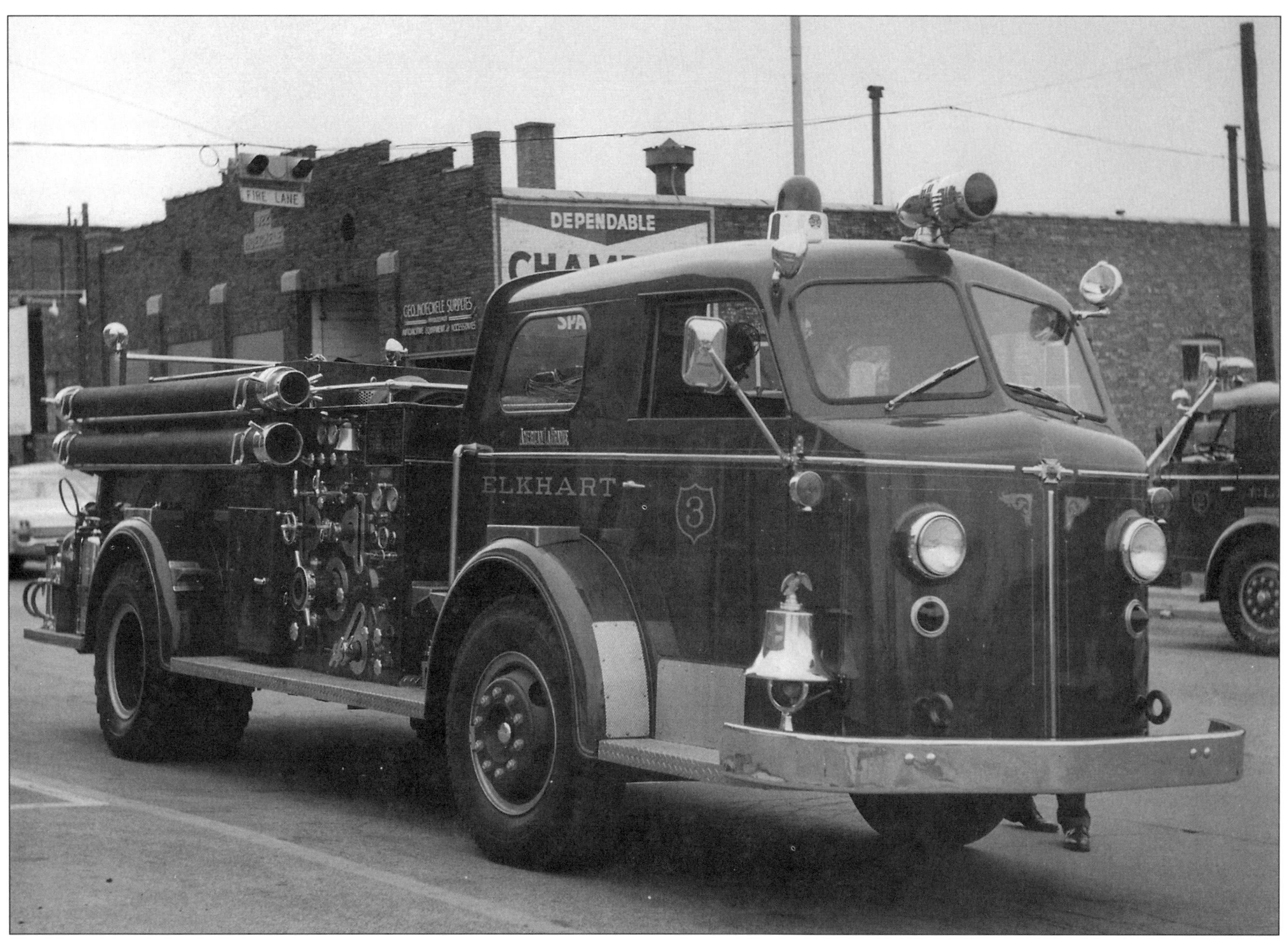

Elkhart, IN - 12/22/54; Model 710-PJC-L: Serial # L-5158 - The very first two 700 Series Pumpers were delivered to Elkhart back in 1947, and they came back to Elmira for another in 1954. The front of one of the original two can be seen in the background across the street.

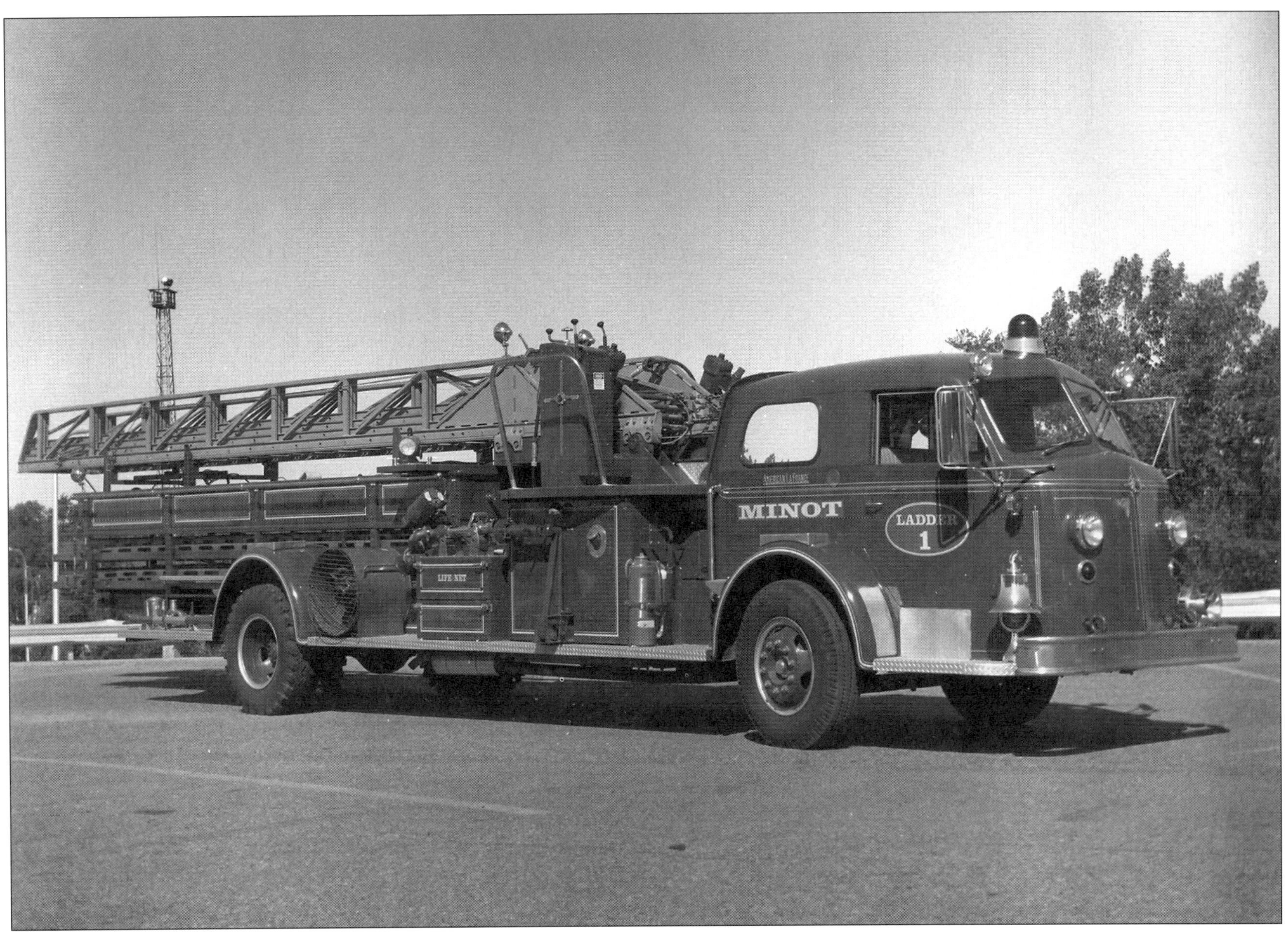

Minot, ND - 12/27/54; Model 7-100-AEC; Serial # 9381 - At the time this was delivered, Minot became only the third fire department in the whole state of North Dakota to have a 100' aerial ladder. Strangely enough, American LaFrance protected the other two cities of Fargo and Jamestown, as well.

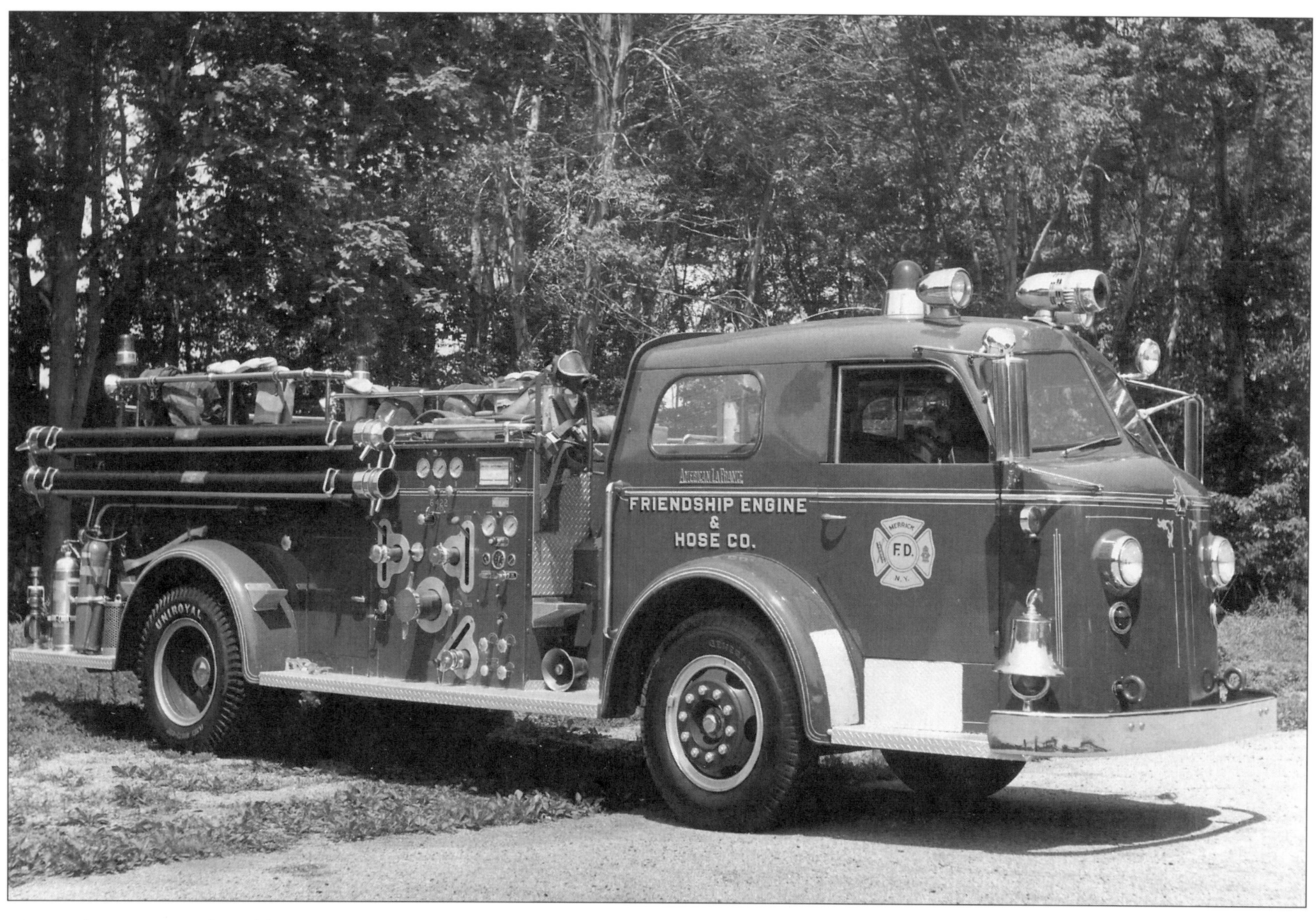

Merrick, NY - 12/30/54; Model 705-PGC; Serial # L-5169 - Additions to this pumper after delivery included two Mars 888 Lights on the roof of the cab, a radio speaker for the pump operator on the running board and breathing apparatus in each of the jump seats.

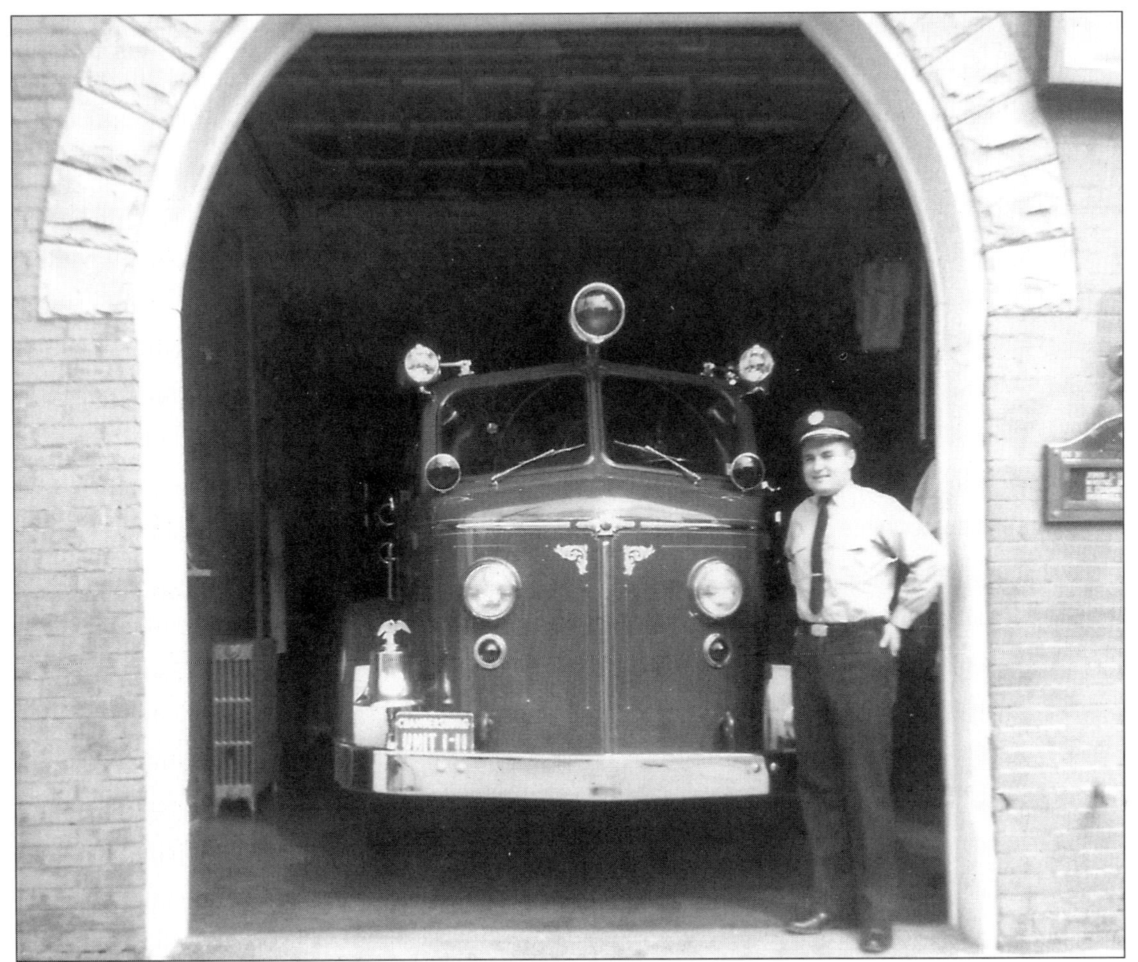

Borough of Chambersburg, PA (Franklin Fire Co.) - 12/28/54; Model 775-PJO-H; Serial # L-5163 - 'Normal' people try to have their picture taken next to some famous celebrity; in the Fire Service, you try to get your picture taken next to some famous fire truck. Here, Jackson H. Gerhart poses with Chambersburg's 1954 700 Series Pumper back in 1962. Jack stated that this unit was delivered by rail to Chambersburg to await acceptance testing. Jack also shared that this pumper, at a cost of $16,430.00, replaced an older 1923 American LaFrance 600 GPM Pumper.

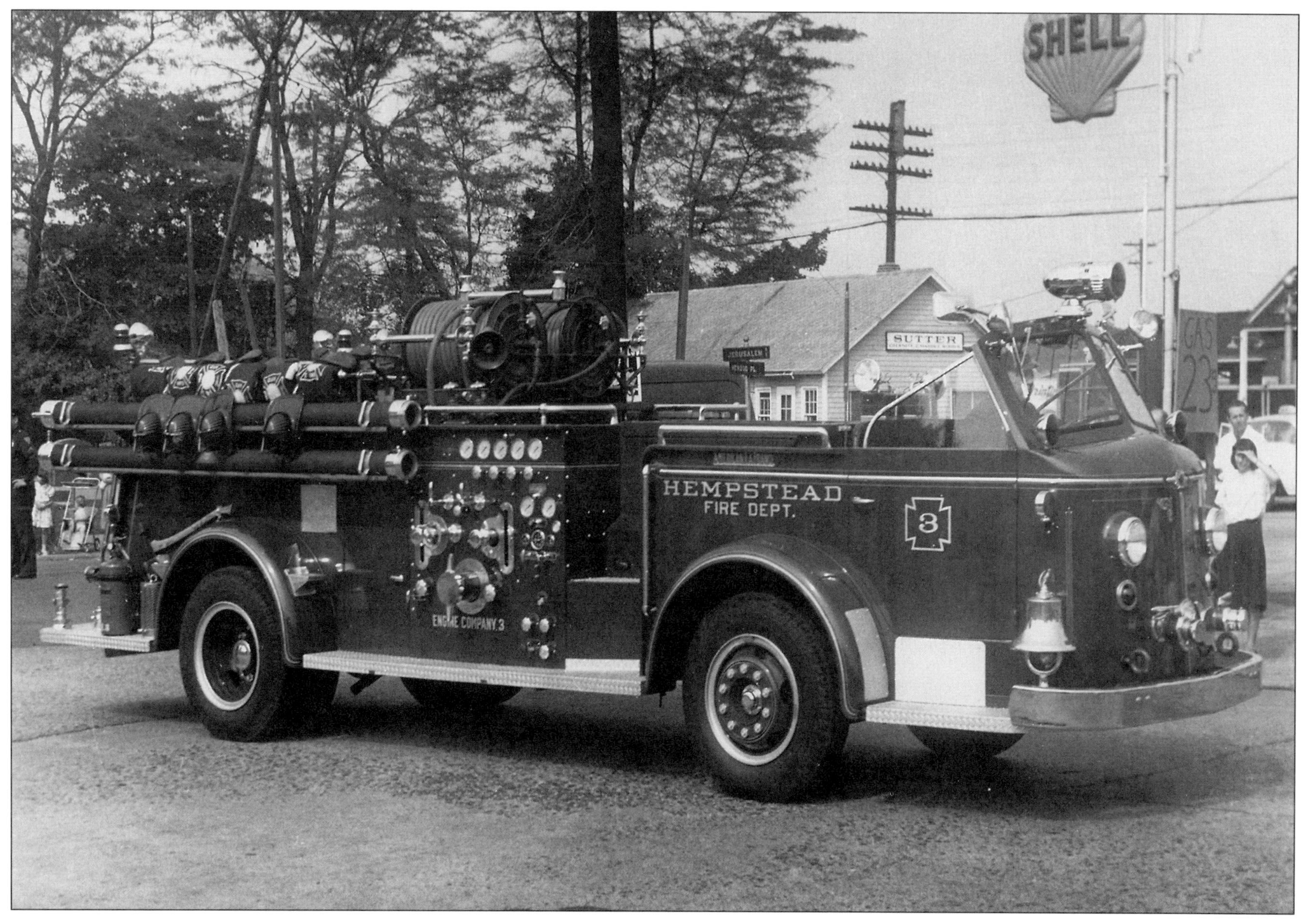

Hempstead, NY - 03/30/55; Model 775-PJO-H; Serial #L-5212 - Hempstead went back to American LaFrance again for additional pumpers, and this is one of them. Note the unusual twin gated auxiliary suction inlets just above the front bumper.

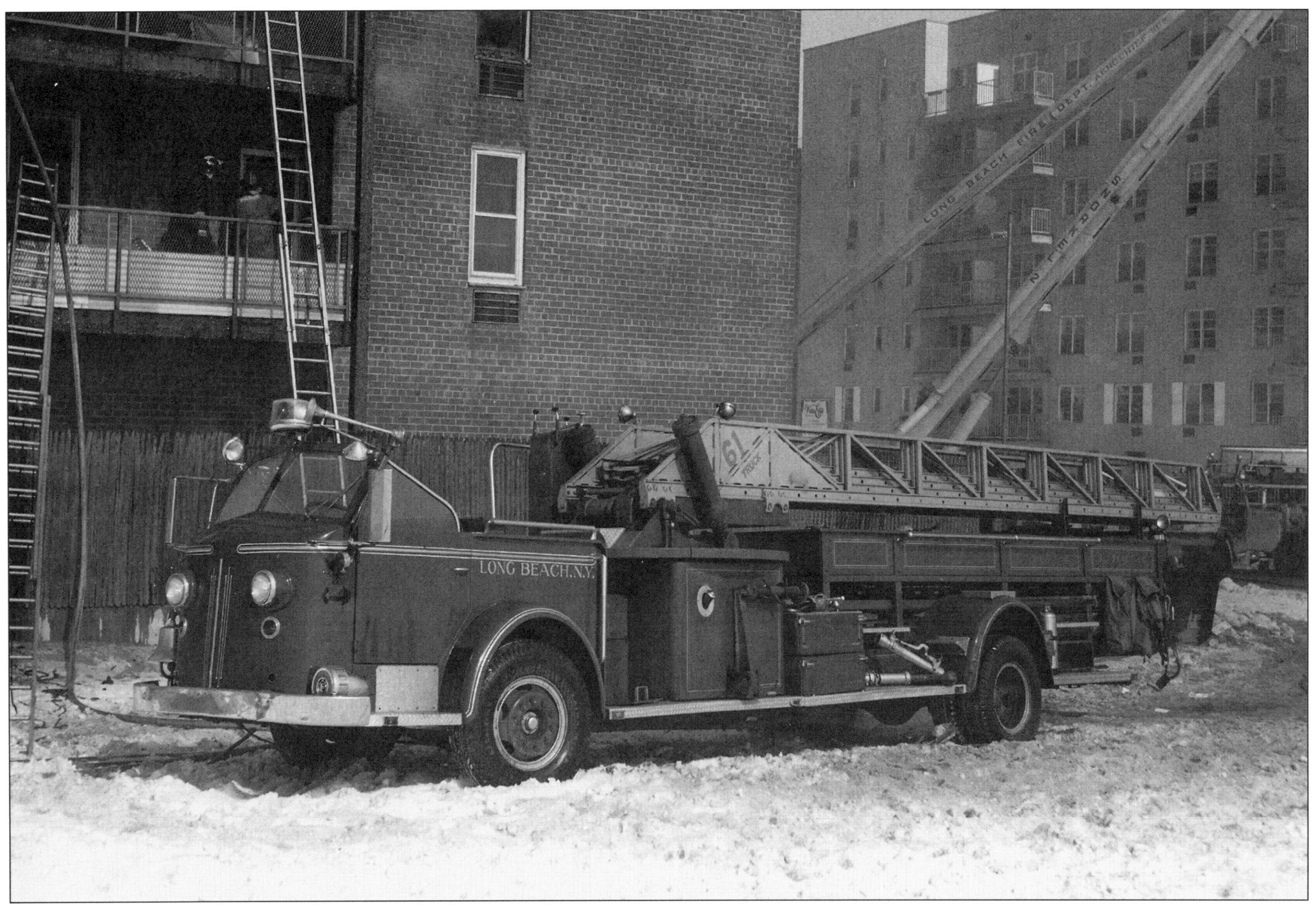

Long Beach, NY - 02/25/55; Model 7-100-AEO; Serial # 9393 - Long Beach, NY was an avid American LaFrance customer. This winter fire scene shows their 700 Series Aerial Ladder in position, ready to be raised if necessary. If you look closely, you can see the boom of their 90' Aero Chief working in the background.

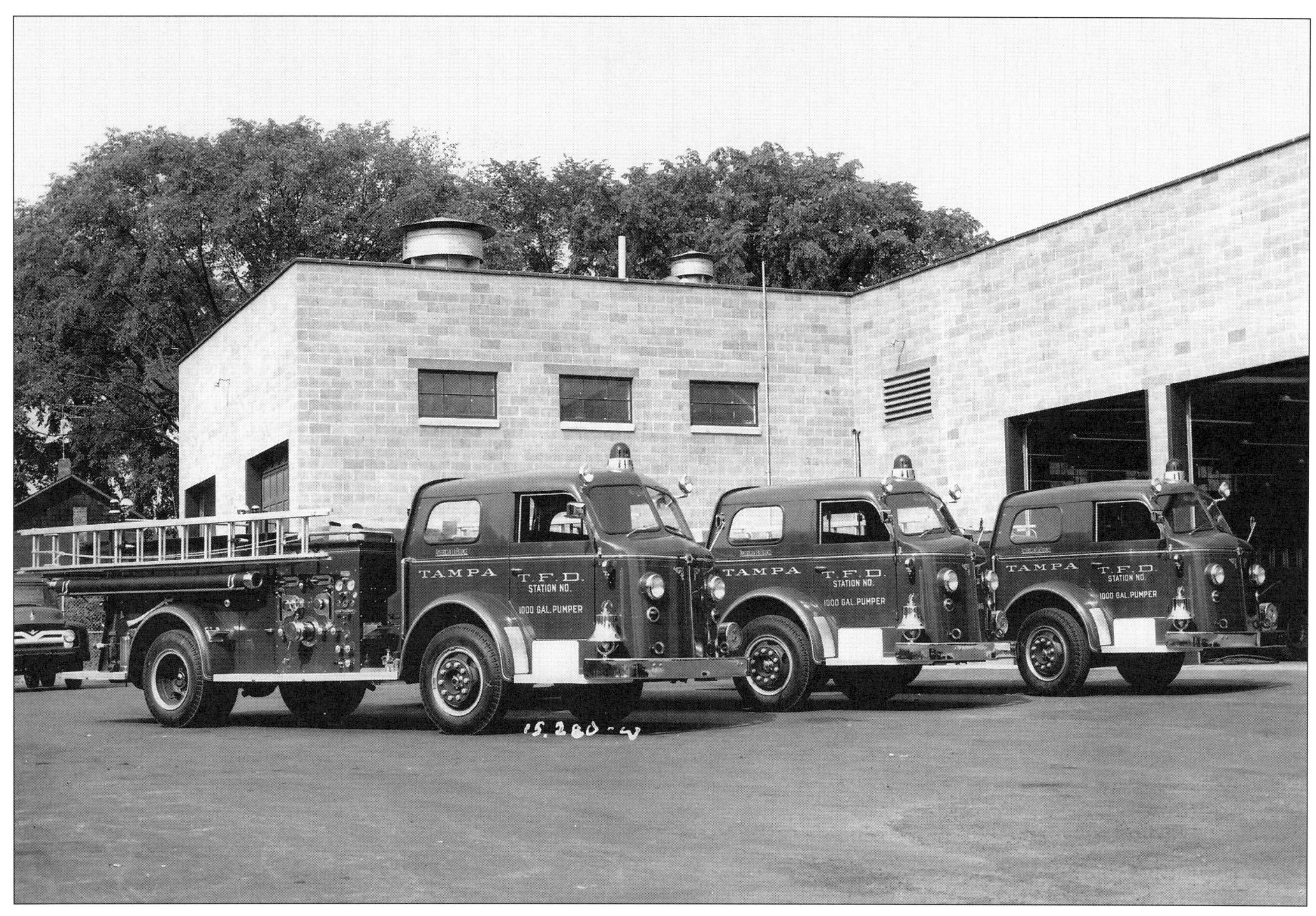

Tampa, FL - 06/30/55; Model 710-PJC; Serial #'s L-5254 through L-5256 - Tampa purchased three 700 Series Pumpers in 1955, all with their rated pump capacity gold-leafed on each front door. In addition, the driver's side discharge valve control handles matched those on the officer's side.

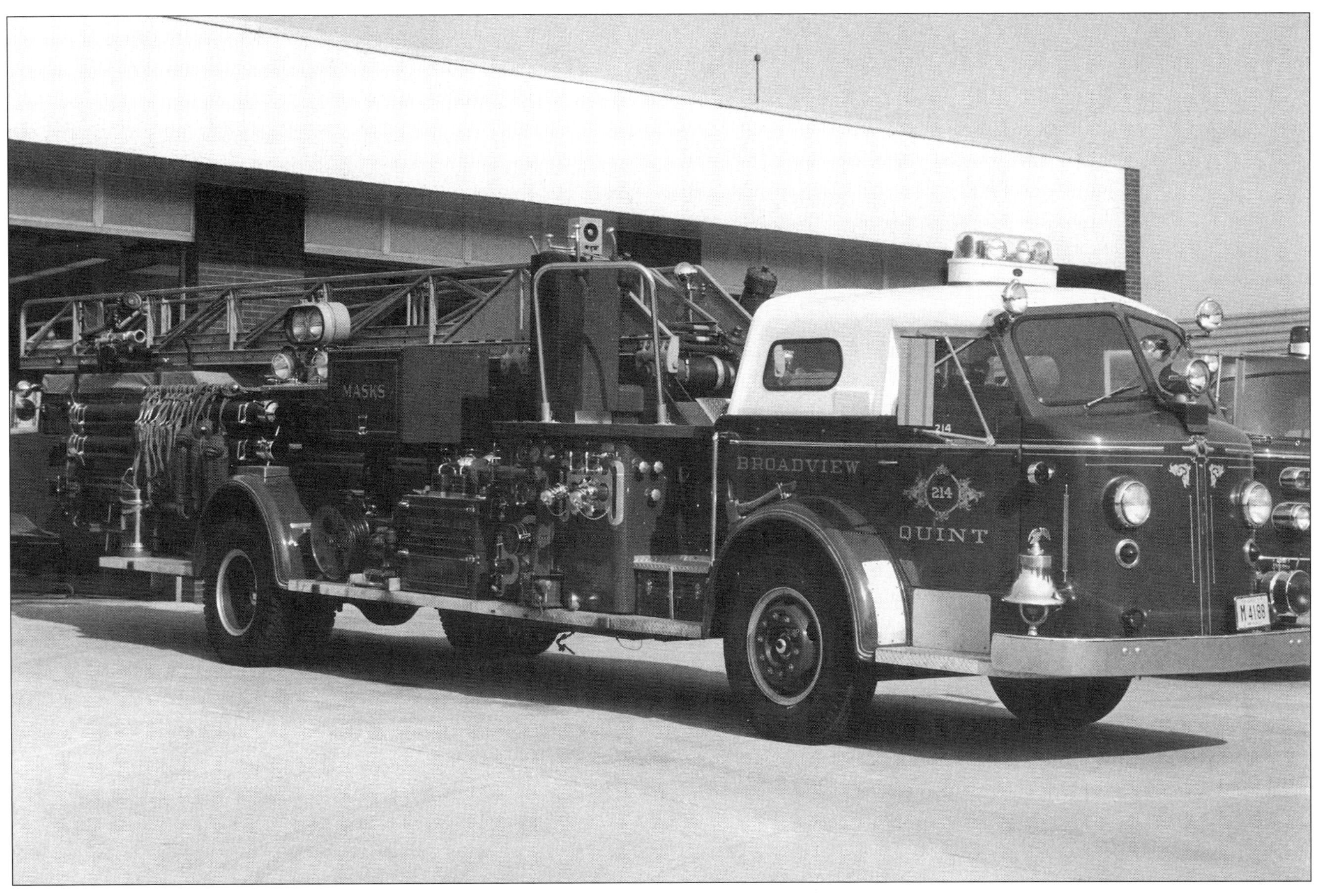

Broadview, IL - 11/28/55; Model 710-QEO-85; Serial # 9421 - Broadview's quint was loaded with just about everything you could think of, and then some. The white fiberglass top was an add-on, made in the mid-1970s by Witten's in California. It was made available nationally through the (then) American LaFrance Service Center in Burlingame, California at a cost of approximately $1,000.00.

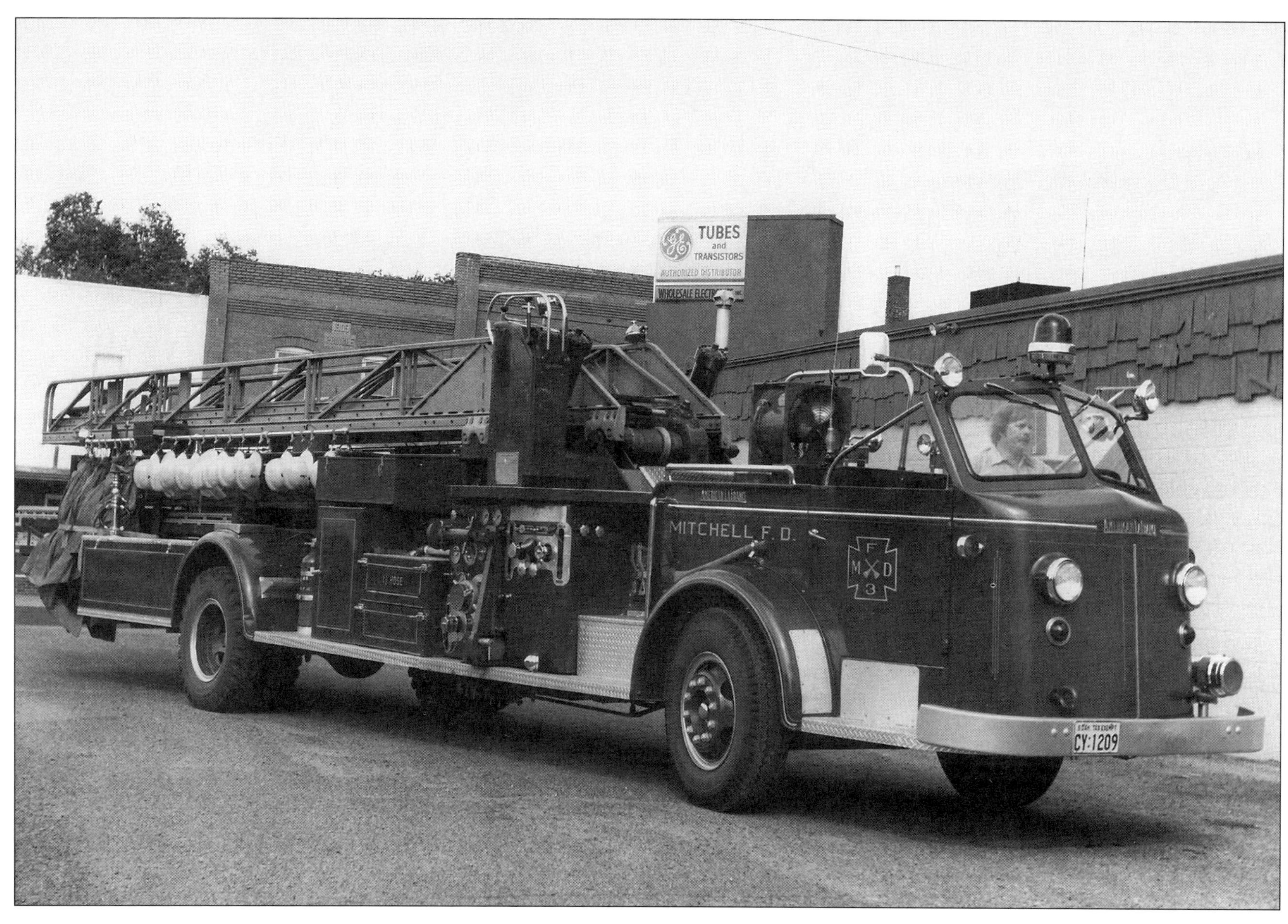

Mitchell, SD - 02/10/56; Model 710-QJO-85; Serial # L-5354 - Mitchell is a combination volunteer and paid fire department. The outside, exposed protective clothing on the side of the truck suggests that when this photograph was taken, the volunteers responded to the fire scene and dressed when they arrived.

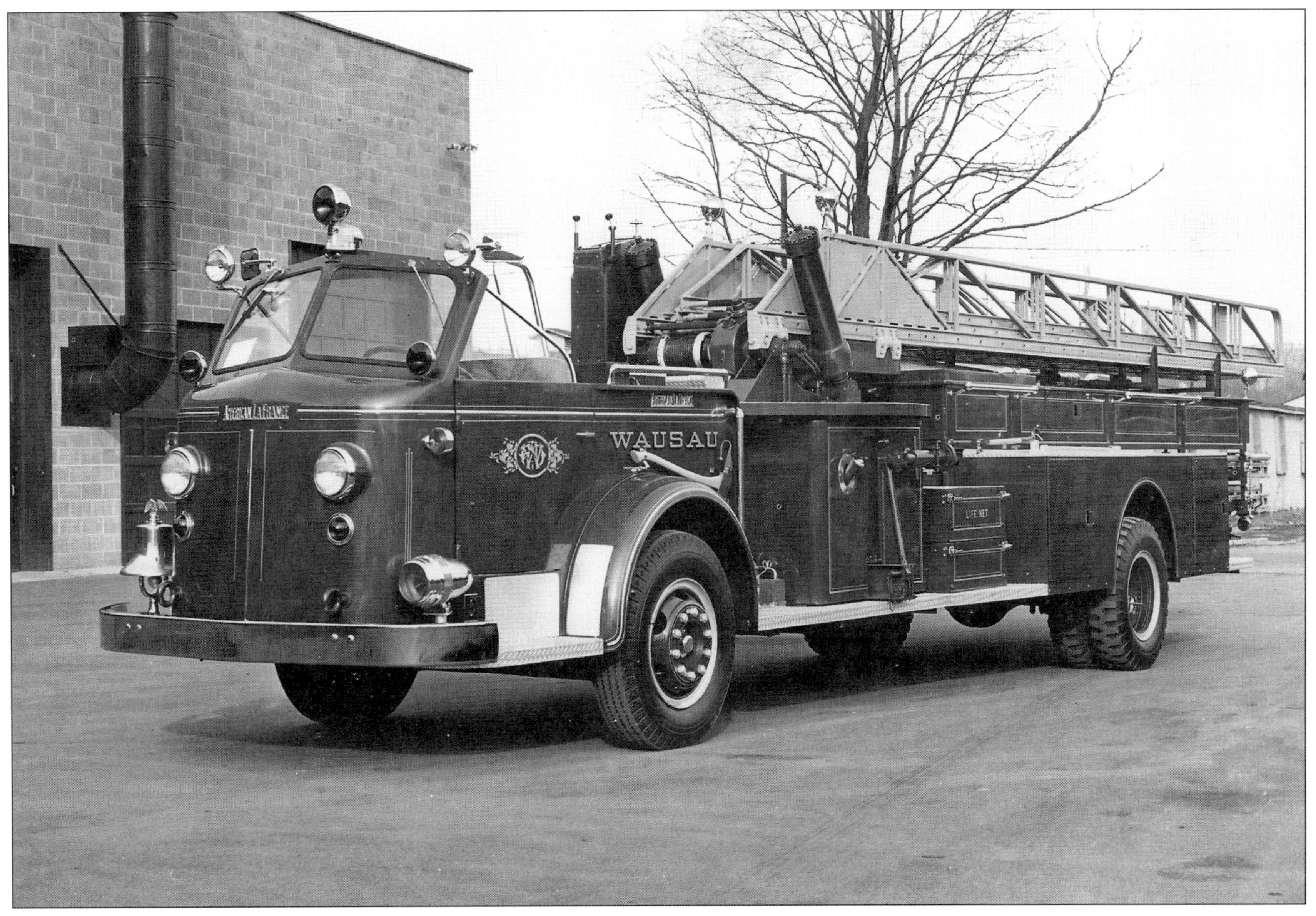

Wausau, WI - 01/16/56; Model 7-85-ALO; Serial # N-47 - In preparation for the upcoming American LaFrance 800 Series of fire apparatus, some of the pumpers and ladders would start showing up with full, rear compartmentation. Remember, however, just the pumpers would receive the 800 Series designation. All other apparatus, like Wausau's Aerial Ladder, would go from the 700 Series straight to the 900 Series.

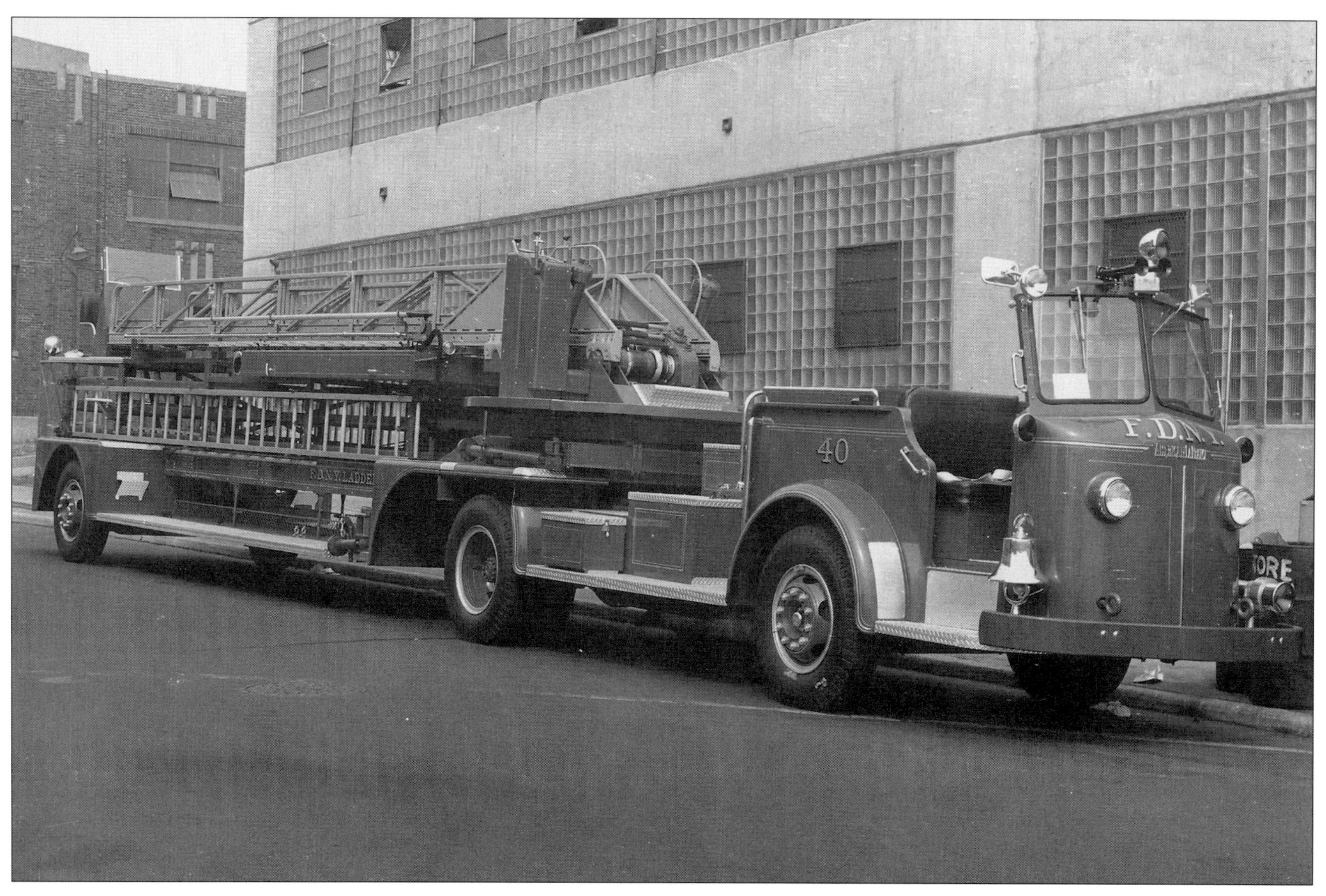

New York City, NY - 02/23/56 through 04/25/56; Model # 7-85-TLO; Serial #'s N-51 through N-61 - F.D.N.Y. purchased eleven of these, all with typical F.D.N.Y. Truck Company equipment. The raised and more 'forward' windshield frame made them really stand out from all other 700 Series apparatus ever produced. Truck #40 is a Manhattan (West Harlem) Company.

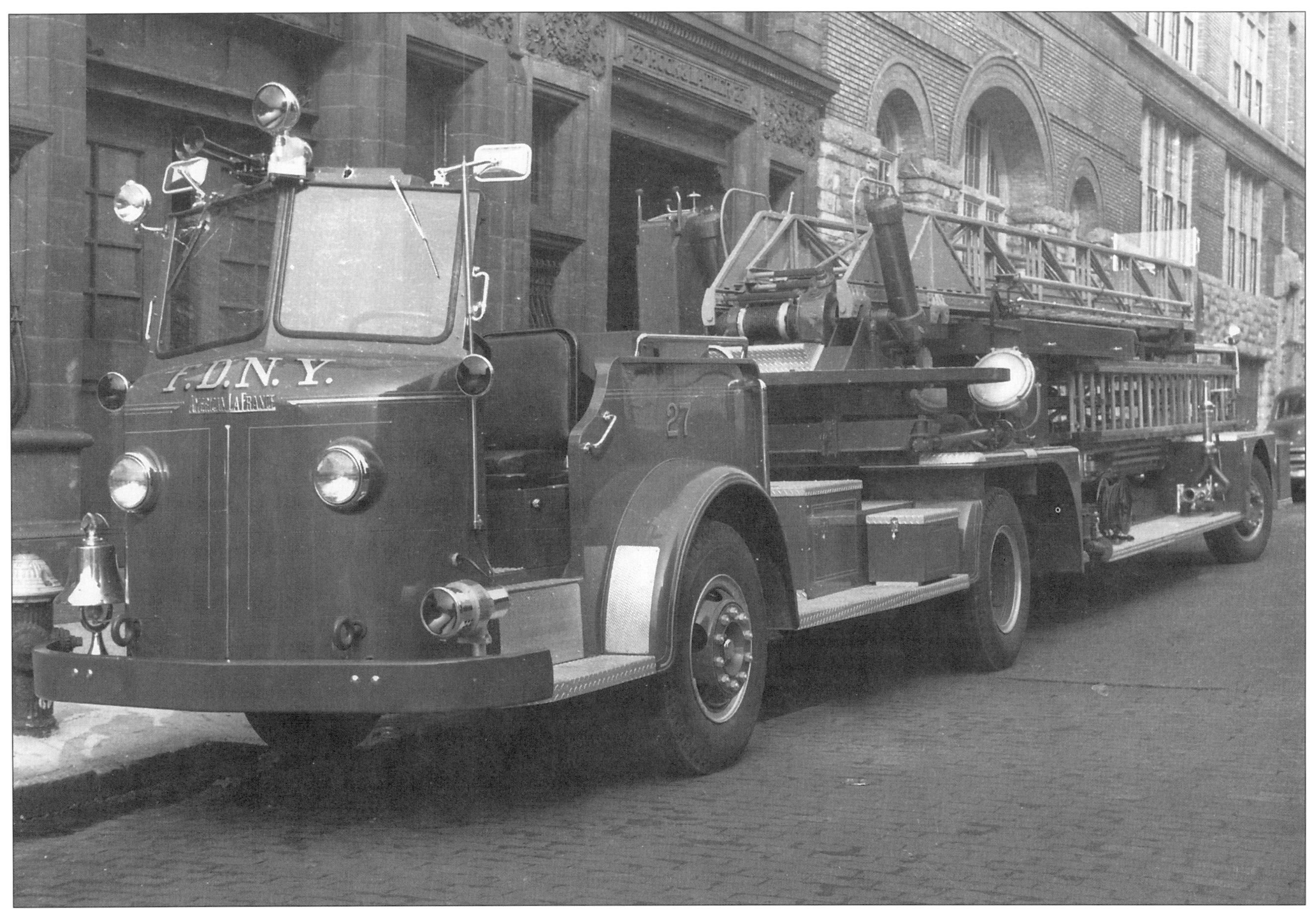

New York City, NY - 02/23/56 through 04/25/56: Model # 7-85-TLO; Serial #'s N-51 through N-61 - Besides the difference of the raised windshields, other F.D.N.Y. 'firsts' included factory installed electric/air horns above the windshield next to the Mars light and a driver's side front step mounted flashing siren light. Truck # 27 is a Bronx Company.

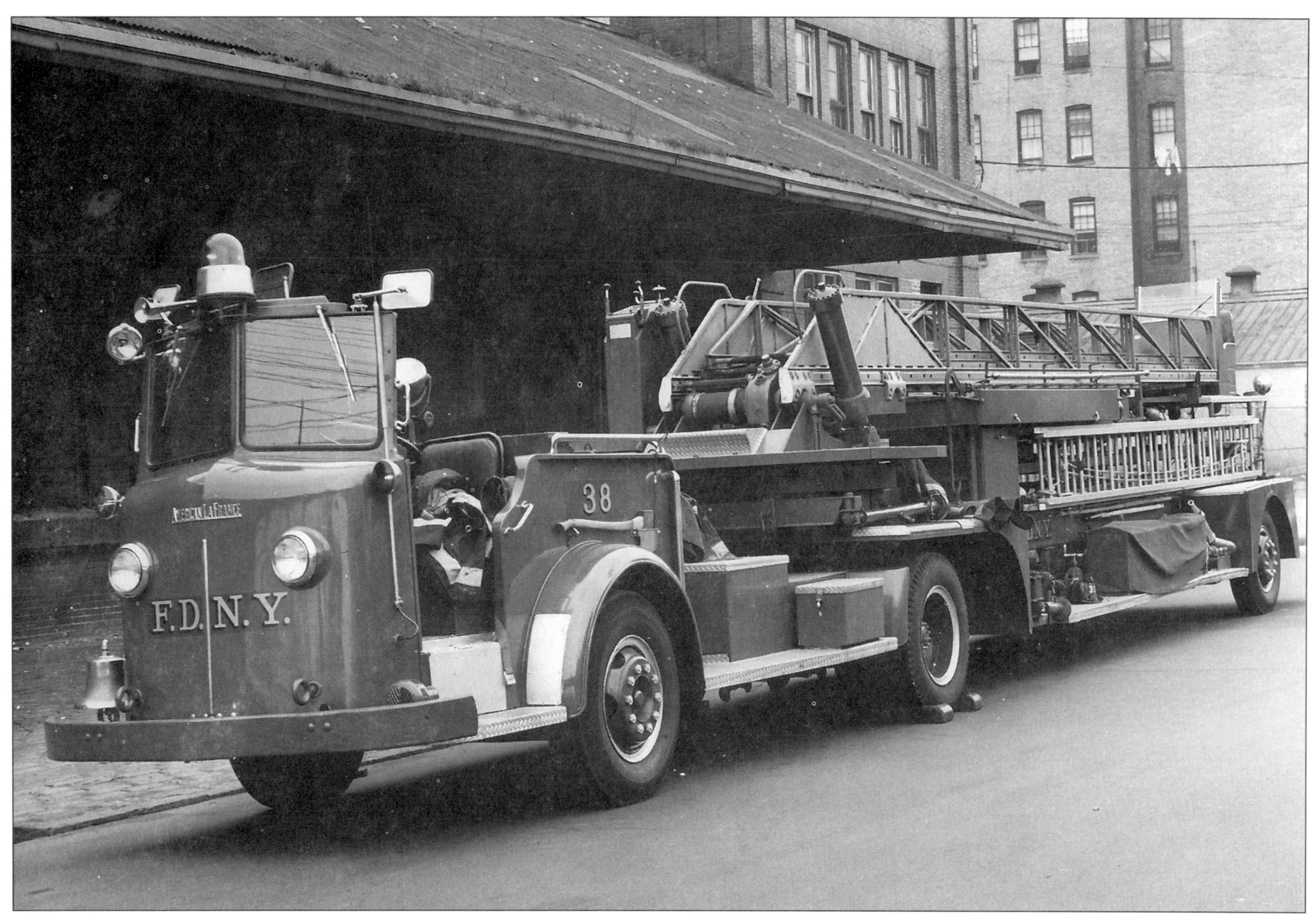

New York City, NY - 02/23/56 through 04/25/56: Model # 7-85-TLO; Serial #'s N-51 through N-61 - After being repainted by the F.D.N.Y. shops, Truck #38's original Mars Light was replaced by a Federal Model 17 Beacon Ray. Truck # 38 is in the Bronx. Original F.D.N.Y. Truck Company assignments for the eleven pieces went to Truck #'s 1; 3; 18; 27; 40; 42; 47; 107; 108; 120; and 127. Truck #1's rig eventually ended up with FDNY's Division of Training.

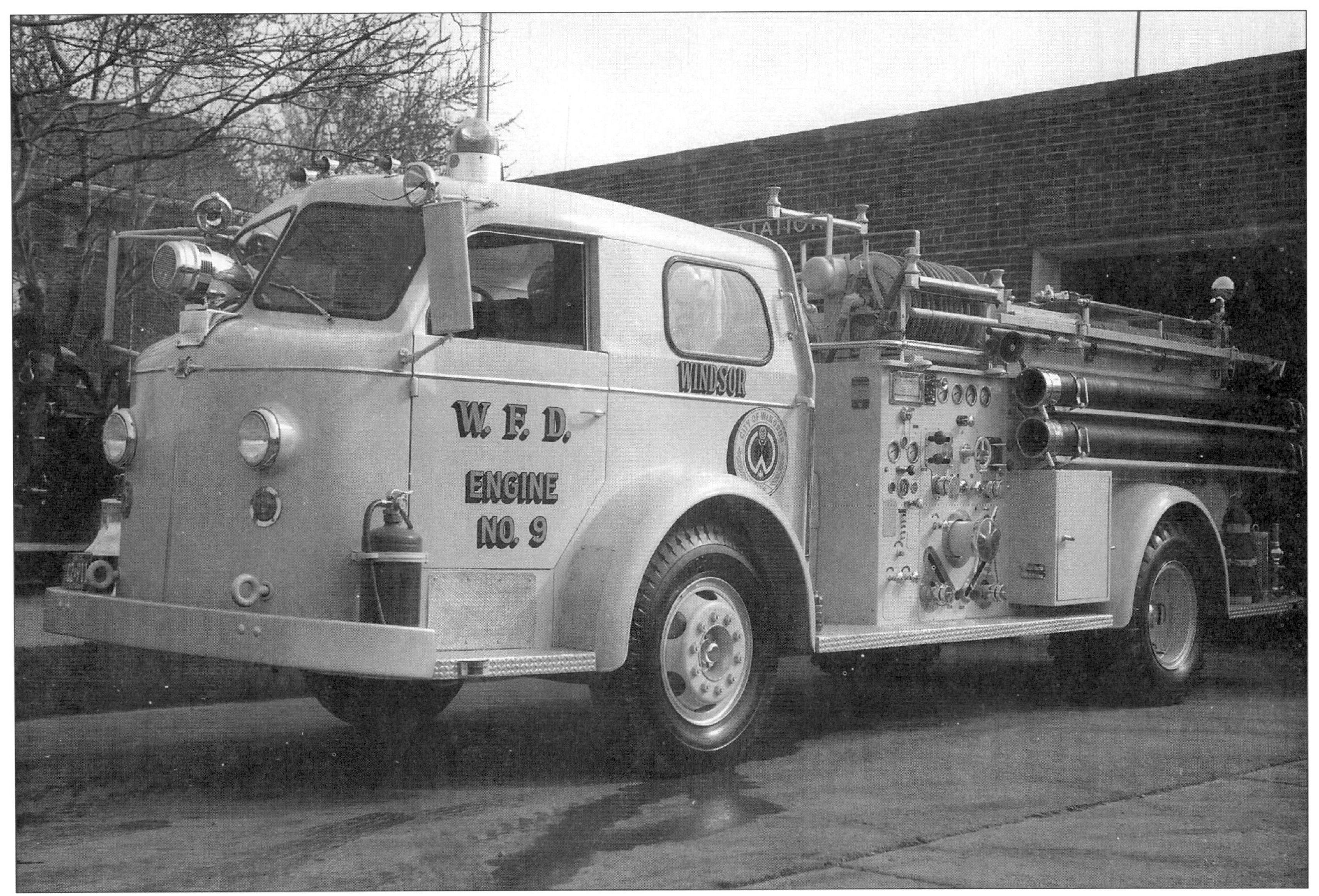

Windsor, Ontario, Canada - 02/29/56; Model # 710-PJC; Serial # L-5323 - Originally purchased by Riverside, Ontario, this 840 IGPM pumper with a 400 gallon water tank was repainted from factory red to lime green. In addition, the original factory motor was replaced with a Ford 534 CID V-8.

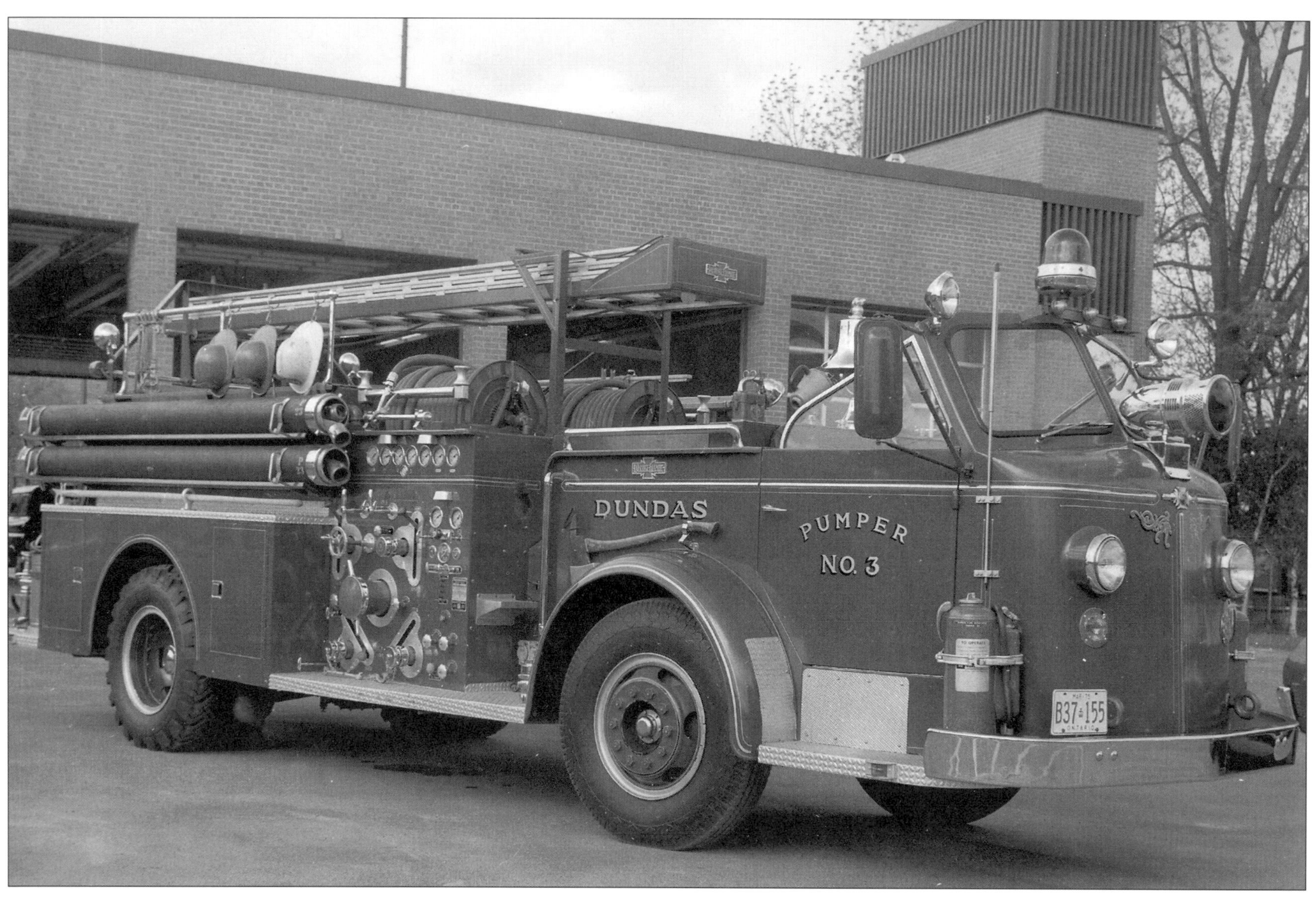

Dundas, Ontario, Canada - 02/24/56; Model 710-PJO: Serial # L-5317 - Some new standard features (including full rear compartmentation) were starting to be included on what could be called 'late' 700 Series Pumpers. The overhead ladder rack was stock from the factory. Due to the location of the dual Ansul Cartridge Fire Extinguishers just ahead of each front step, the Sterling Model 30 Siren was mounted on the cab's nose while the bell (with the Canadian Beaver instead of the American Eagle) wound up, centered, just above and behind the front seat.

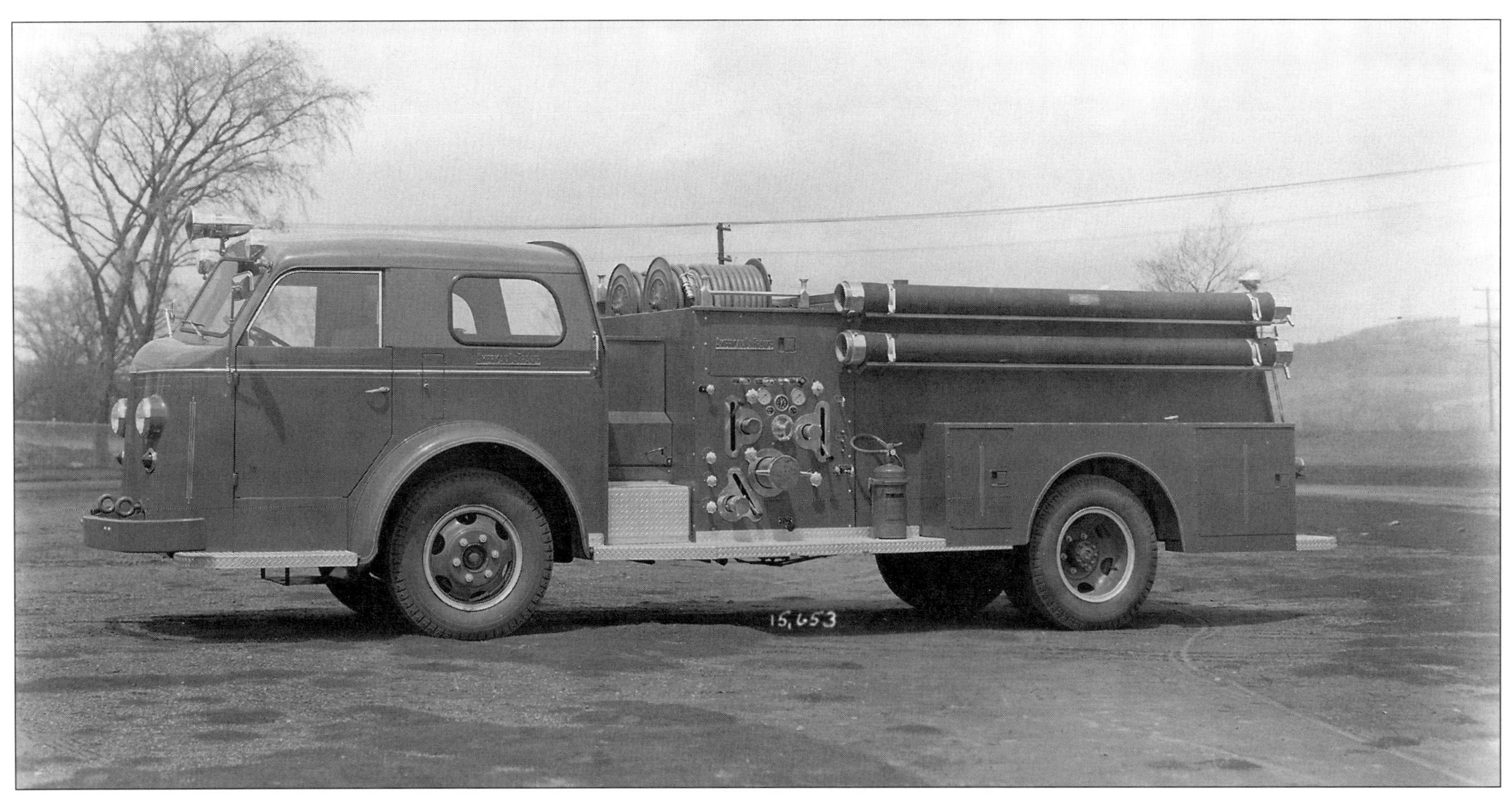

American LaFrance Sales Car - 04/00/56; Model 800 Series Demo - Serial # Not Recorded - Even after extensive research by several fire apparatus historians, not much information could be located about this particular piece of apparatus. It is believed to be one of the first, if not the first, 800 Series Pumpers built for American LaFrance evaluation. While keeping the highly recognized and accepted 700 Series body style design, the most radical change was the relocation of the pump panel from the officer's side to the driver's side.

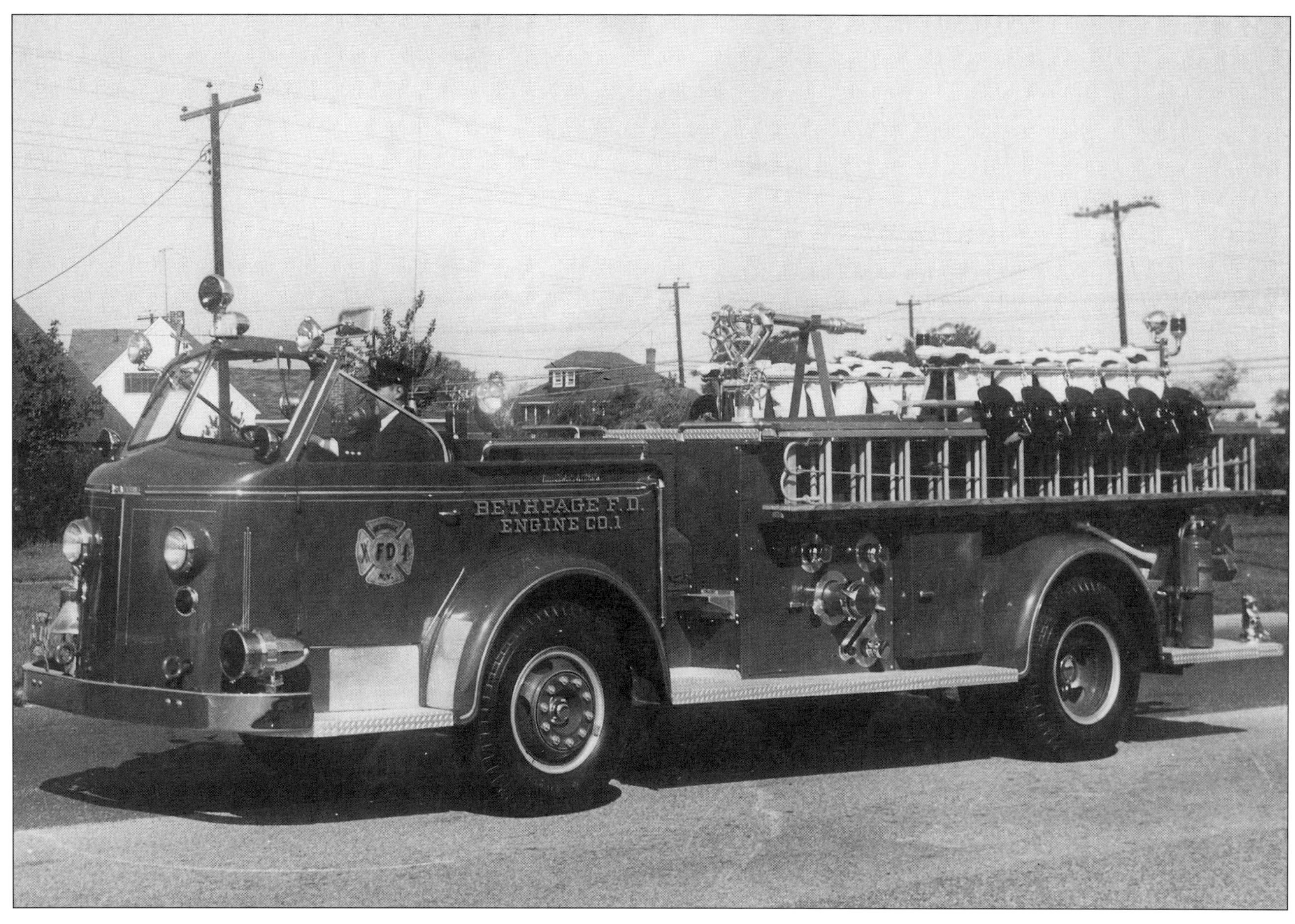

Bethpage, NY - 04/26/56; Model 710-PJOH; Serial #'s L-5389, L-5390 - The F.D.N.Y. influence is easy to spot on these 700 Series Pumpers. Bethpage had (and still has) a number of F.D.N.Y. career firefighters on their volunteer department who helped draw up the specs for these. Both of these pumpers appear on the book's cover, together, in full color, while assigned to Engine Company # 5.

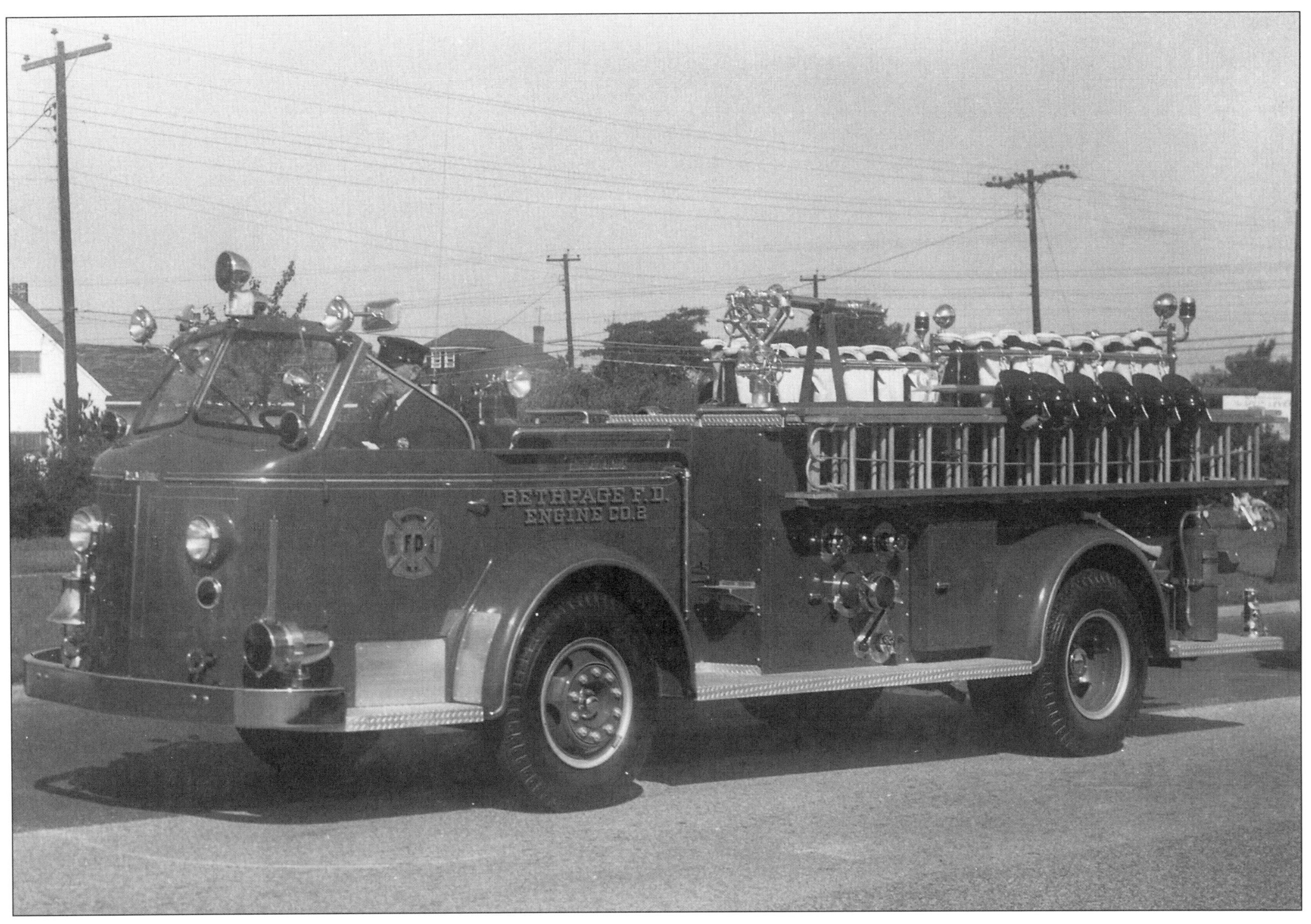

Bethpage, NY - 04/26/56; Model 710-PJOH; Serial #'s L-5389, L-5390 - These 700 Series Pumpers were assigned to Engine Company #'s 1 and 2. They were equipped with 1,000 GPM pumps and 300 gallon water tanks. Although the protective clothing was mounted on the rig, Bethpage firefighters geared up in the Firehouse (and still do) before rolling out.

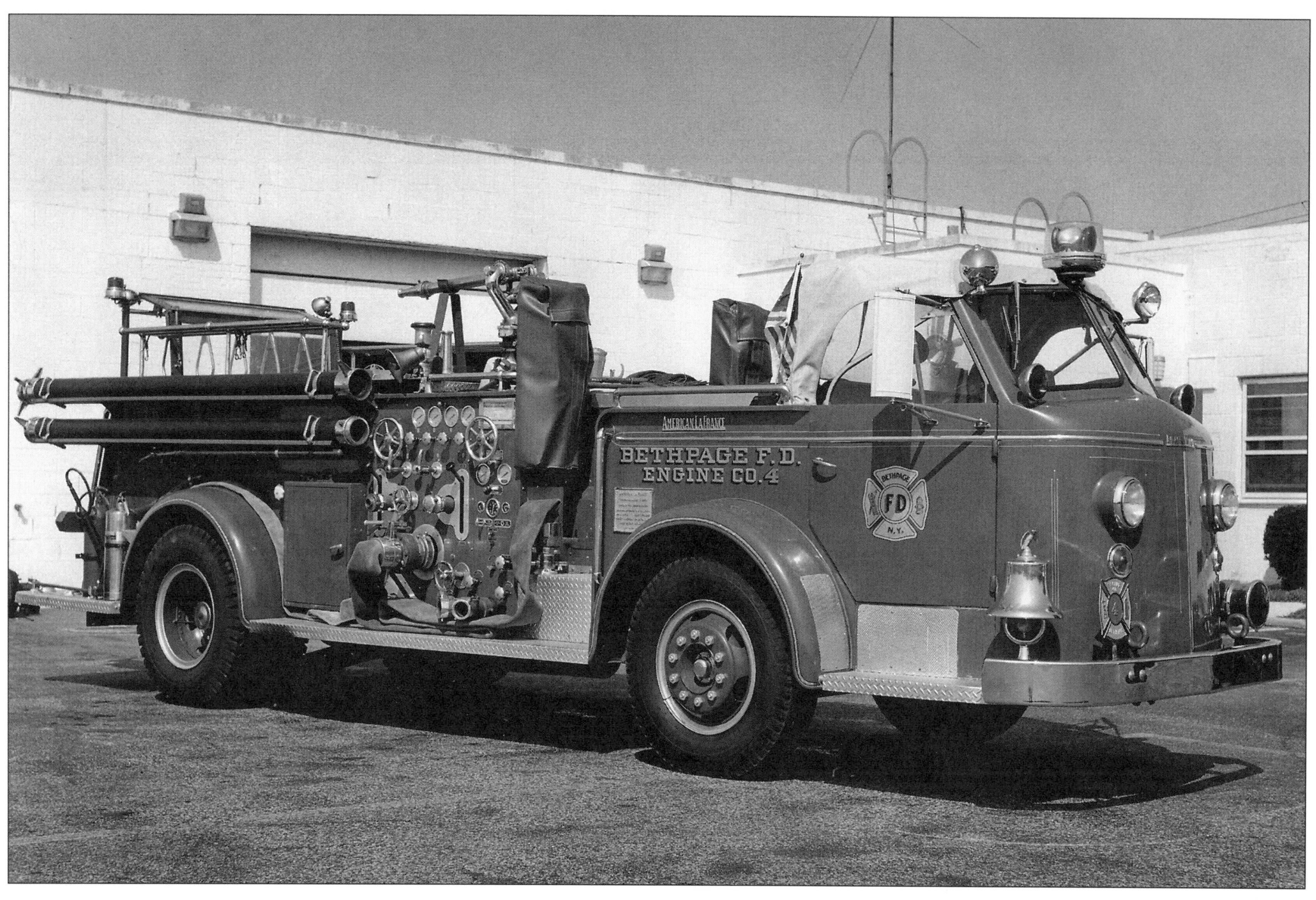

Bethpage, NY - 04/26/56; Model 710-PJOH; Serial #'s L-5389, L-5390 - Both Bethpage's 700 Series Pumpers led quite a life, serving in Engine Company #'s 1, 2, 4, and 5. While in service at Company #4, this half of the 'twins' sported a protective canvas cab top; west coast mirrors; air masks mounted in the jump seats; preconnected master and auxiliary suction lines, and a rear windshield. A Dietz 'Over/Under-White/Red' 4-Beacon Light replaced the factory installed Mars Light over the windshield.

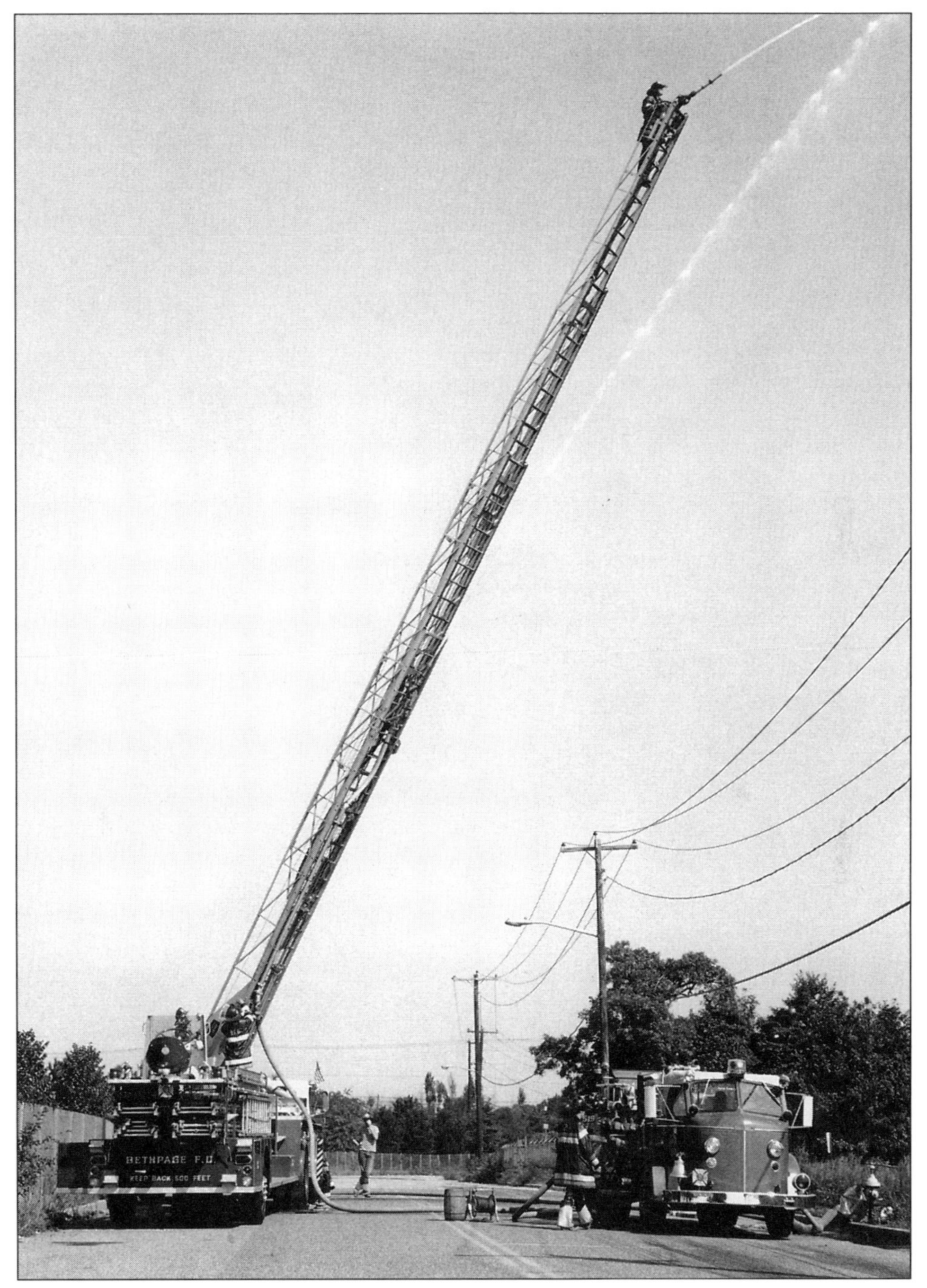

Bethpage, NY - 04/26/56; Model 710-PJOH; Serial #'s L-5389, L-5390 - In this photograph, one of Bethpage's 700 Series Pumpers provides the ladder pipe water supply for Bethpage Ladder # 3, a 1969 100' Maxim TDA. Both of Bethpage's 700 Series Pumpers were re-powered with Detroit Diesels during their long careers with the department.

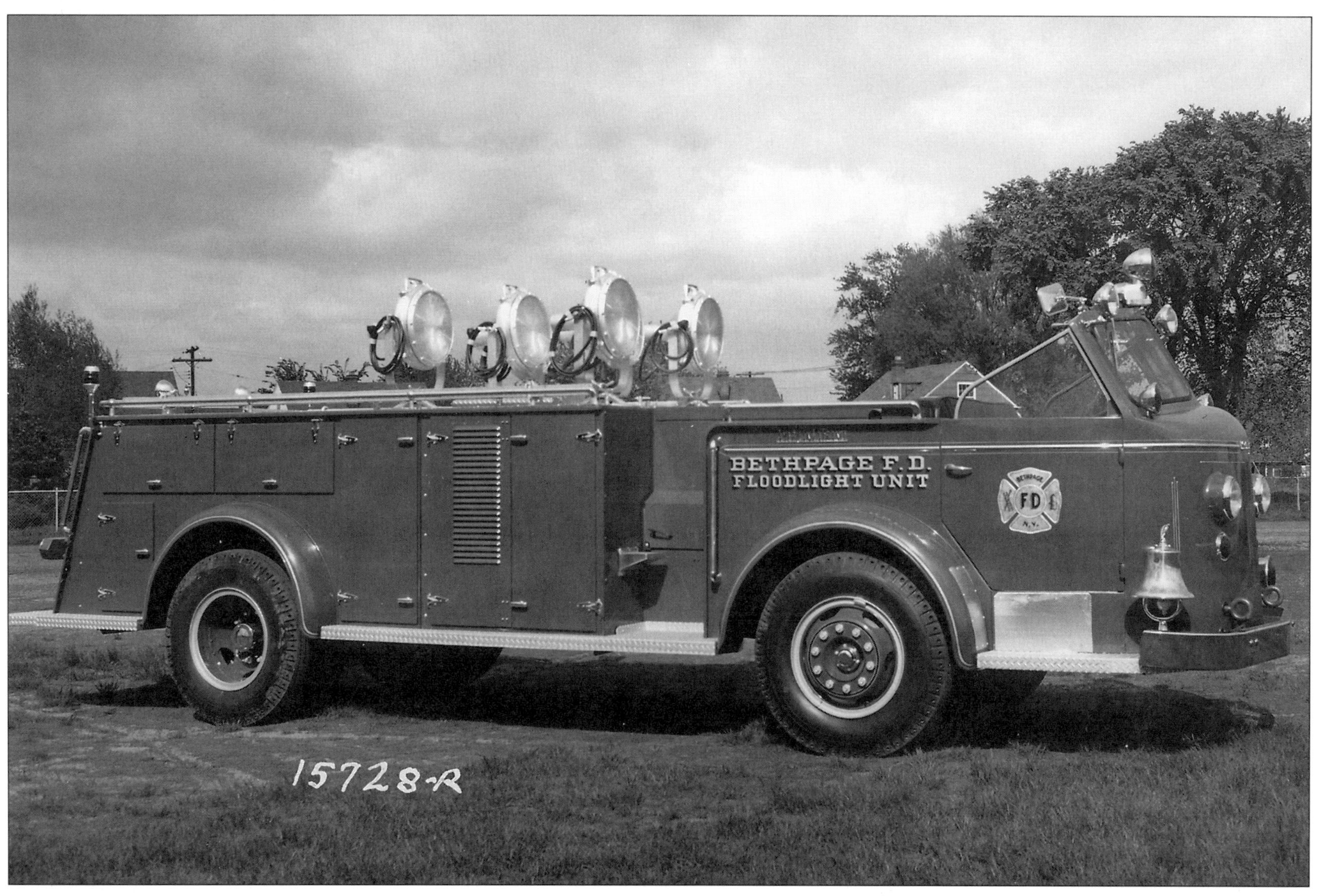

Bethpage, NY - 05/28/56; Model 700-JO-SQUAD; Serial # L-5401 - Bethpage took the distinctive body style of the previously built Toronto, Ontario, Canada, and Hyattsville, MD, Squad Units and added to it by installing six large floodlights on the top deck. The power came from the generator located immediately beneath them; the air intake for the generator can be seen cut out in the louvered compartment door in the center of the rear body. The price for this rig was $22,000.00.

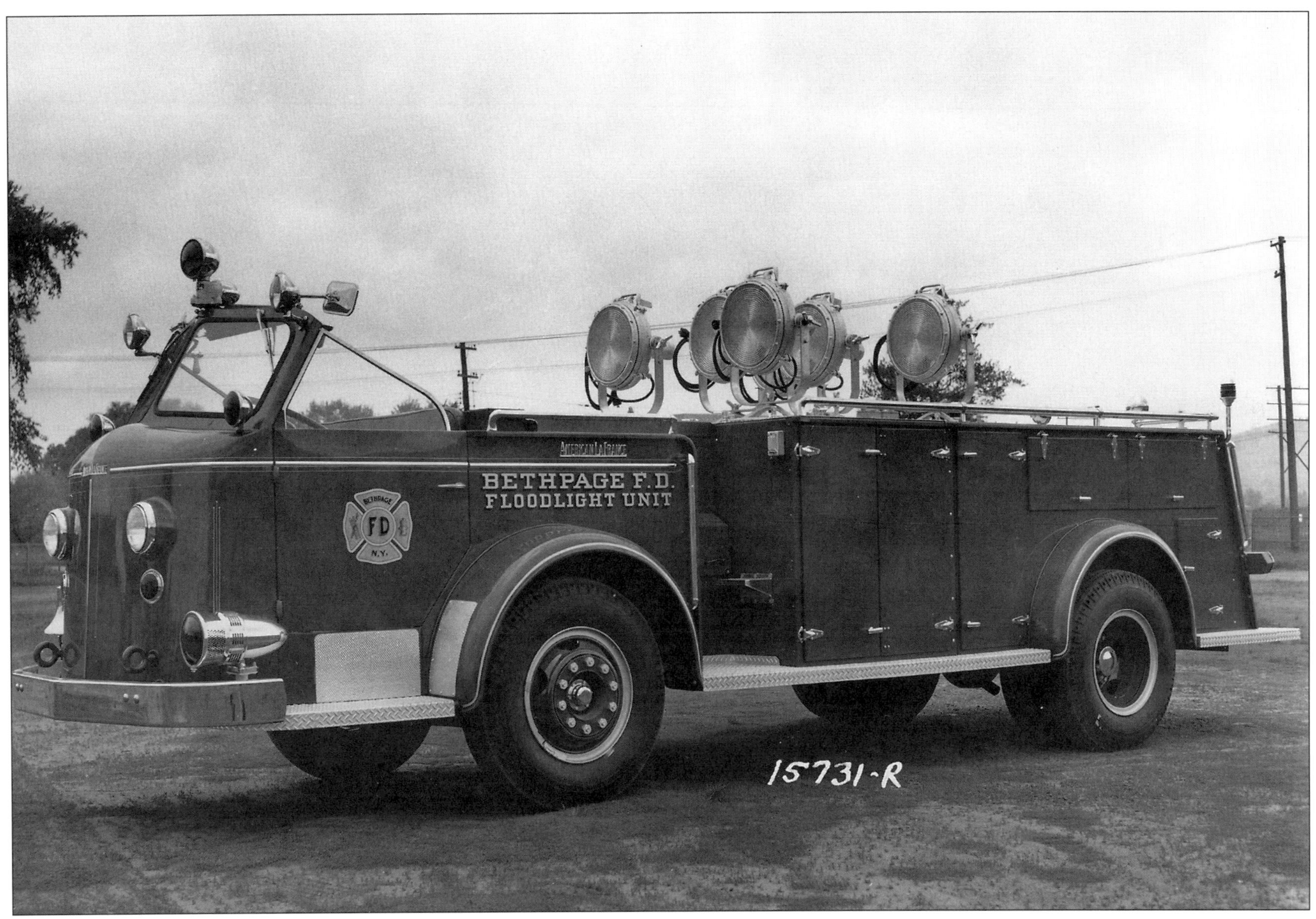

Bethpage, NY - 05/28/56; Model 700-JO-SQUAD; Serial # L-5401 - The main power switch box for the top deck mounted floodlights can be seen on the back of the jump seat wall, just ahead of the first vertical rear body compartment door. When not used for assisting at night fires or where auxiliary power was needed, the Floodlight Unit was used to transport extra needed firefighters to daytime fire scenes.

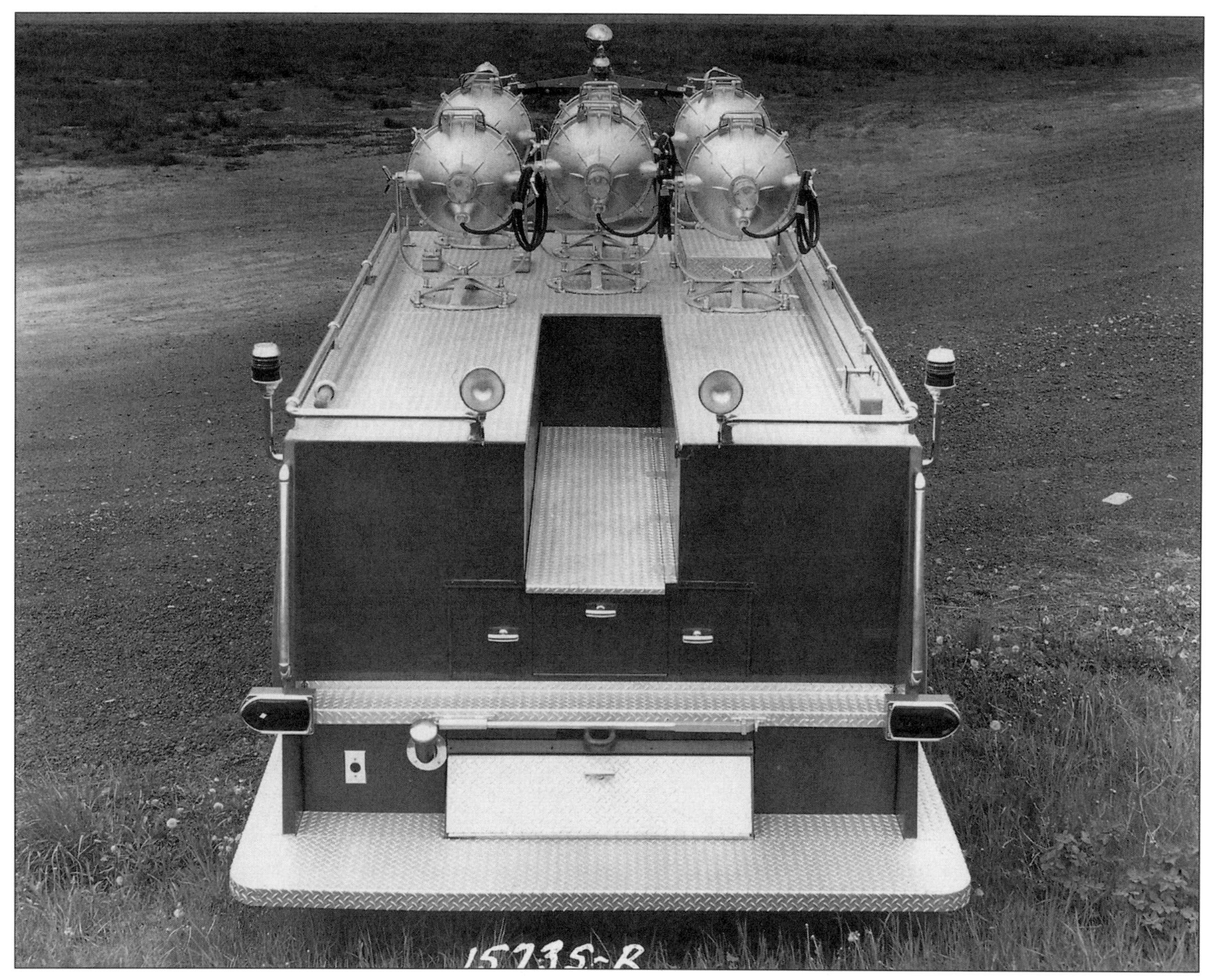

Bethpage, NY - 05/28/56; Model 700-JO-SQUAD; Serial # L-5401 - A pike pole was mounted on the upper left side of the rear body while a folding attic ladder was mounted on the right. The Floodlight Unit was assigned to Bethpage's Truck Company and ran as Nassau County, NY, Unit # 9013. Note the fold-down door covering the compartment where the booster reel would normally be located on a 700 Series Pumper.

Bethpage, NY - 05/28/56; Model 700-JO-SQUAD; Serial # L-5401 - The Kohler Company (established back in 1873) of Kohler, WI, supplied the internal power plant for the Bethpage Floodlight Unit. Kohler used the Bethpage truck in their national advertising, and promoted the truck in their booth at the International Association of Fire Chiefs Annual Conference held at Grand Rapids, MI.

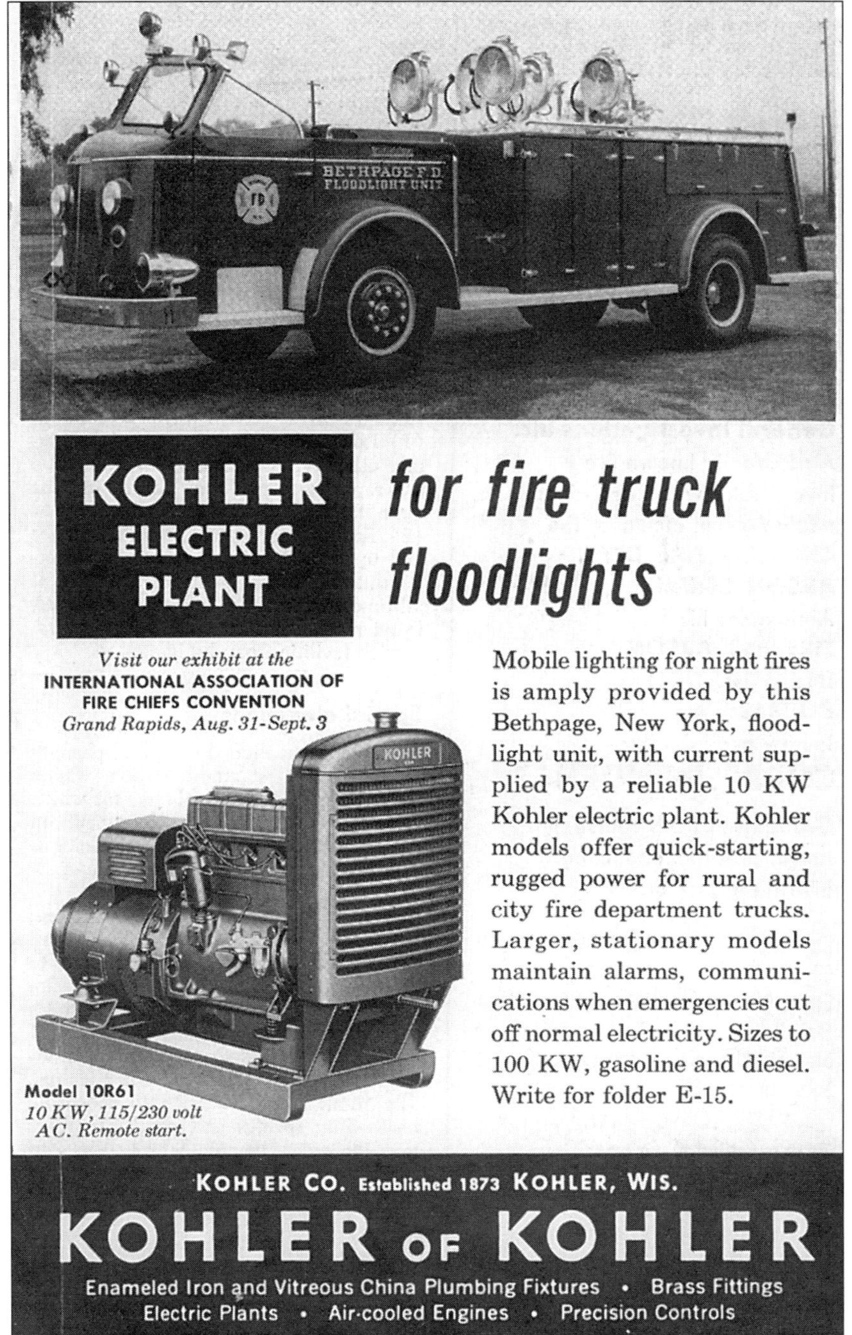

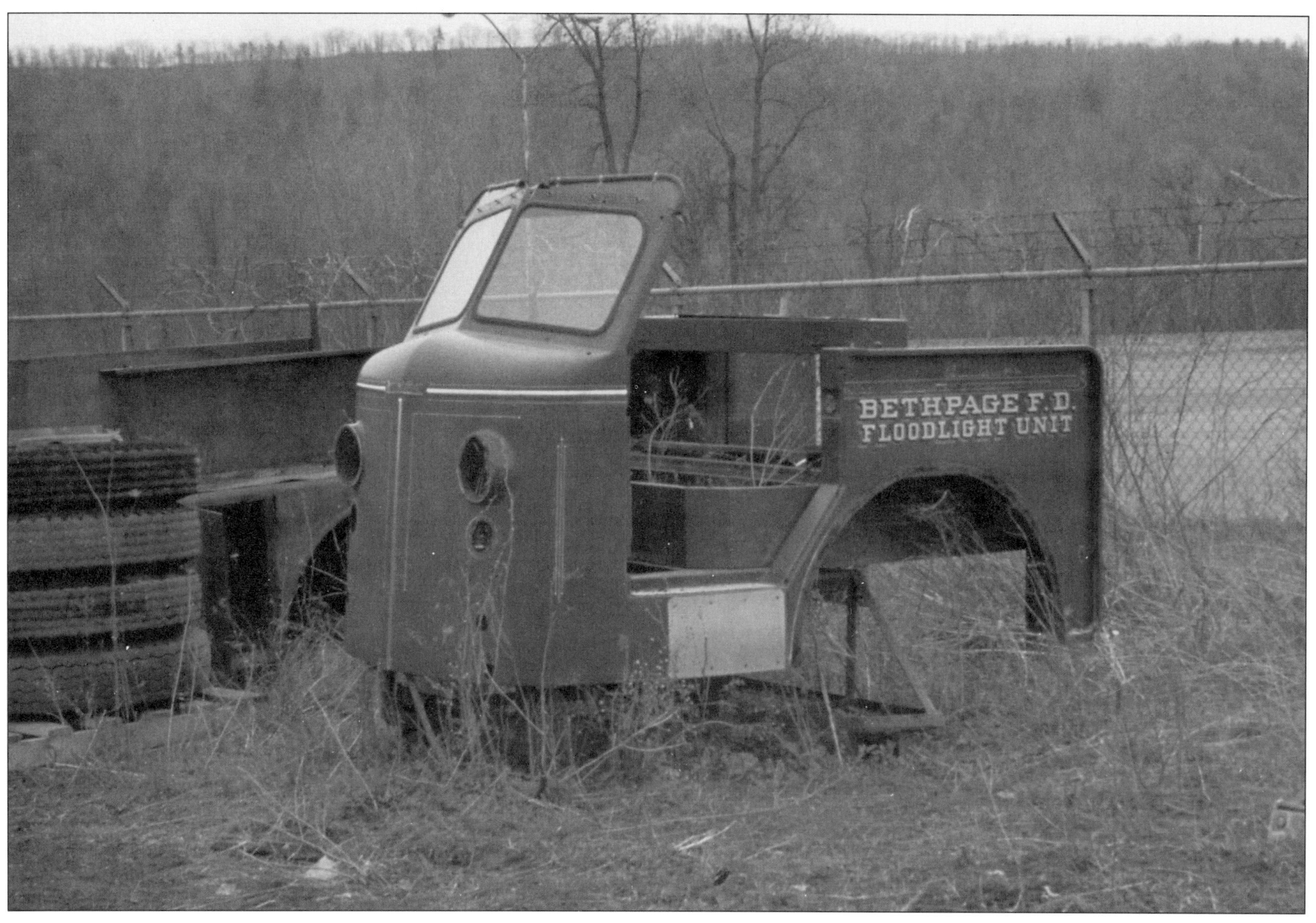

Bethpage, NY - 05/28/56; Model 700-JO-SQUAD; Serial # L-5401 - Taken amongst the weeds at the American LaFrance factory at Elmira, the original factory cab from the Bethpage Floodlight sits on an 700 Series cab frame support which was used to move cabs down the assembly line. Bethpage sent the Floodlight back to Elmira in 1974 for a complete rehab at a cost of $22,400 which included a new 1000 Series closed cab.

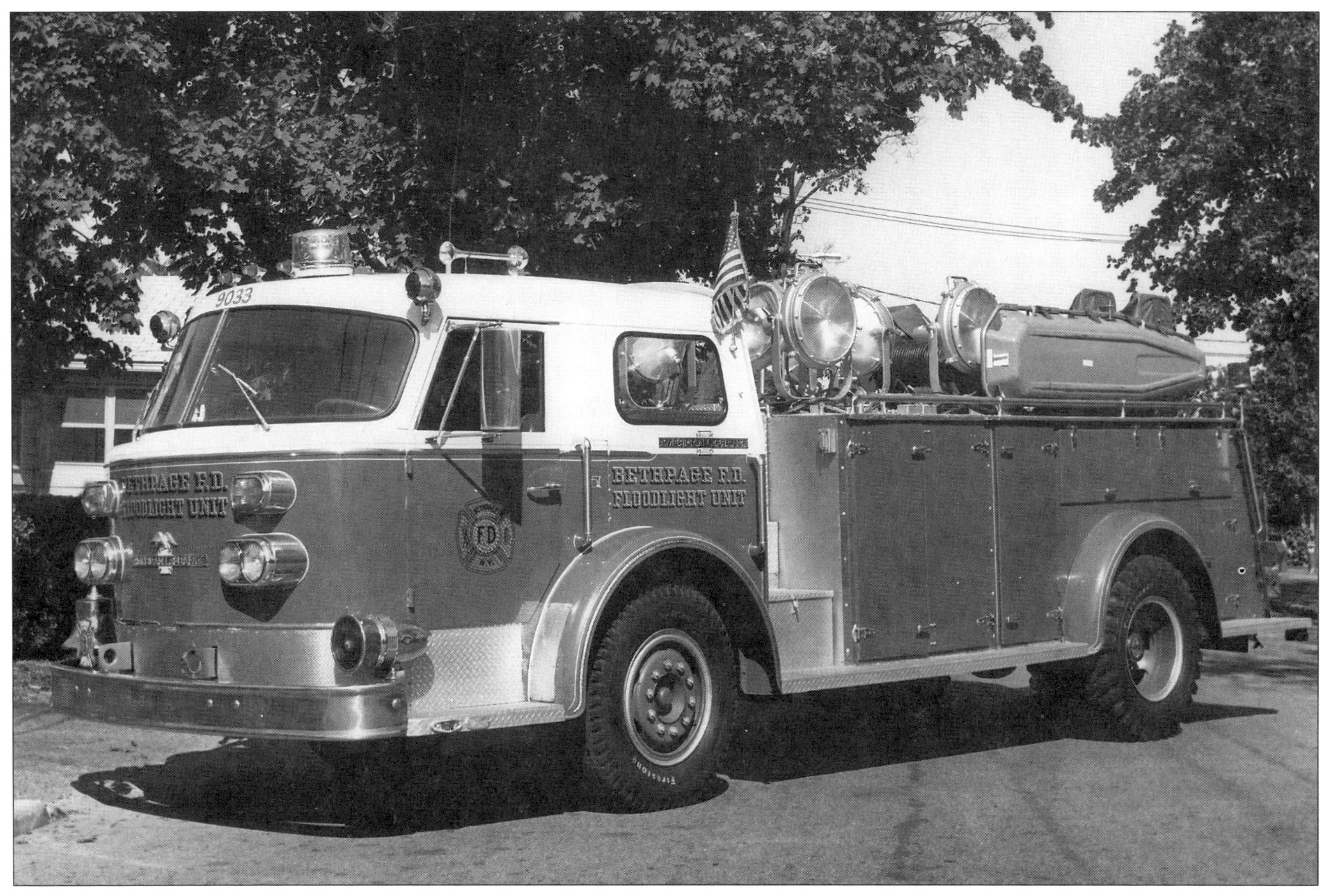

Bethpage, NY - 05/28/56; Model 700-JO-SQUAD; Serial # L-5401 - Now back from Elmira and sporting a 1000 Series cab, the Floodlight Unit also received a Detroit Diesel Motor and an Allison Automatic Transmission. The rear body remained untouched except for the addition of rescue equipment which included a Stokes Basket. The county radio number was also changed from 9013 to 9033. This piece served Bethpage until 1991, when it was replaced by a Pierce Heavy Rescue with its own auxiliary power supply and floodlighting capabilities.

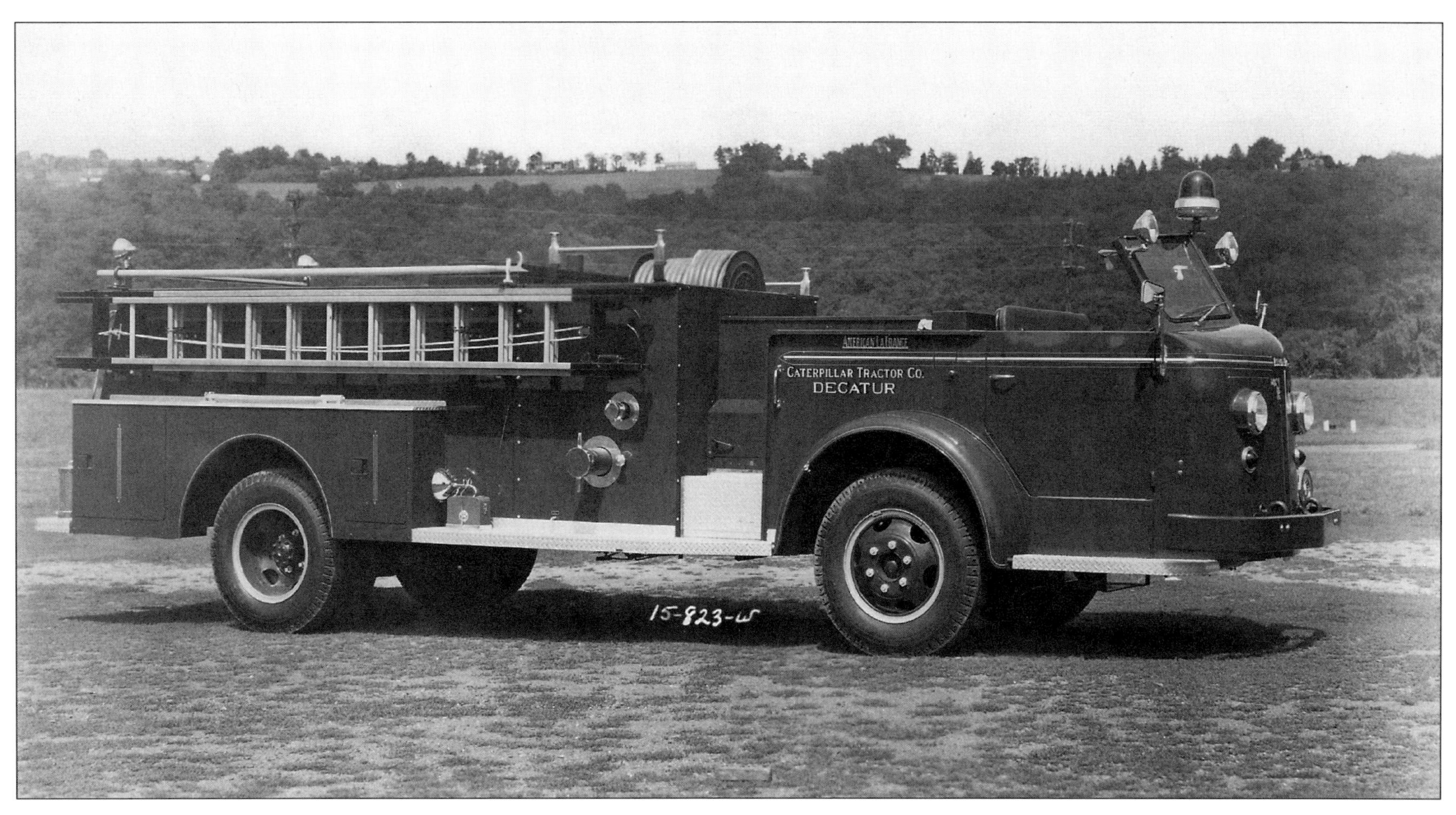

Caterpillar Tractor Co., DeCatur, IL - 07/23/56: Model C-775-PDO; Serial # N-132 - Built for the Caterpillar Tractor Company's private Fire Brigade, this was one of the first 800 Series Pumpers to come off the line.

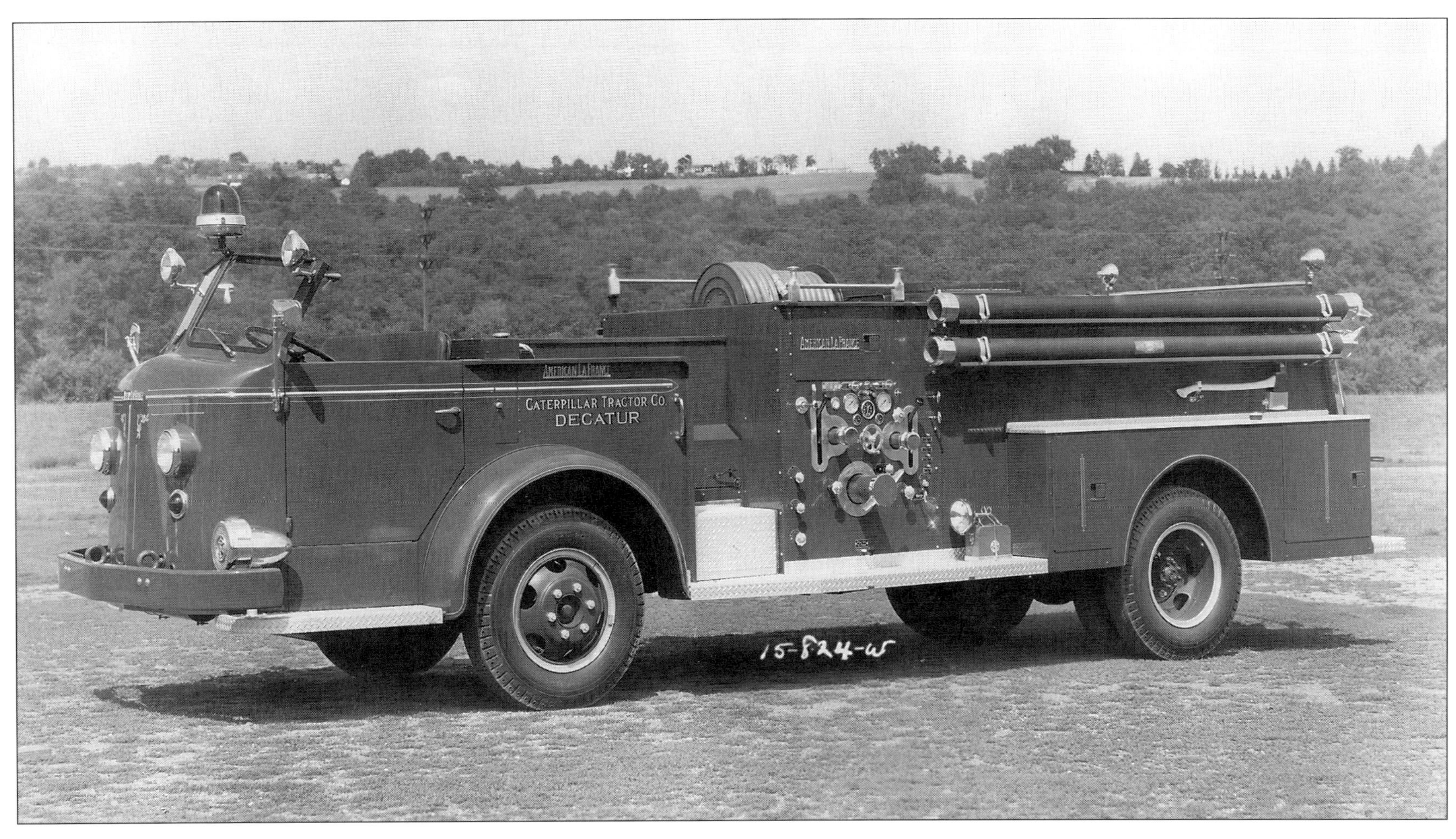

Caterpillar Tractor Co., DeCatur, IL - 07/23/56; Model C-775-PDO; Serial # N-132 - If you look long and hard, it doesn't take much to see the body design changes from the 700 Series to the 800 Series of pumpers. Amongst the obvious are the fully enclosed rear compartments, a raised front bumper, the two-way radio compartment located above the pump panel (behind the nameplate), and the pump panel change from the officer's side to the driver's side of the rig.

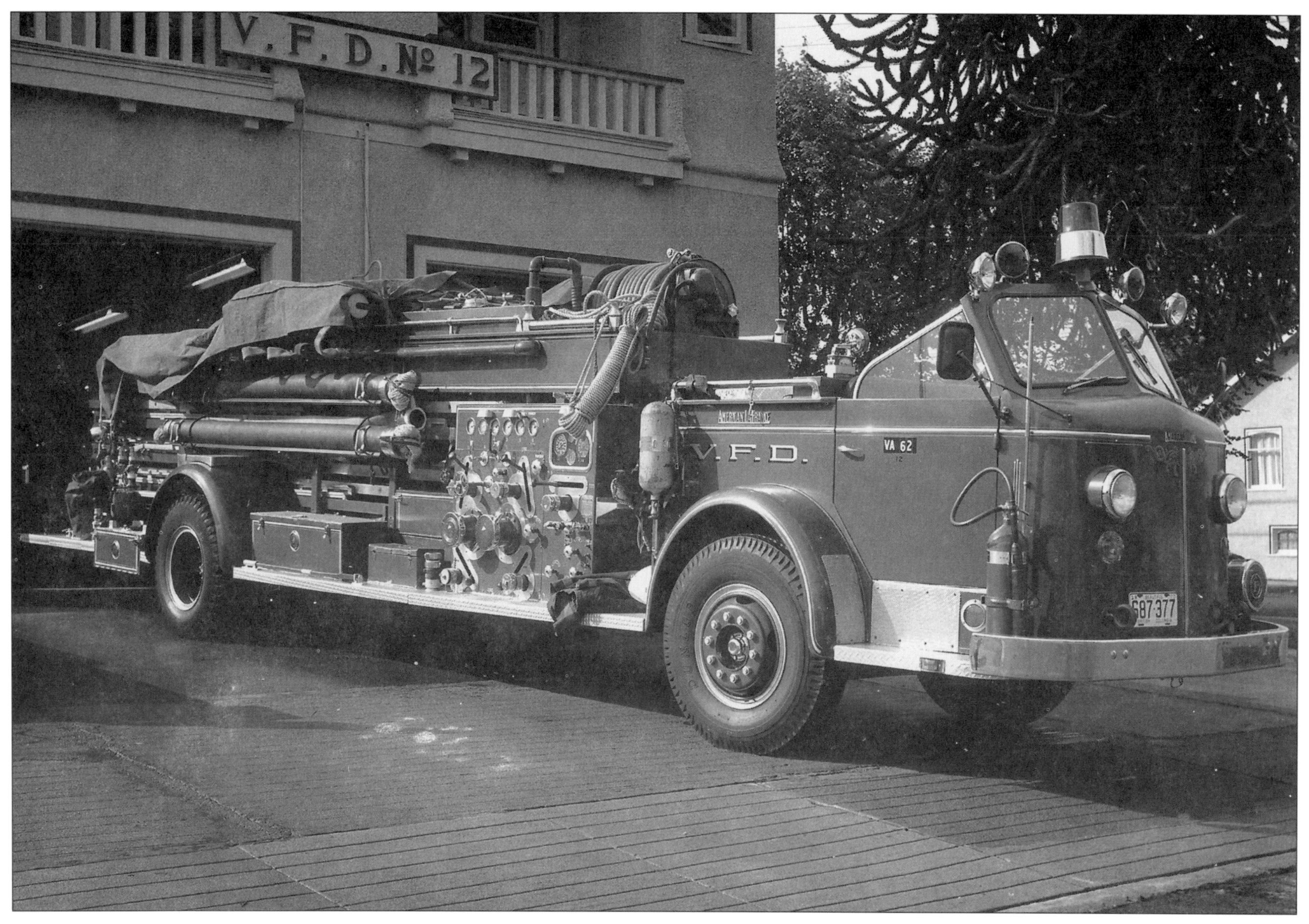

Vancouver, British Columbia, Canada - 08/30/56, 09/12/56; Model 715-PMO, Serial #'s N-96, N-97 - Vancouver ordered two of these Quads, each rated at 1250 IGPM (1500 GPM-US). Fire Department specifications for each Quad also required dual 6" intakes which were then wyed together into the pump.

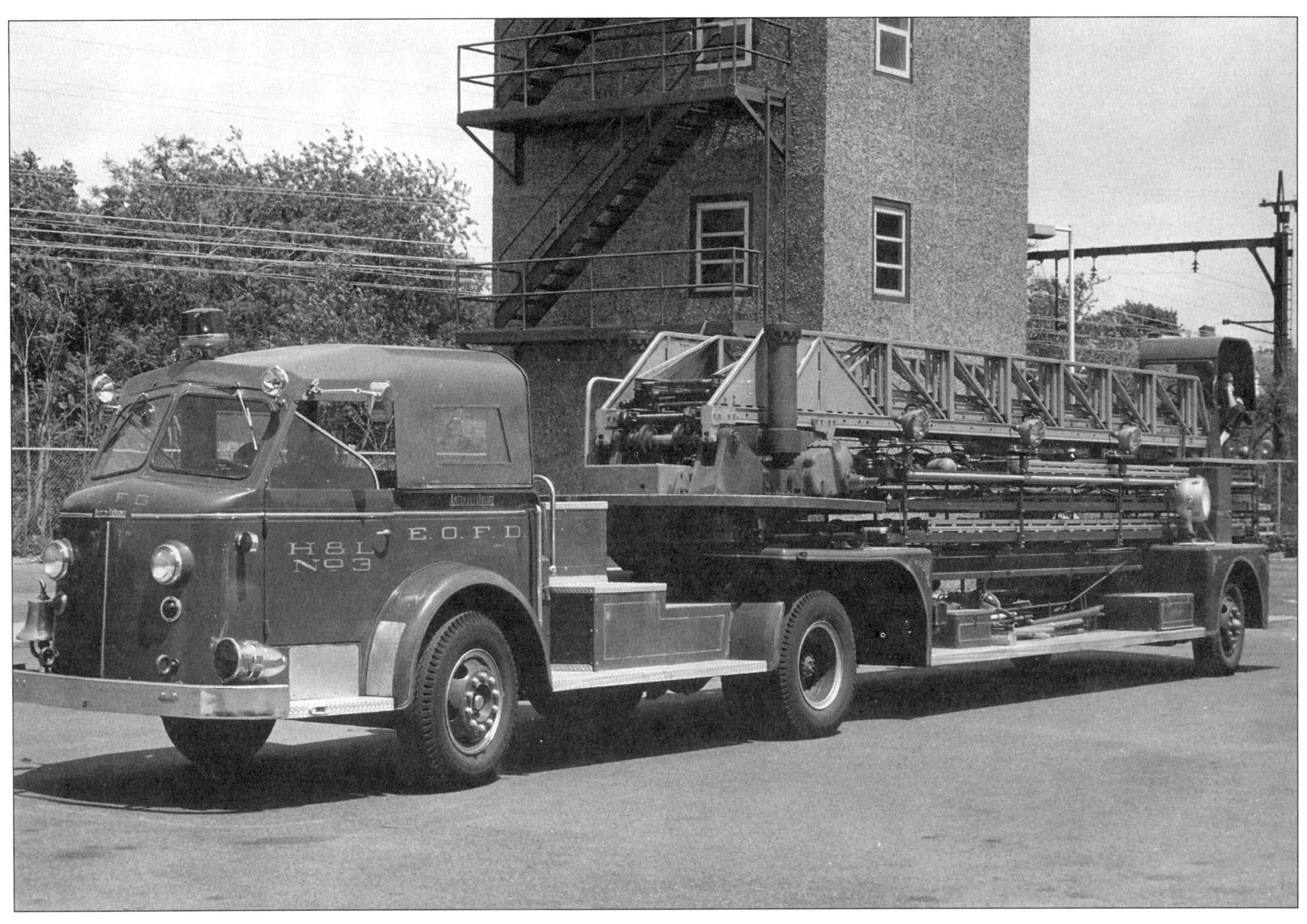

East Orange, NJ - 09/10/56; Model 7-100-TKO; Serial # N-144 - East Orange ordered three TDA's from American LaFrance; Serial # 8173 in 1944; Serial # 9133 in 1948; and Serial # N-144 in 1956. It is believed that this photograph shows the 1956 tractor pulling the 1944 trailer.

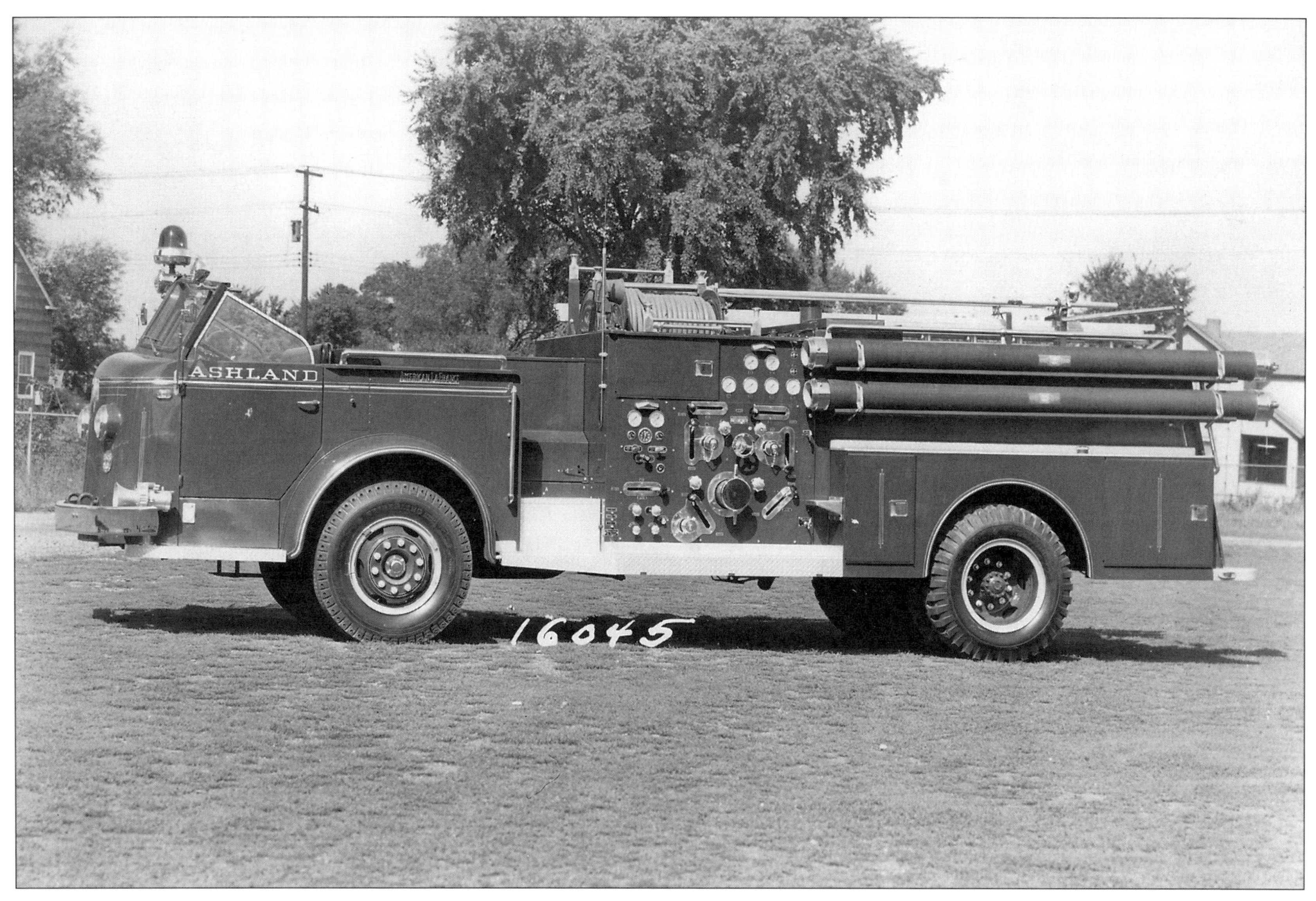

Ashland, OR - 09/25/56; Model C-810-PLO; Serial # N-156 - The evidence of the standard two-way radio compartment located just above the pump panel on the 800 Series Pumpers can be seen by the radio's antenna mounted at the rear of the jump seat area, just ahead of the radio compartment's hinged left side.

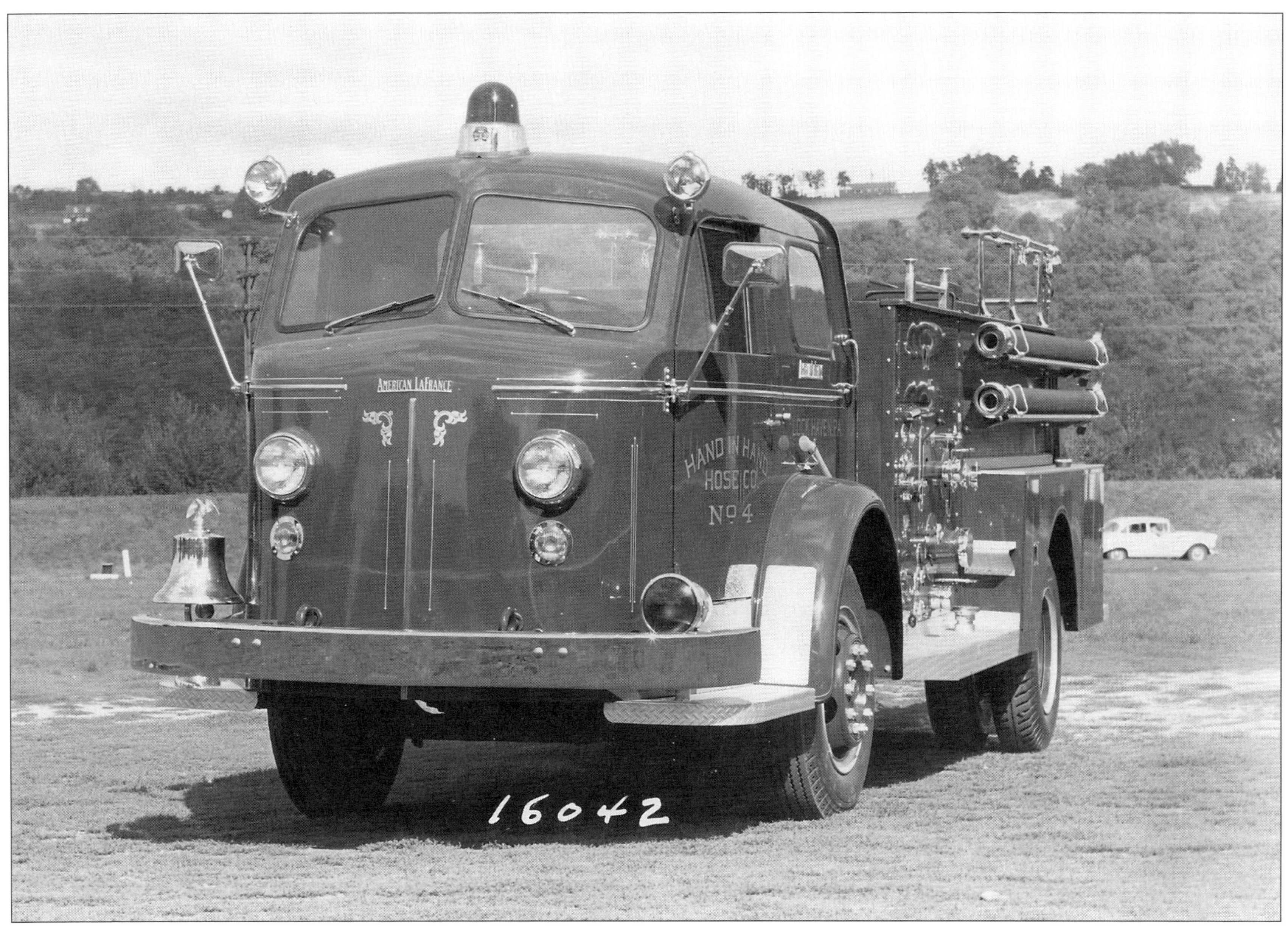

Lock Haven, PA - 10/01/56; Model S-875-PKO; Serial # N-171 - This delivery photo was taken to accentuate the front end of the 800 Series Pumpers. Again, the most noticeable feature besides the pump panel (side) change is the raised front bumper.

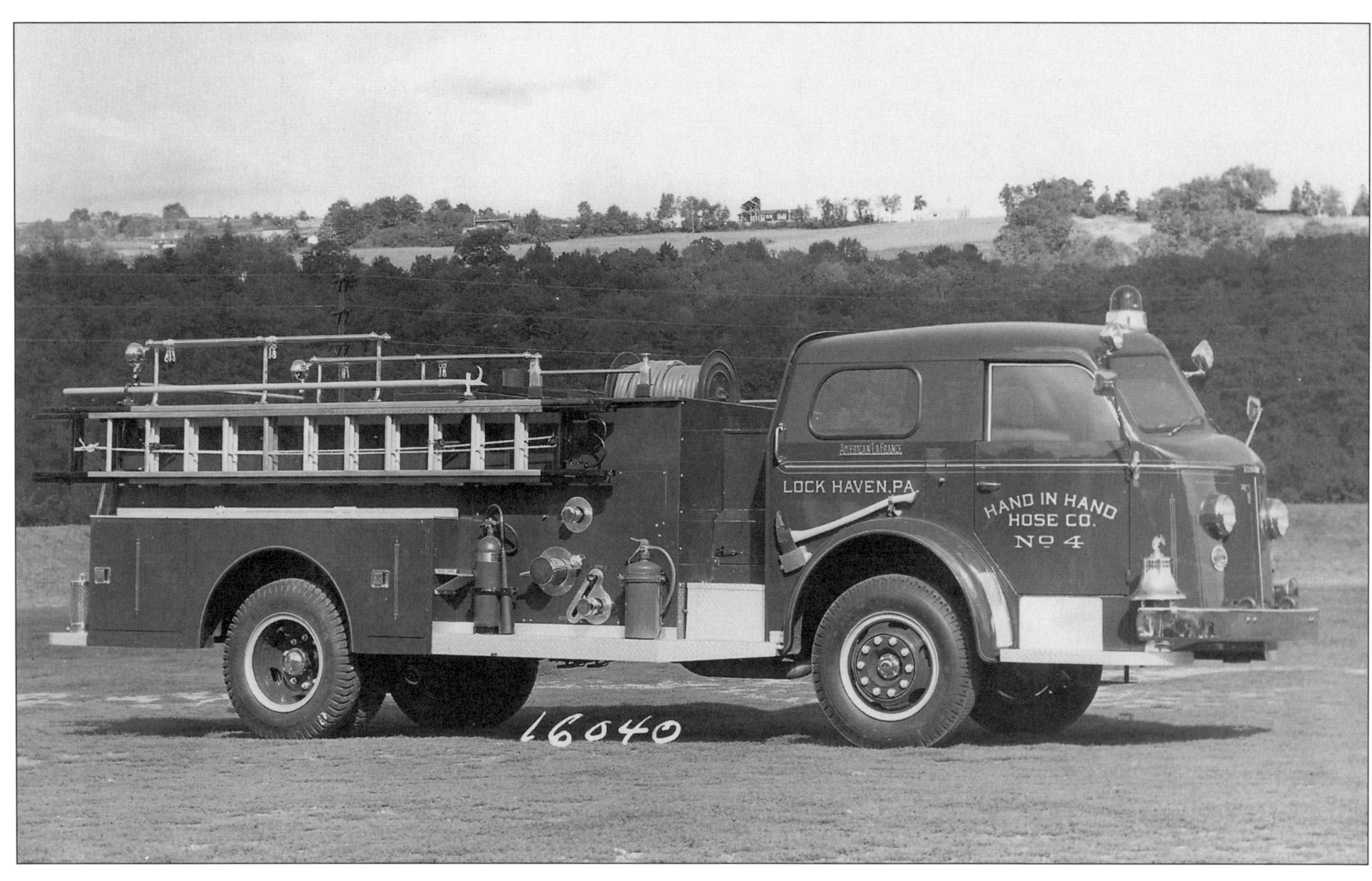

Lock Haven, PA - 10/01/56; Model S-875-PKO; Serial # N-171 - Lock Haven's Pumper was a standard 800 Series 750 GPM Pumper and featured high coat and boot rails on each rear side.

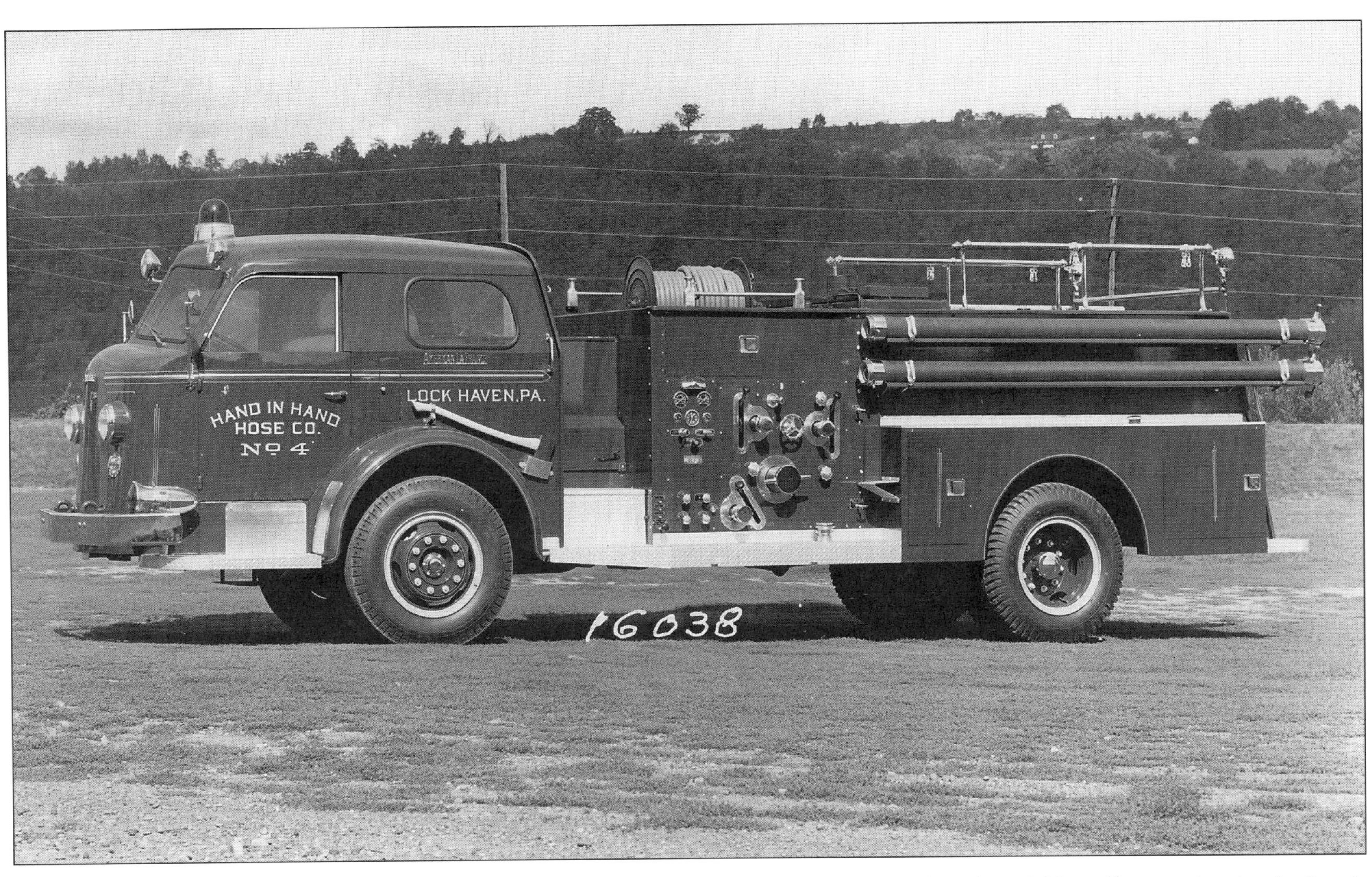

Lock Haven, PA - 10/01/56; Model S-875-PKO; Serial # N-171 - Equipped with a 300 gallon water tank, Lock Haven's pumper had axes located just above each front fender. This would become the standard location (unless otherwise specified) for factory installed axes on the 900 Series as well.

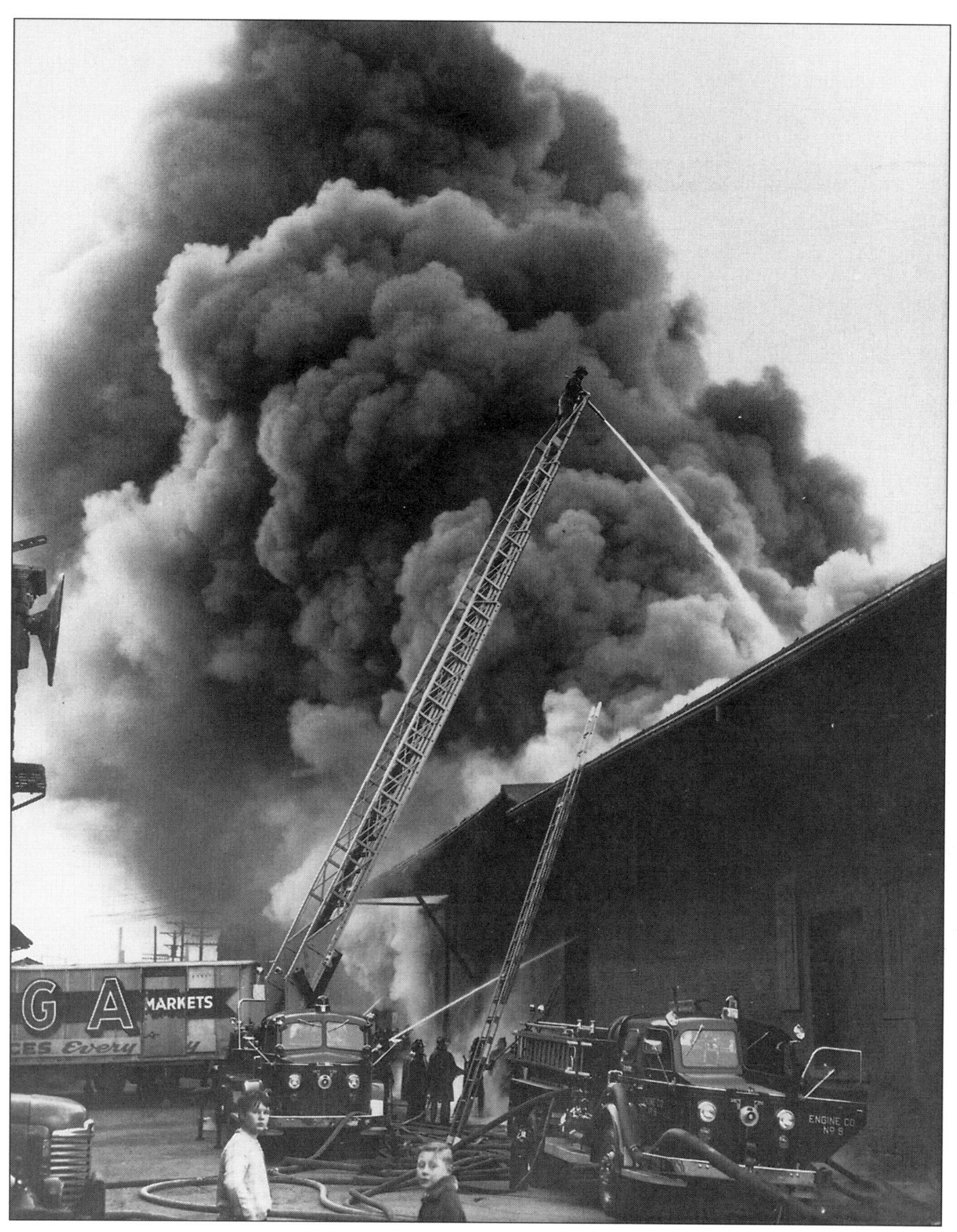

St. Louis, MO - A 5-Alarm fire at the Grocers Terminal Warehouse (Building # 5) at 101 Monroe St. on January 4, 1958 brought both St. Louis Engine Company # 9 (1,000 GPM/N-163) and Ladder Company # 7 (100' TDA/N-189) from the same Firehouse located at 814 LaBeaume Street to work the action.

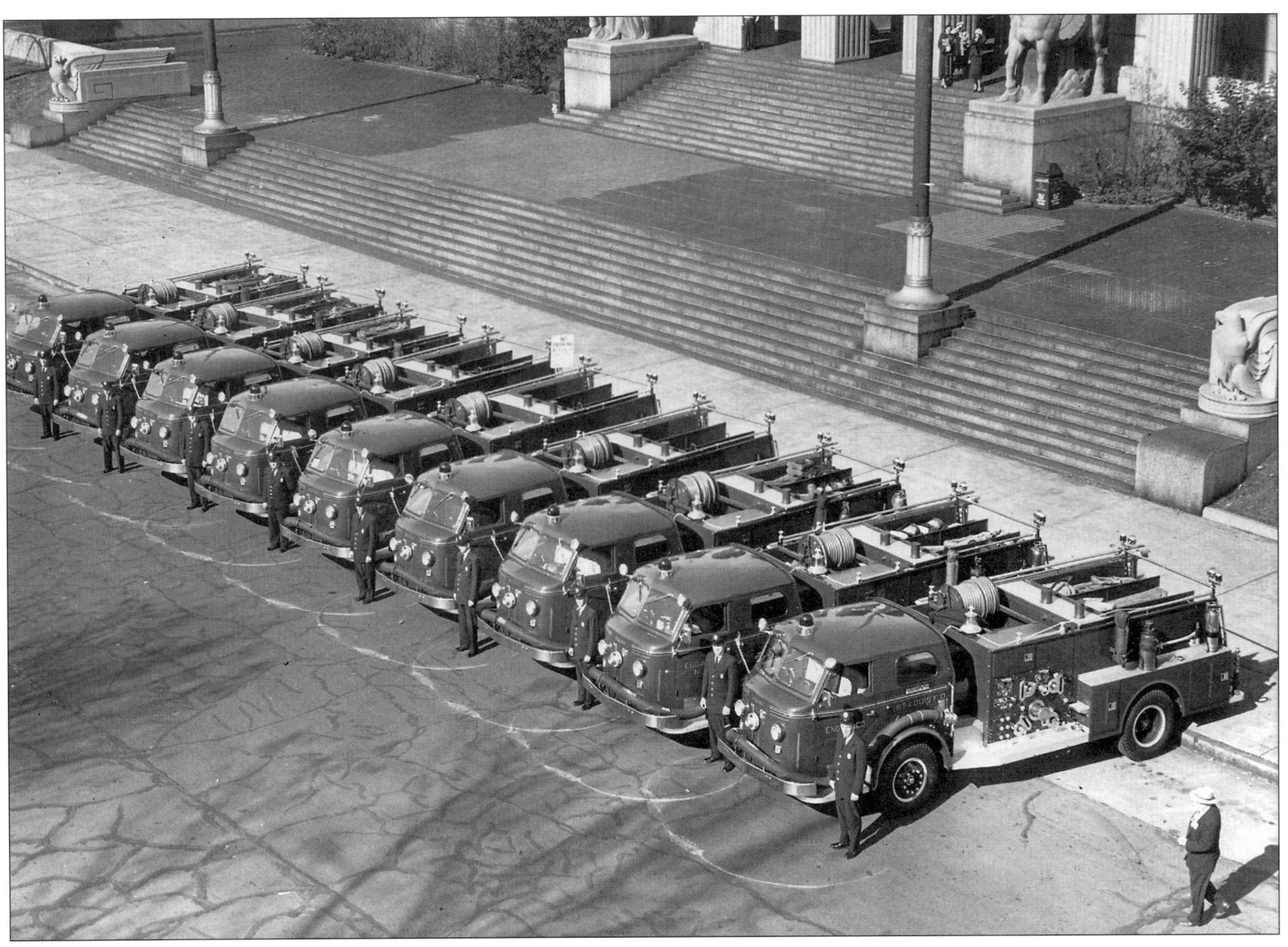

St. Louis, MO - 10/18/56 through 11/03/56; Model(s) D-810-PKC, D-815-PKC; Serial #'s N-161 (1,500 GPM), N-162 through N-169 (1,000 GPM) - Taken on November 14, 1956 in front of the St. Louis Soldier's Memorial, these nine new 800 Series Pumpers cost St. Louis a total of $130,000. Six of the pumpers were purchased with 1955 Bond Issue Funds while the other three were bought with General Revenue Funds.

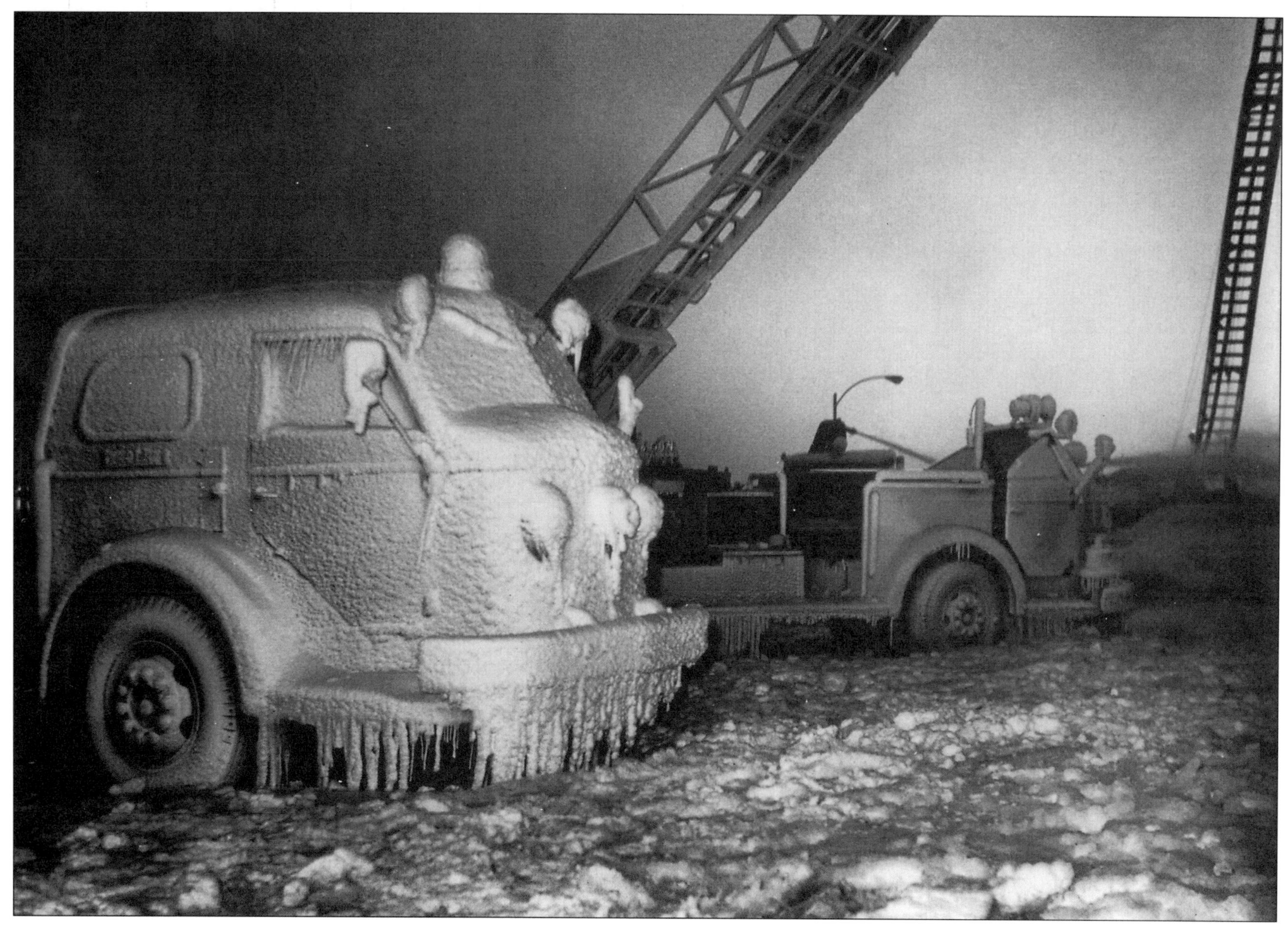

St. Louis, MO - 11/03/56; Model D-810-PKC; Serial # N-169 - You can feel the cold come right through this page as St. Louis Engine Company # 7 continues to pump, although totally encrusted in ice, at the Ralston-Purina fire back in 1962. Truck Company # 13, a 1953 ALF/TDA (Serial # L- 4750) shares the same fate in the background.

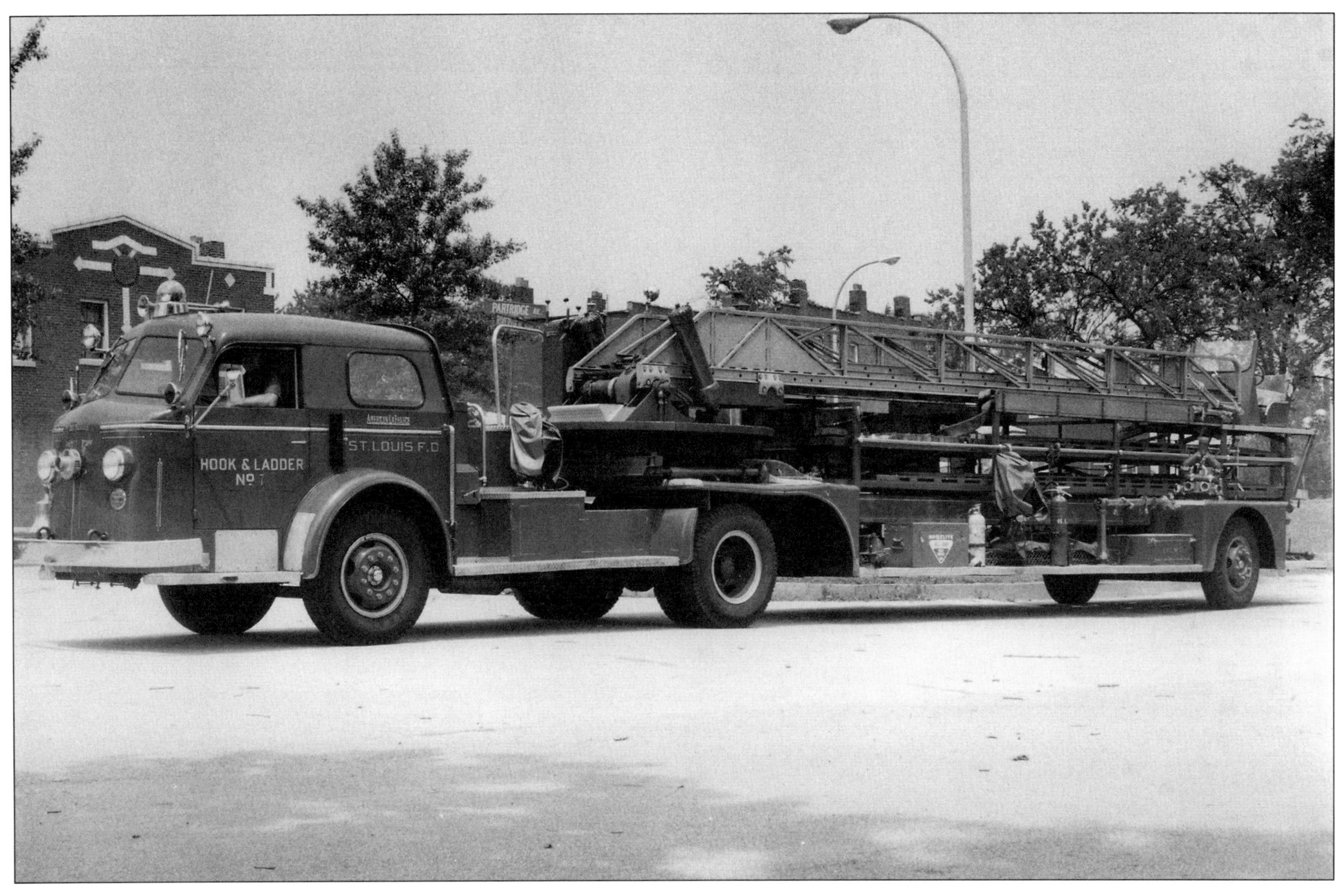

St. Louis, MO - 12/10/56; Model 7-85-TKC; Serial #'s N-184 through N-188 - St. Louis ordered five of these TDA's in 1956. Even though the front of the tractor cab had the 800 Series identity features, American LaFrance still classified it as a 700 Series model.

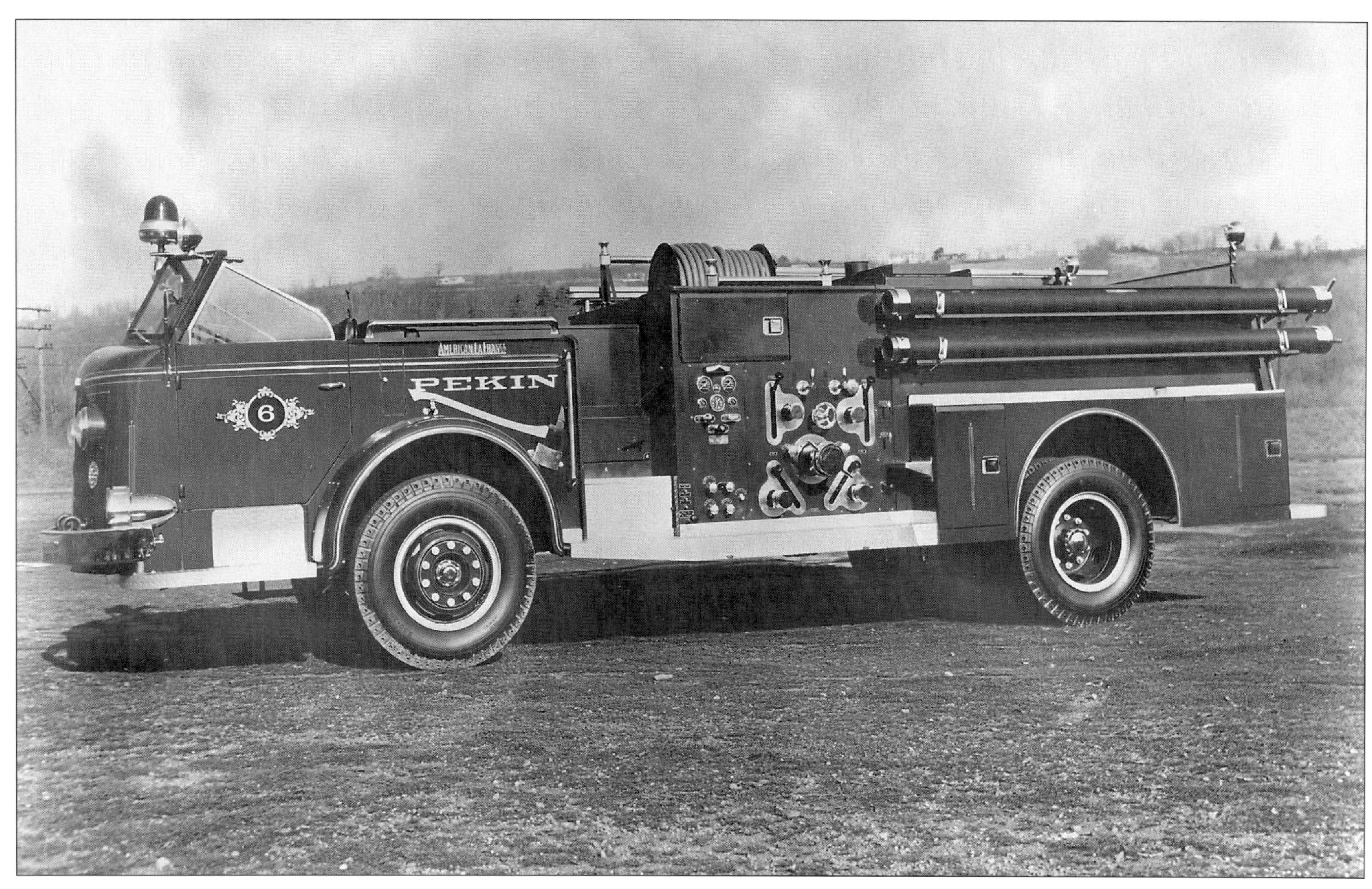

Pekin, IL - 11/15/56; Model 810-PJO; Serial # L-5448 - Pekin's 800 Series Pumper was rated at 1,000 GPM, but was equipped with only the two master compound gauges on the pump panel. The rear enclosed compartment was larger than the front one.

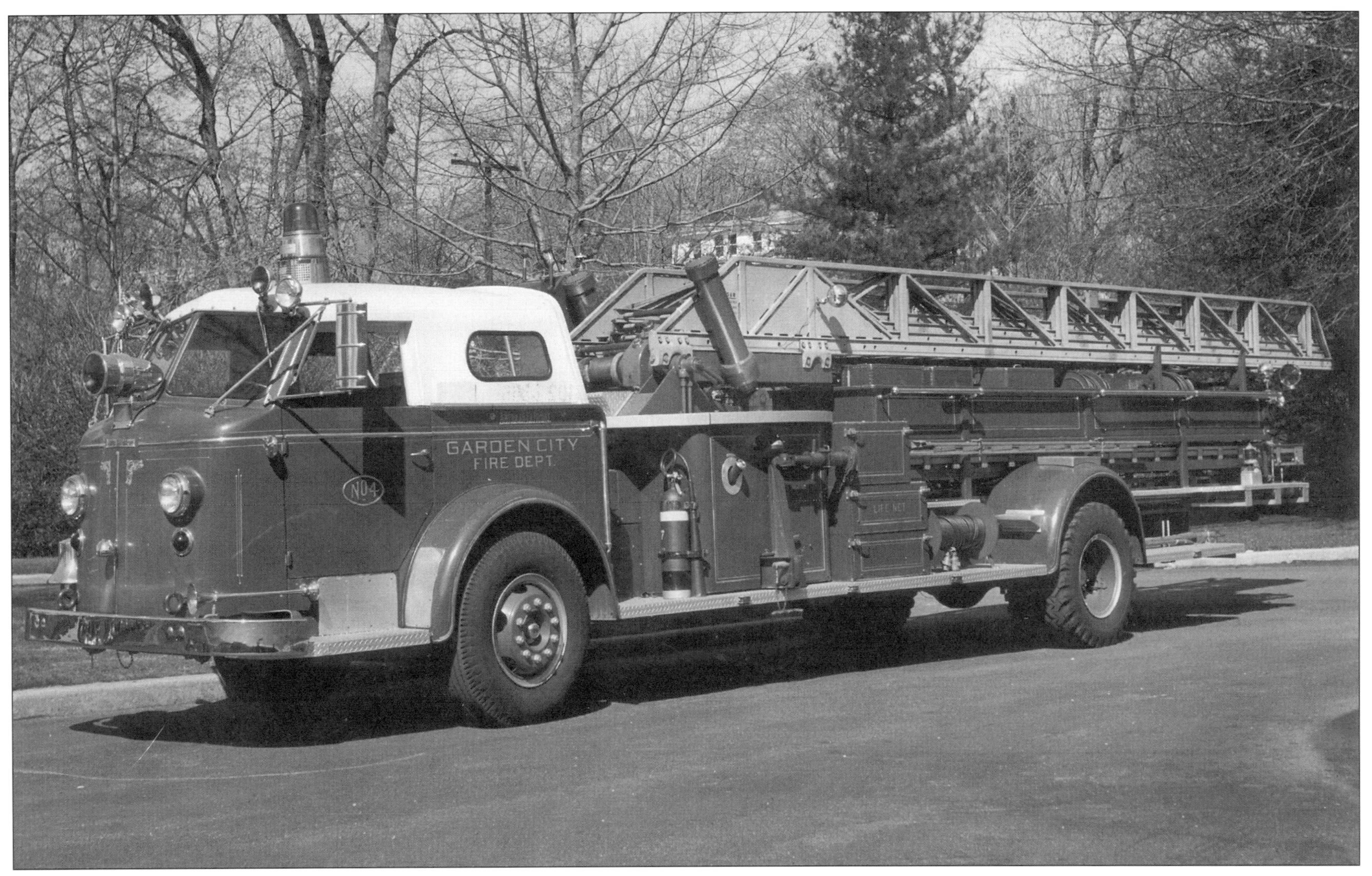

Garden City, NY - 10/03/56; Model 7-100-AJO; Serial # L-5436 - A typical 700 Series ladder truck, it was equipped with a small generator to provide power for the cable reels on each running board. The fiberglass cab top, electronic siren/strobe light combination and air horn were all fire department additions.

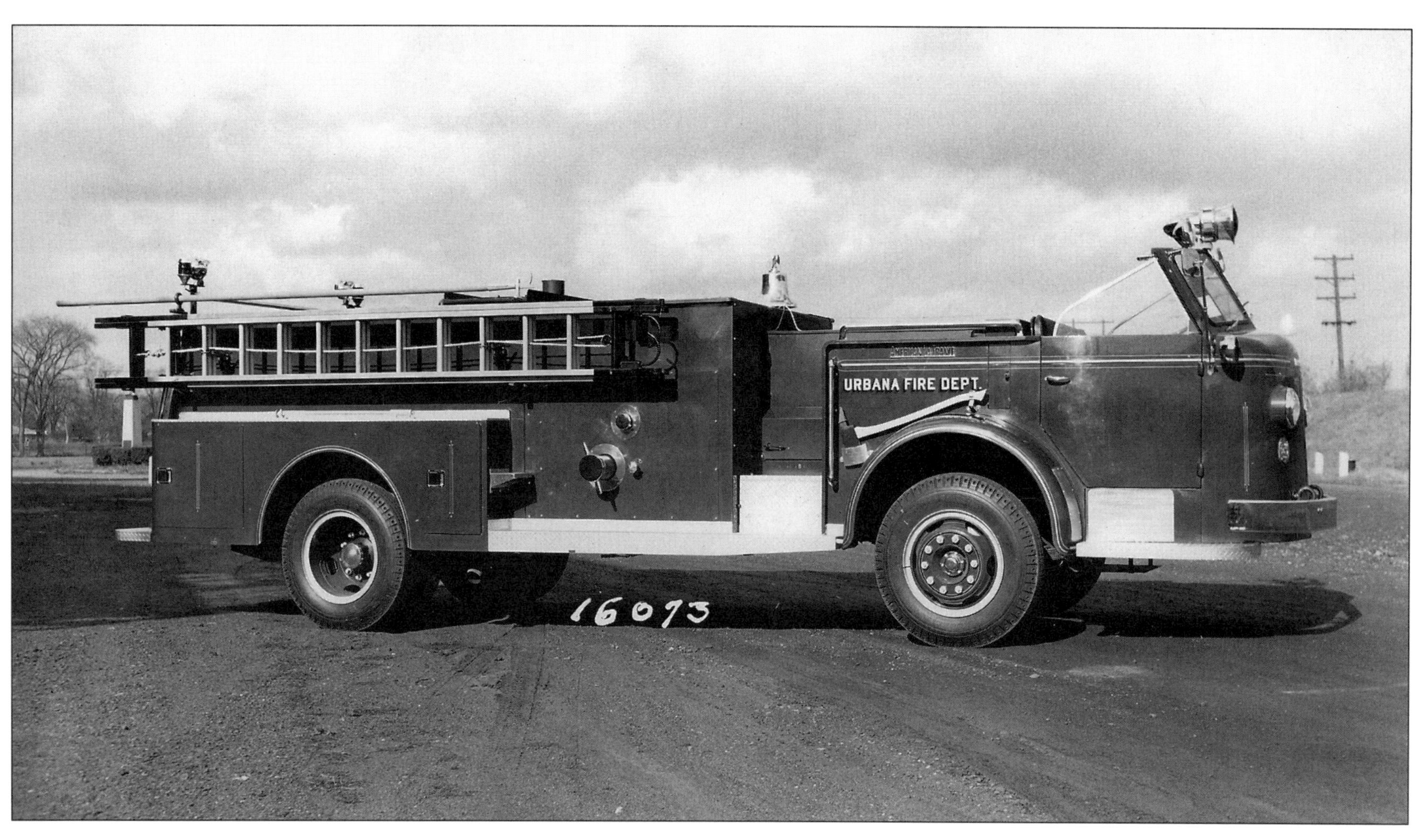

Urbana, OH - 11/01/56; Model D-875-PJO; Serial # L-5446 - Urbana's pump was rated at 750 GPM. What you are looking at here is basically a 700 Series front end with a 900 Series body.

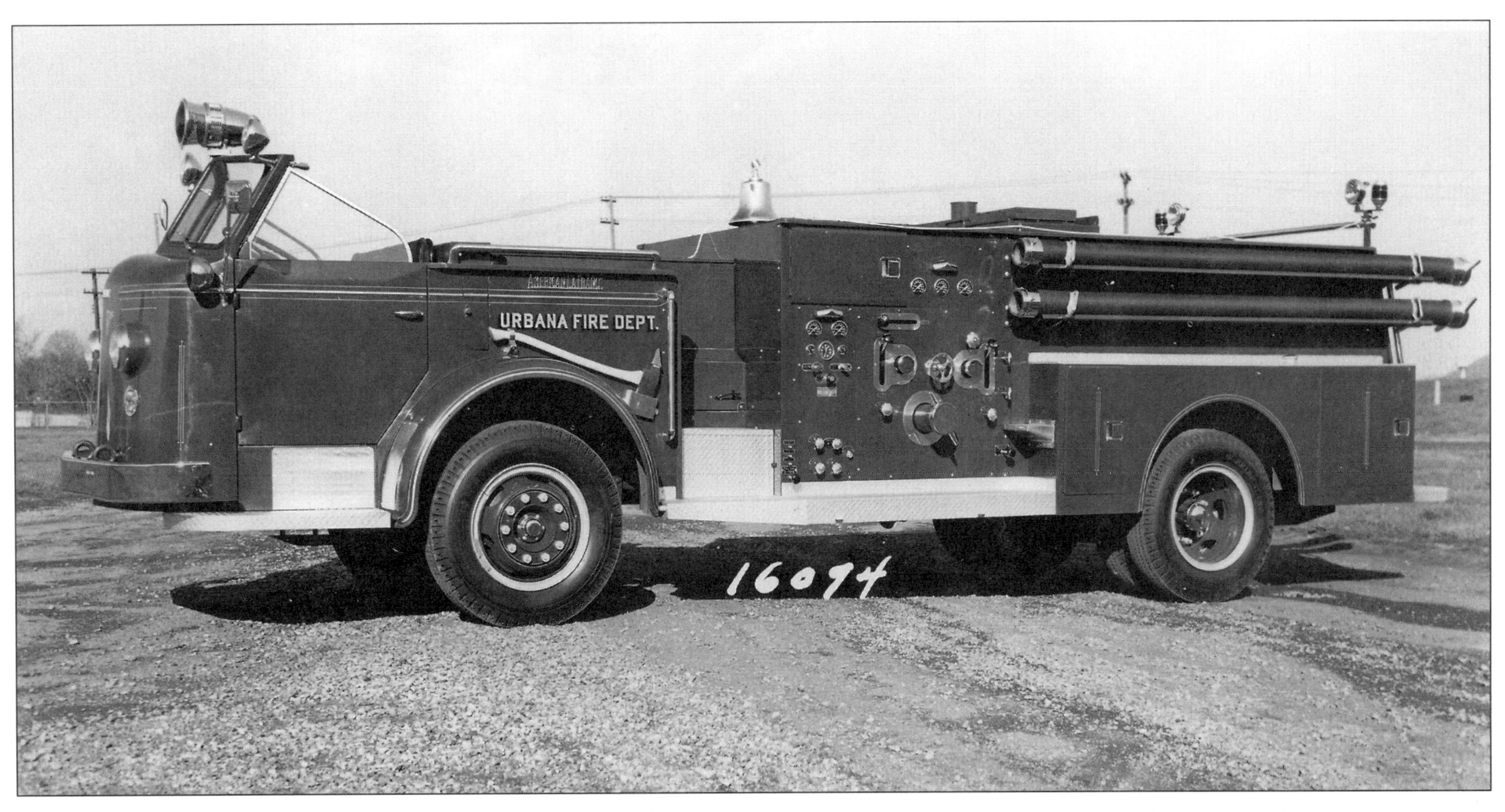

Urbana, OH - 11/01/56; Model D-875-PJO; Serial # L- 5446 - Urbana chose to mount their bell above and behind the 'dog house' (motor compartment) as some other 800 users did also. The die was now cast for the 900 Series; all that was left was to get the 'bugs' out of the 800 Series and redesign the front end.

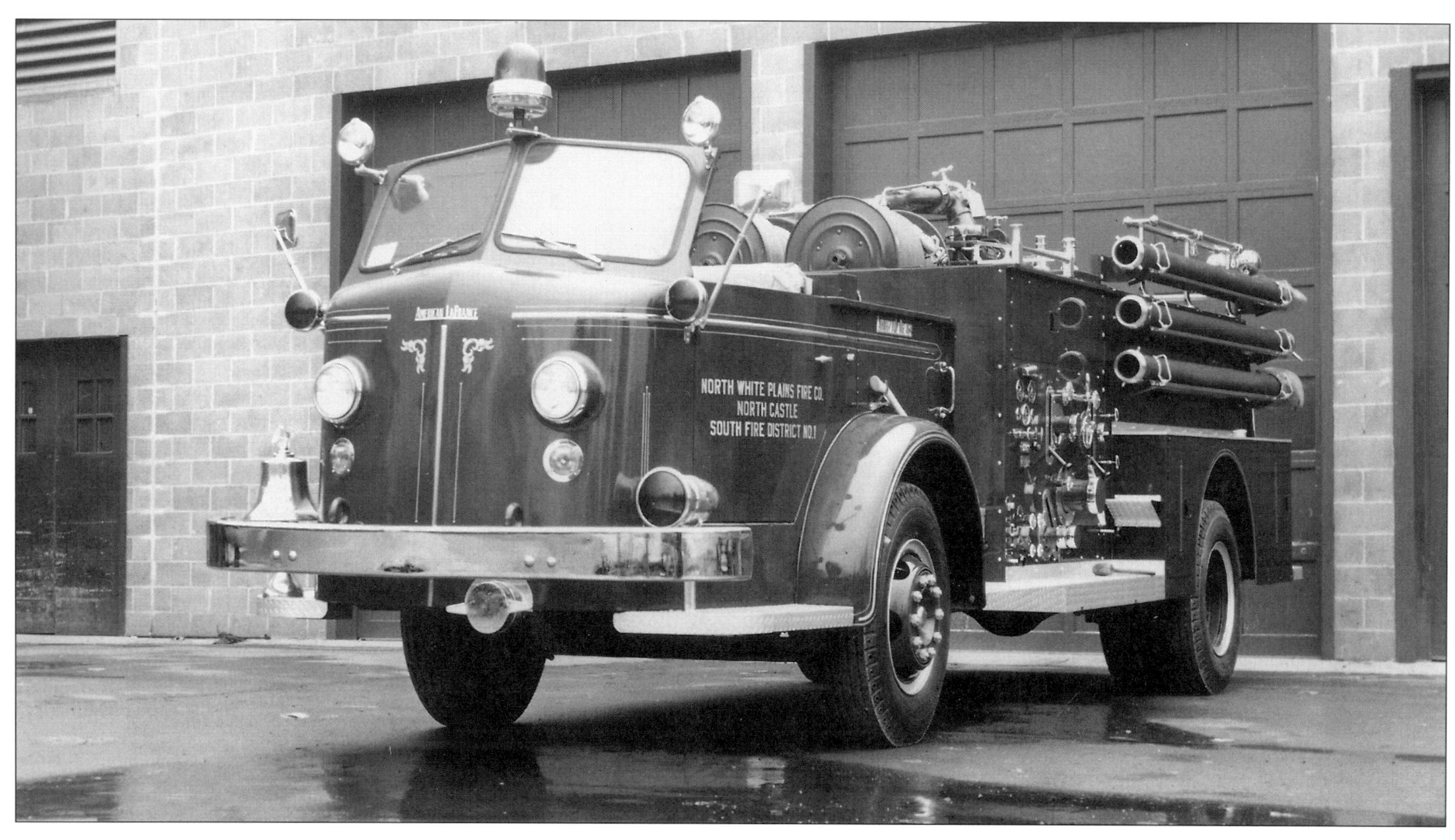

North White Plains, NY - 12/26/56; Model C-875-PKO; Serial # N-195 - The South Fire District # 1 operated this 800 Series Pumper. It was equipped with a front suction option which was gated at the pump panel.

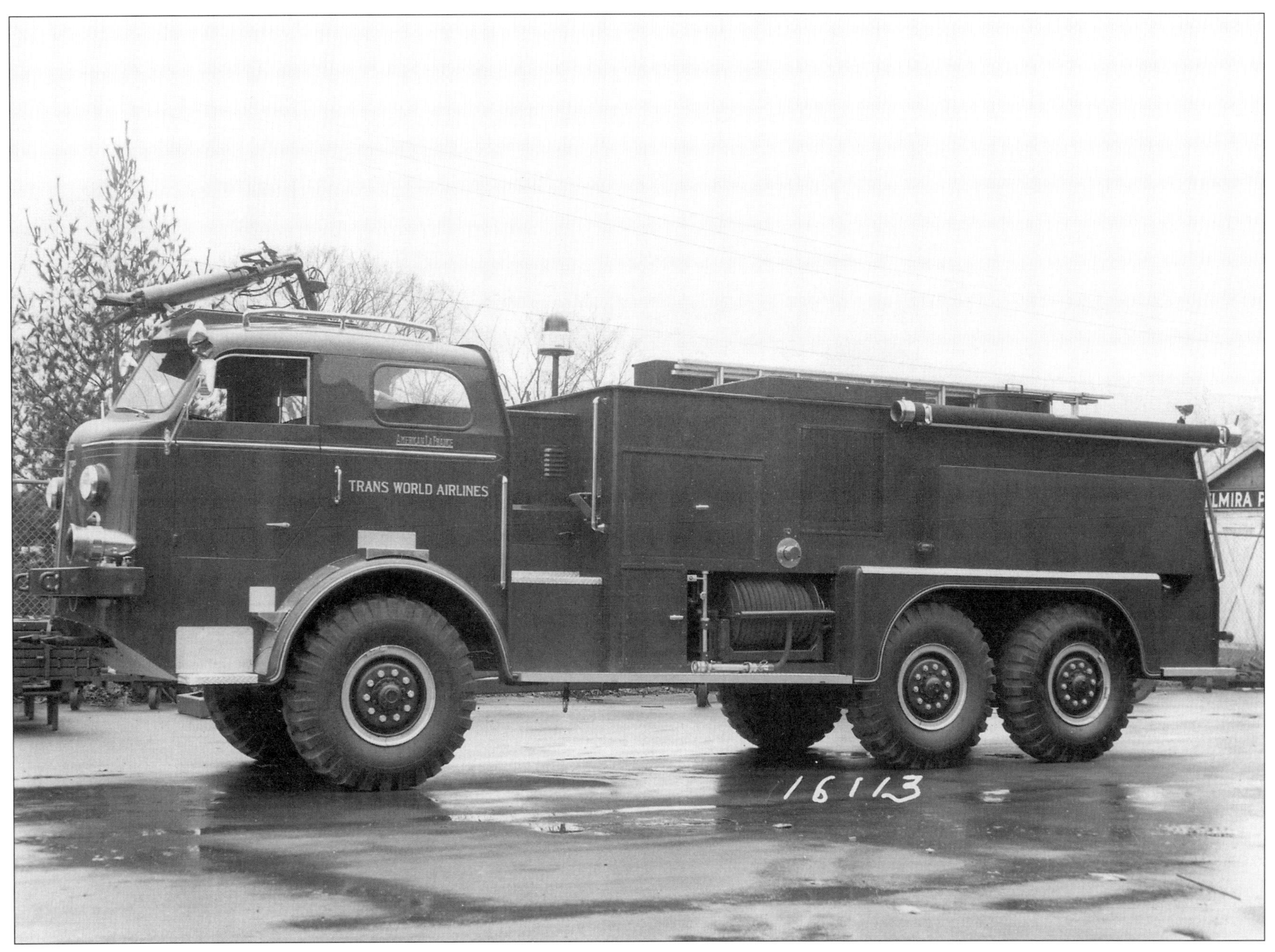

Kansas City, KS - Trans World Airlines - 12/24/56; Model 6 X 6-CFR; Serial # N-191 - TWA ordered this piece with a 750 GPM pump, 1,000 gallon water tank, 4,500 GPM turret, and 6 X 6 drive and pump & roll capabilities.

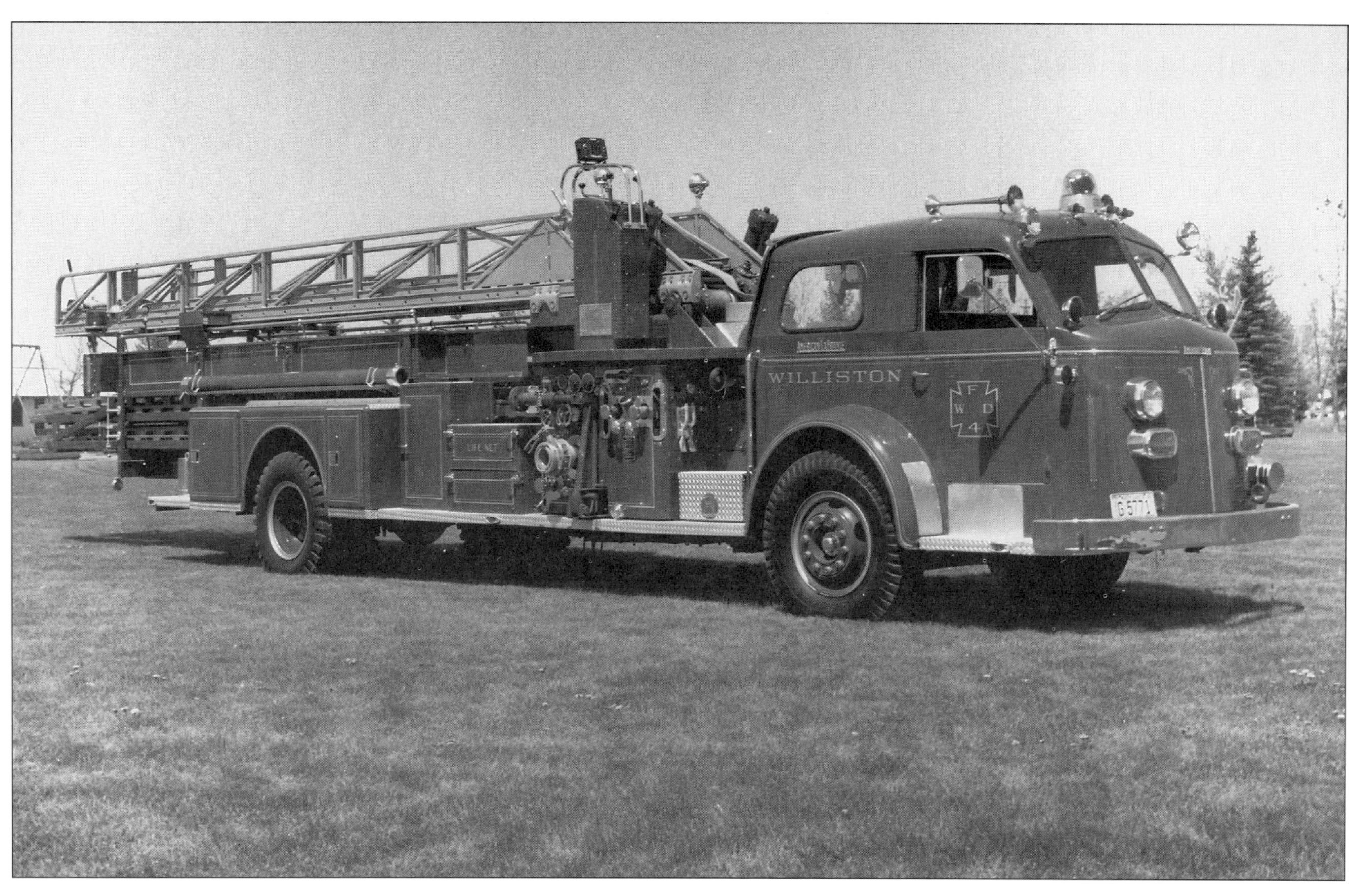

Williston, ND - 01/23/57 - Model 775-QJC-85; Serial # L-5472 - After years of service, this 700 Series Aerial Ladder went back to an ALF Service Facility for a pump overhaul, new aerial, diesel motor, and complete air system (brakes). The 1000 Series turn signals were also added at that time.

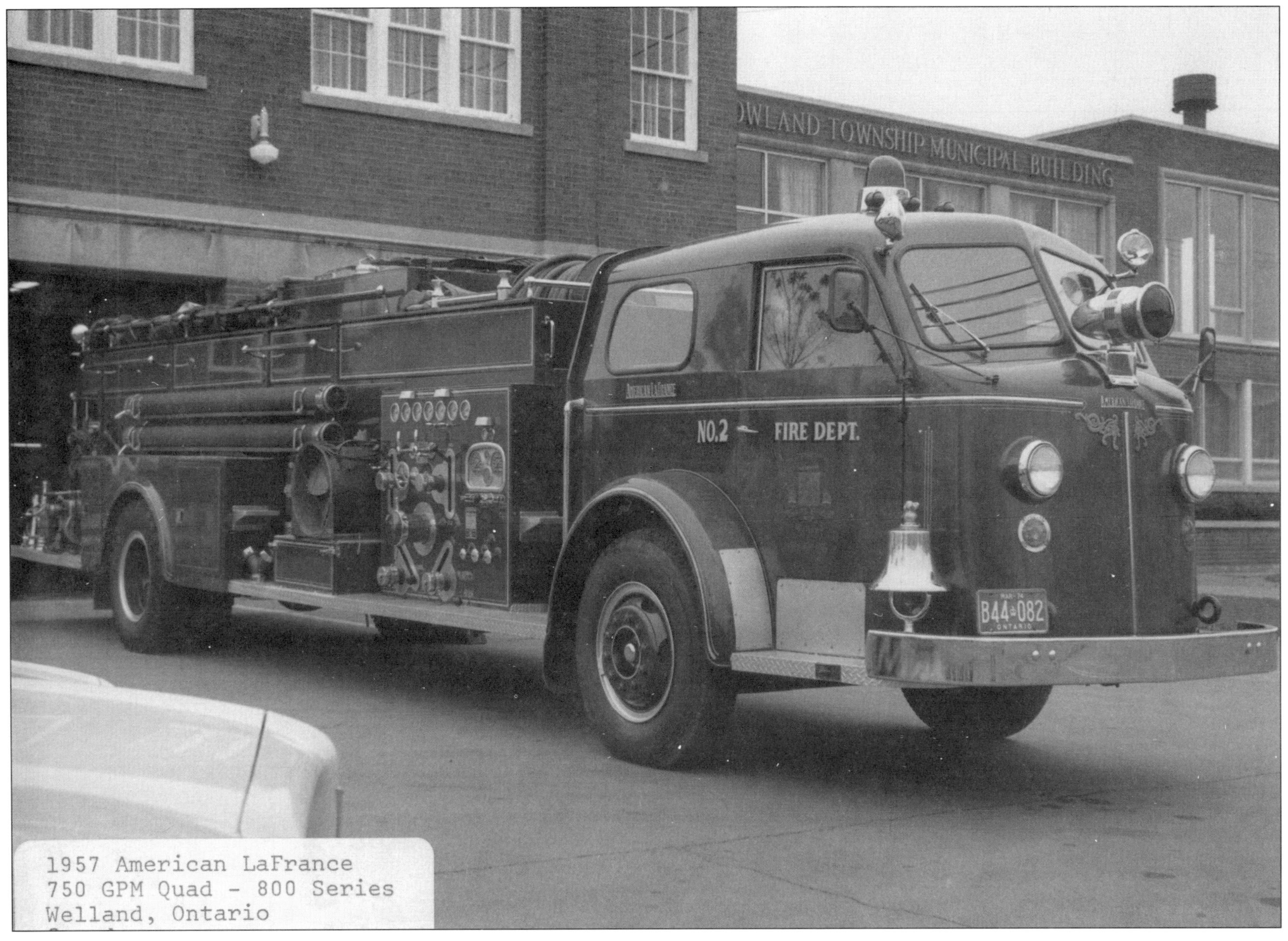

Crowland, Ontario, Canada - 01/31/57; Model 775- QDC; Serial # N-193 - This 700 Series Quad featured fully enclosed rear compartmentation and a separate gauge for each discharge gate, including the booster reel.

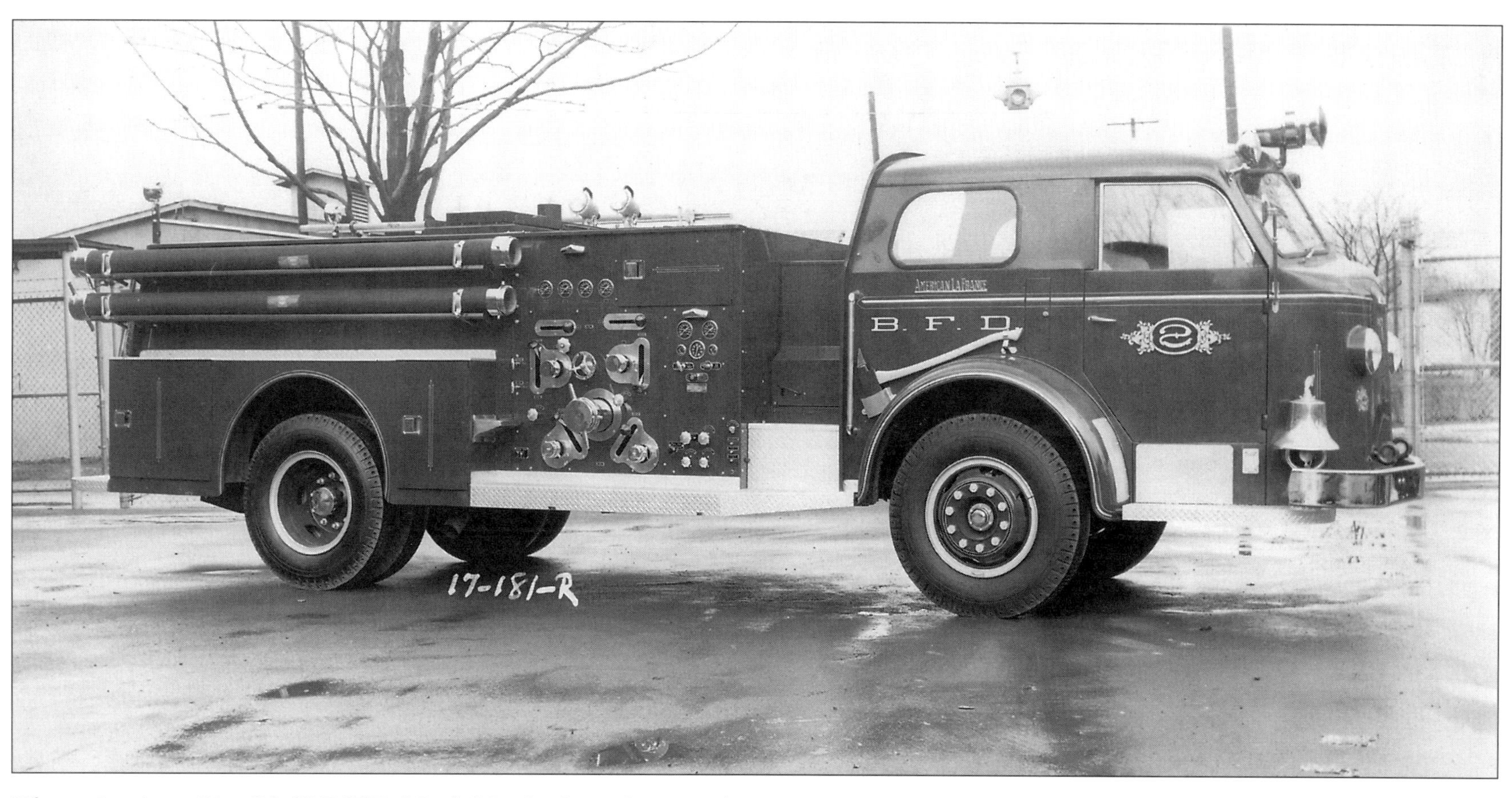

Bloomington, IL - 03/27/57; Model D-810-PJC; Serial #'s L-5489, L-5494 - Bloomington purchased two of these 1,000 GPM Pumpers in 1957.

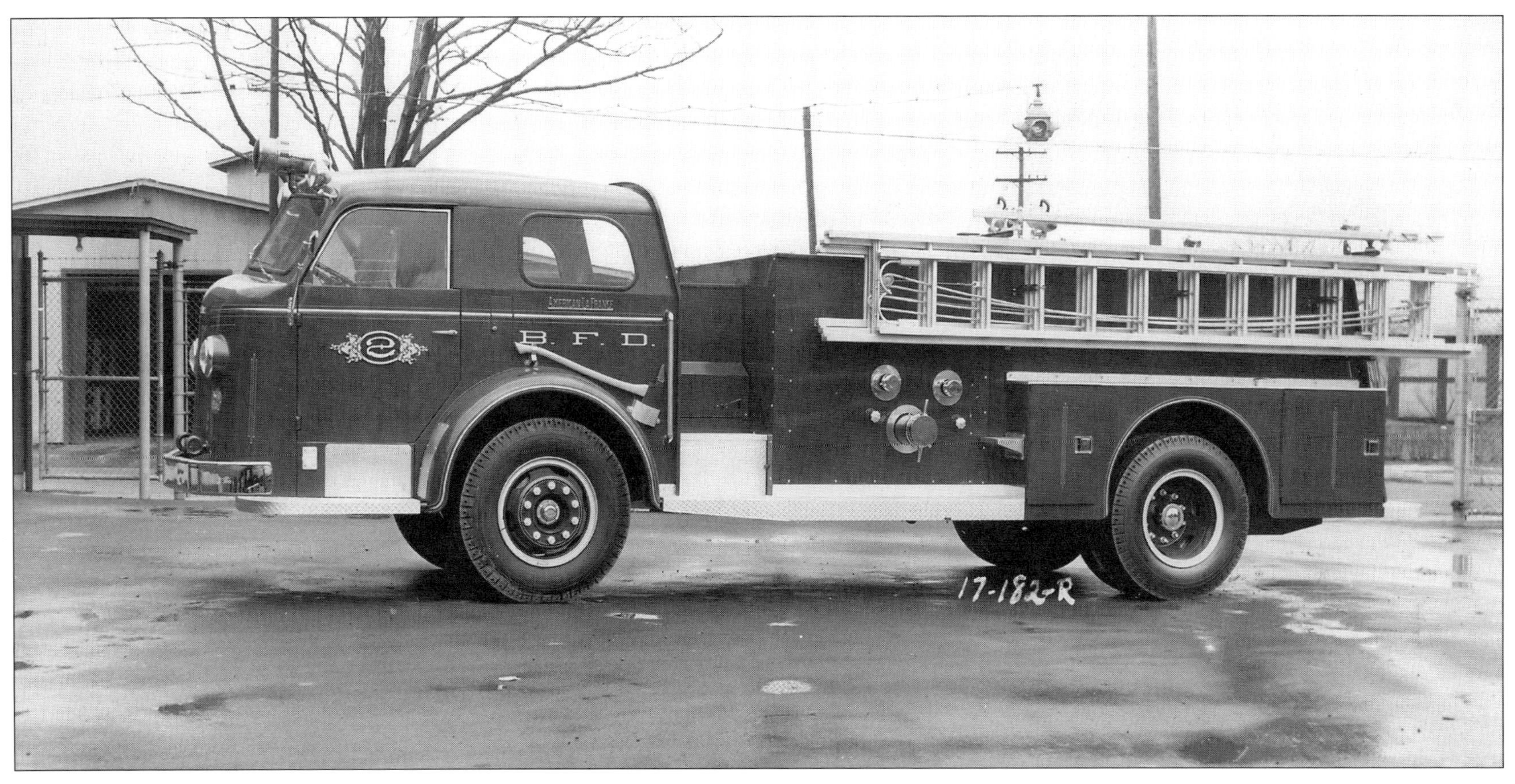

Bloomington, IL - 03/27/57; Model D-810-PJC; Serial #'s L-5489, L-5494 - Although a true 800 Series Pumper, Bloomington specified their pump panel on the officer's side, a regular 700 Series feature.

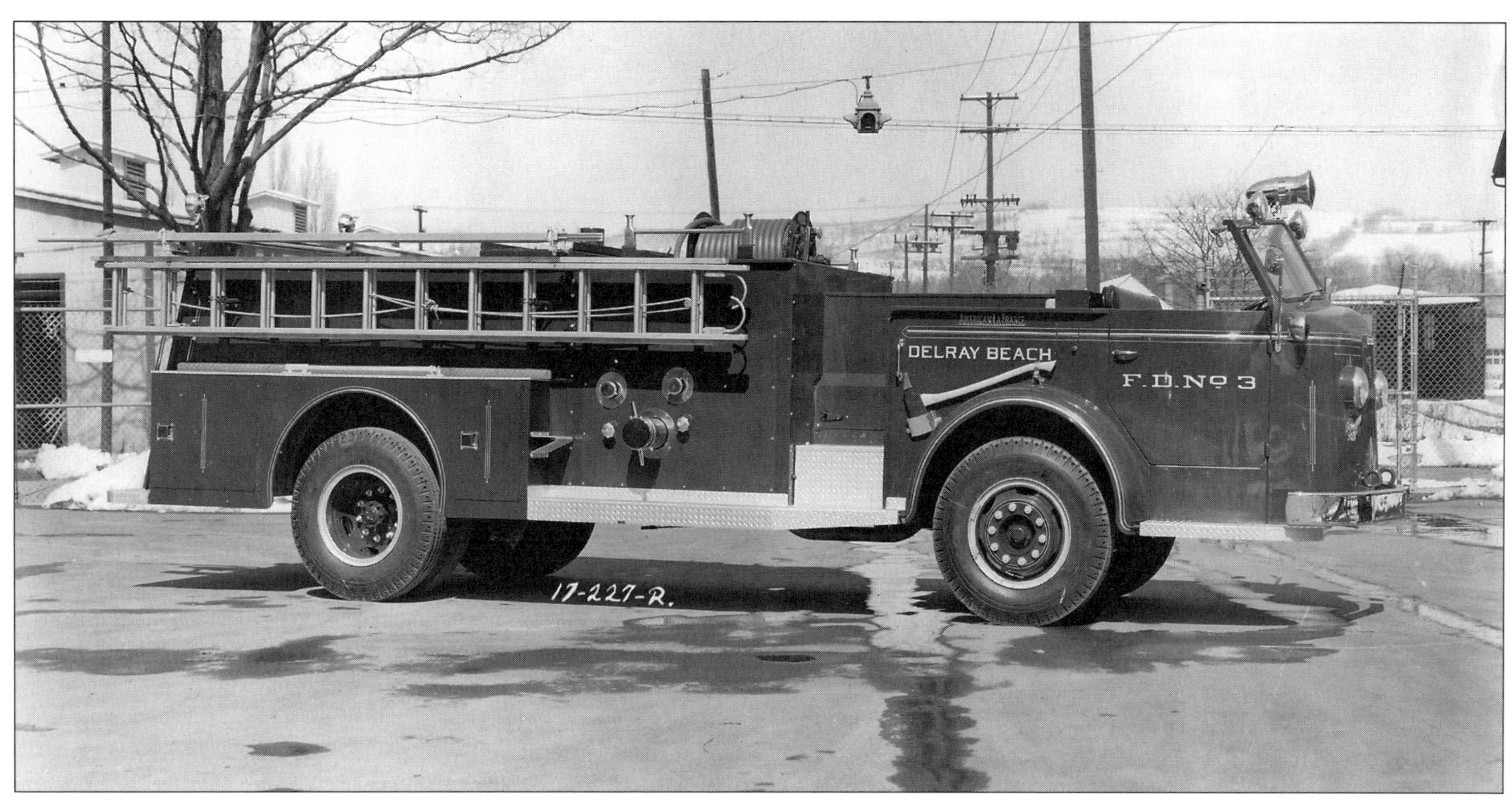

Delray Beach, FL - 04/10/57; Model C-810-PDO; Serial # N-237 - This Pumper featured a 1,000 GPM Pump and a 300 gallon water tank, which was now the standard water tank size unless otherwise specified by the fire department.

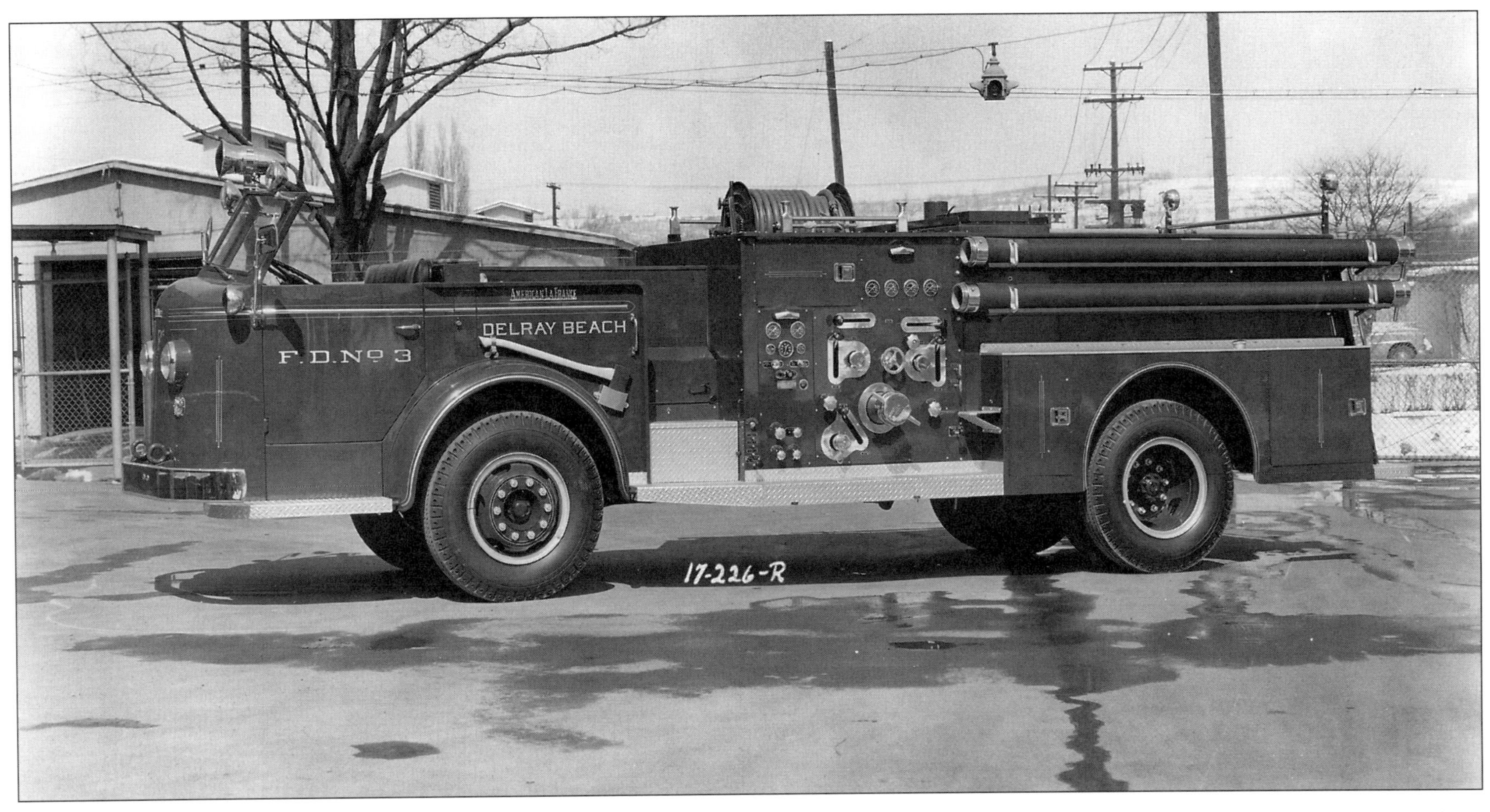

Delray Beach, FL - 04/10/57; Model C-810-PDO; Serial # N-237 - The 900 Series pump panel configuration was starting to take shape on the 800 Series. The two handles below the individual pressure gauges controlled the officer side discharge gates.

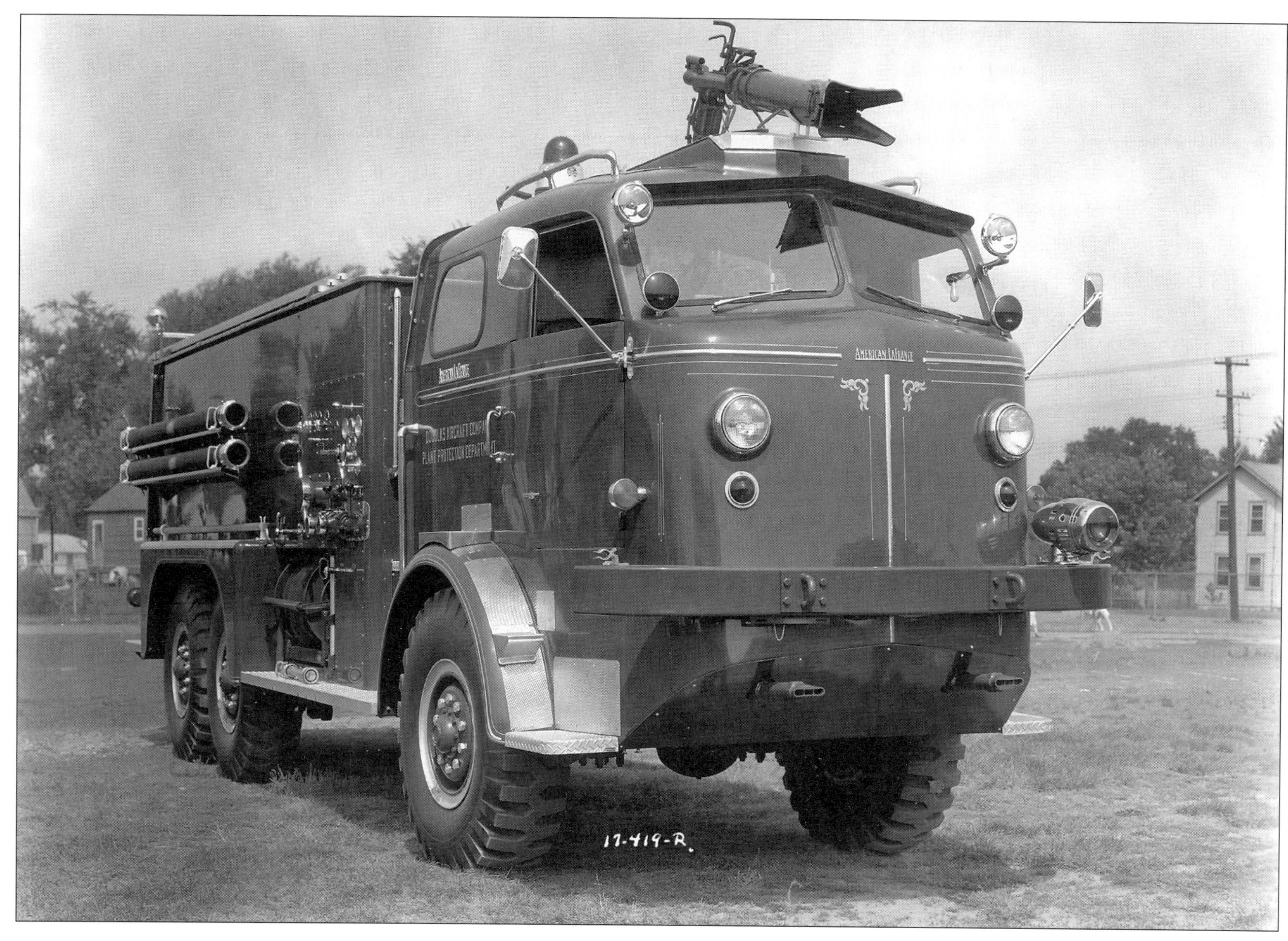

Long Beach, CA - Douglas Aircraft Co. - 07/23/57; Model 6 X 6 CFR; Serial # N-268 - This low front end view reveals the twin ground sweep nozzles located just under each of the tow eyes on the front bumper. All of the Crash Trucks made by ALF featured large water tanks and pump & roll capabilities.

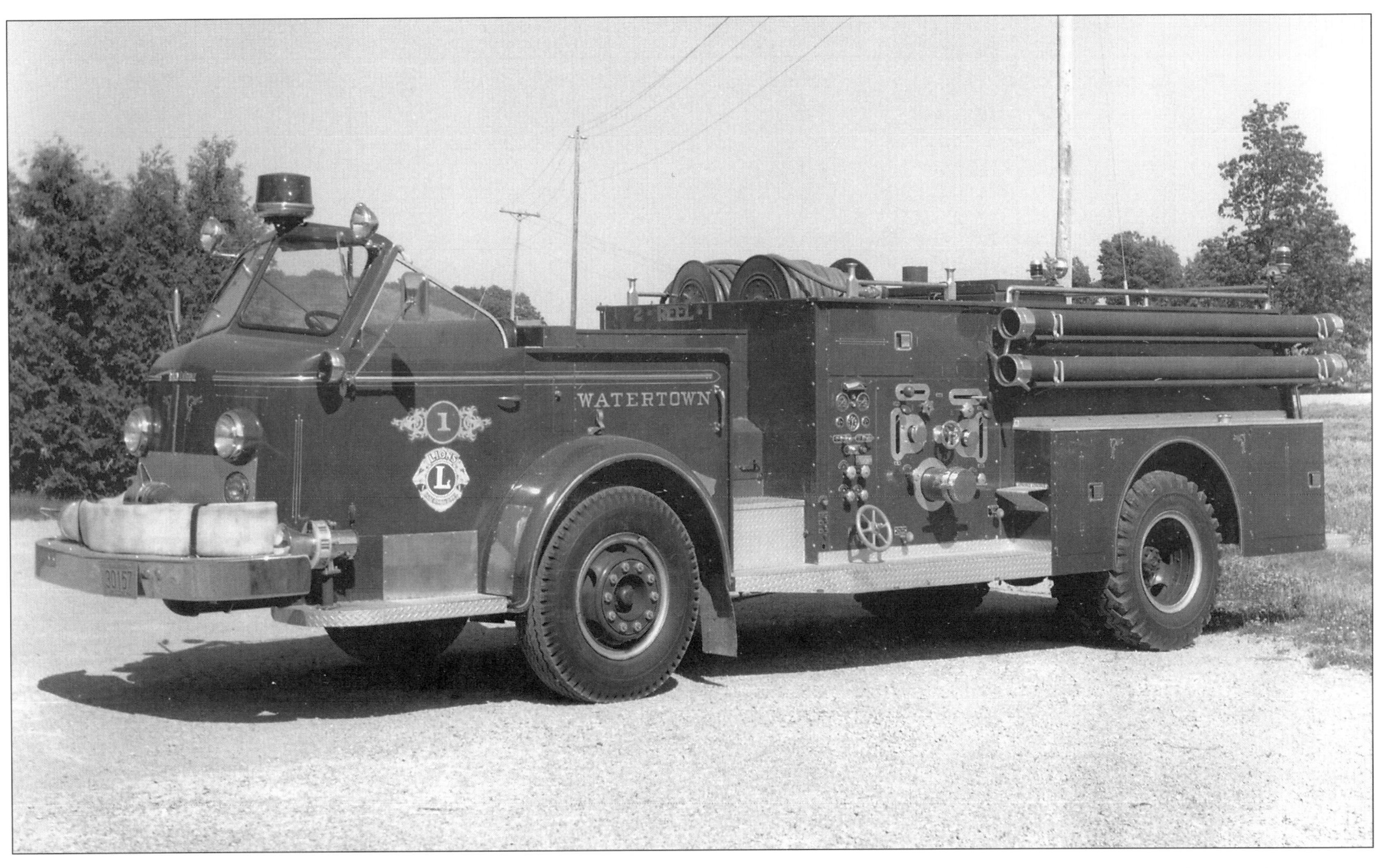

Watertown, WI - 07/17/57; Model C-810-PJO; Serial # L-5534 - The chrome hand wheel just above the pump panel running board is the gate valve control for the preconnected front suction. After leaving active Fire Department service, the local Lions Club acquired this rig for parades, etc.

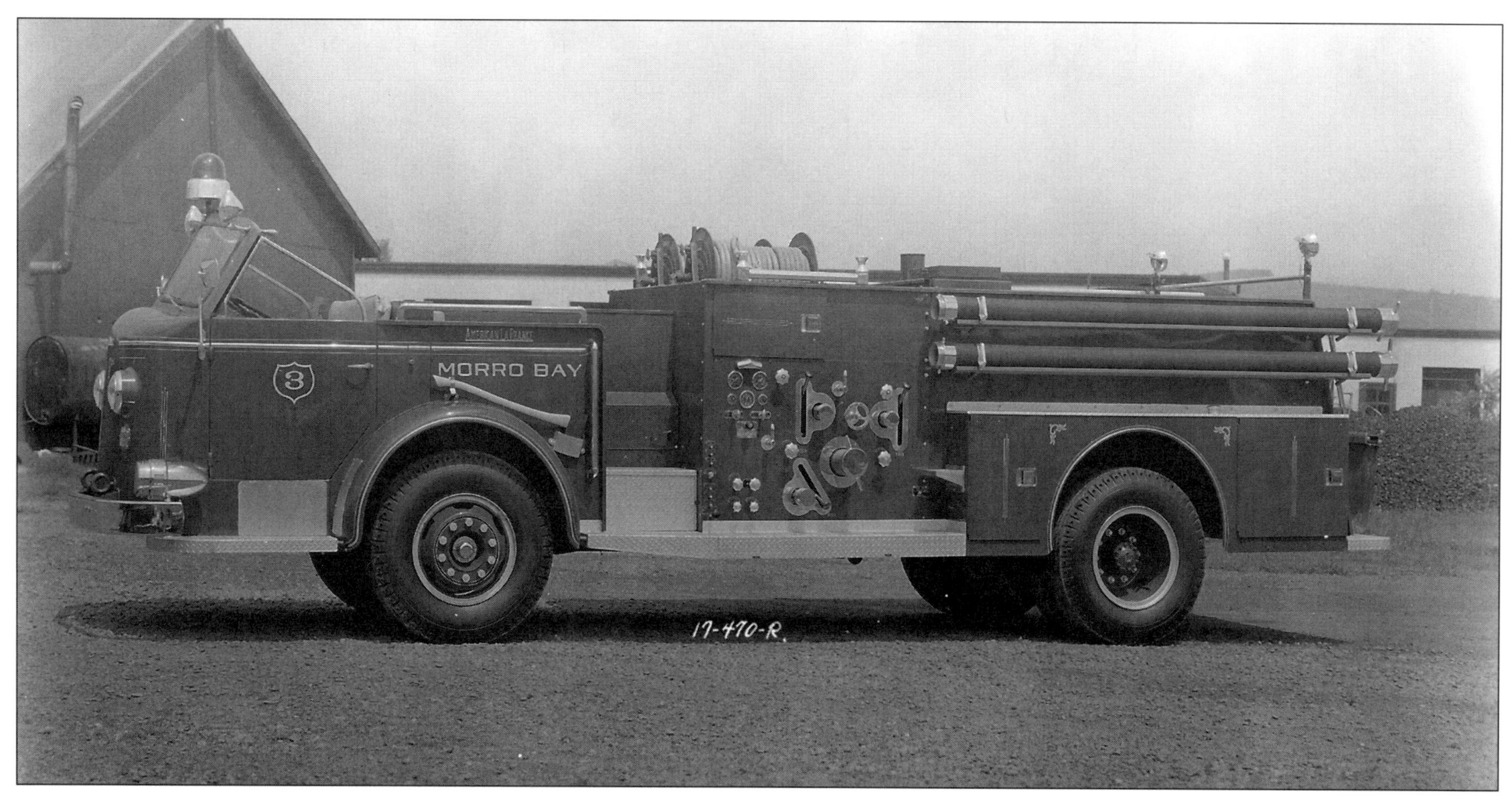

Morro Bay, CA - 08/02/57; Model D-875-PDO; Serial # N-281 - The flat edge of the top of the windshield frame went back to a more curved, 700 Series-like windshield frame on open cab 800 Series Pumpers. Morro Bay's Pumper was rated at 750 GPM.

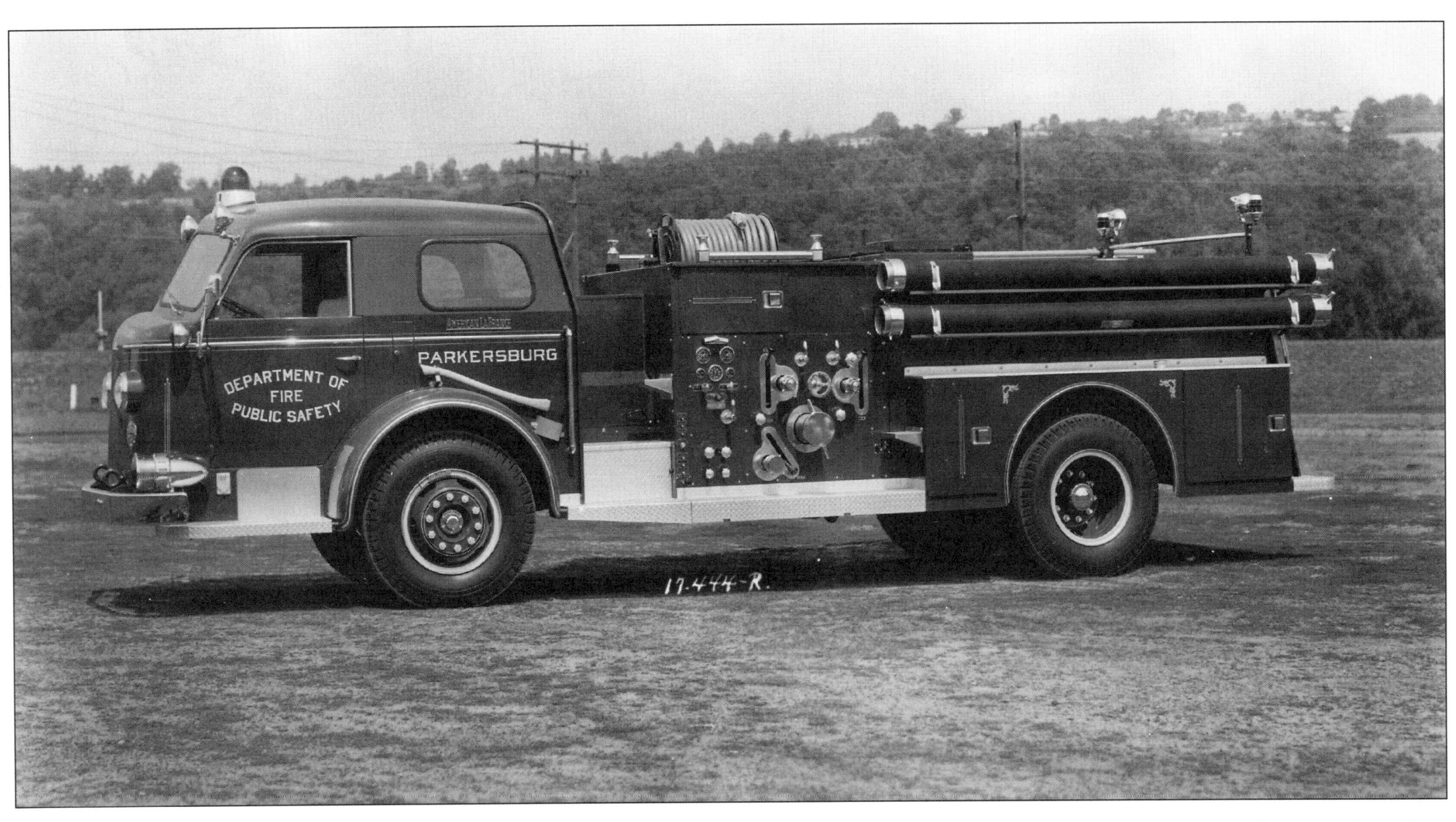

Parkersburg, WV - 08/20/57; Model D-810-PJC; Serial # L-5536 - Some of the 800 Series Pumpers featured amber turn signals in the same location as the two (steady) red lenses on the 700 Series models. The turn signals were plastic amber lenses mounted in a metal chrome plated ring frame. Parkersburg's Pumper was rated at 1,000 GPM.

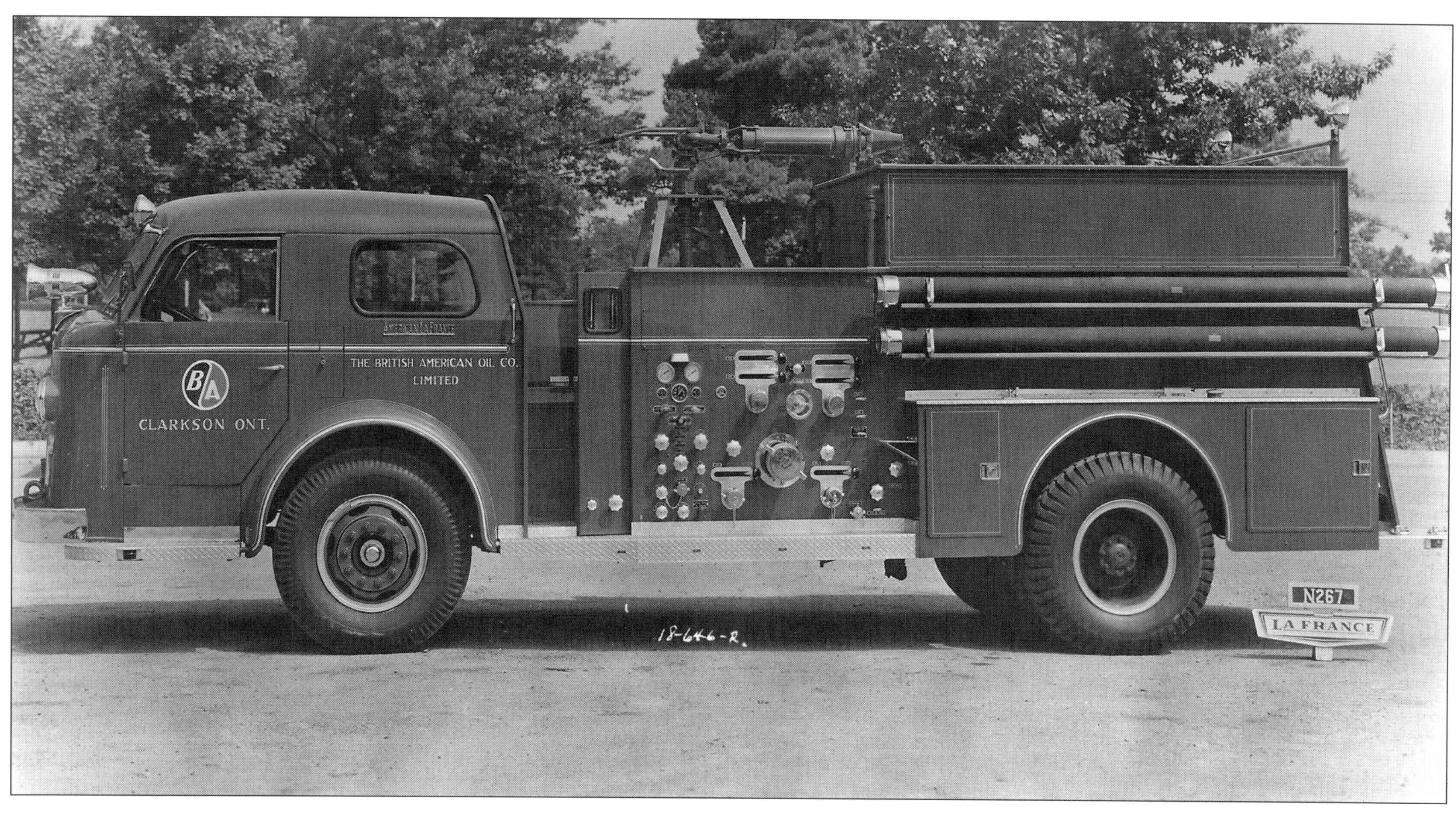

Clarkson, Ontario / British American Oil Co. Ltd. - 08/26/57; Model 810-PNC-FOAM; Serial # N-267 - Rated at 1,000 GPM and with separate water and foam tanks, this 800 Series Pumper provided refinery protection for a private, in-plant fire brigade.

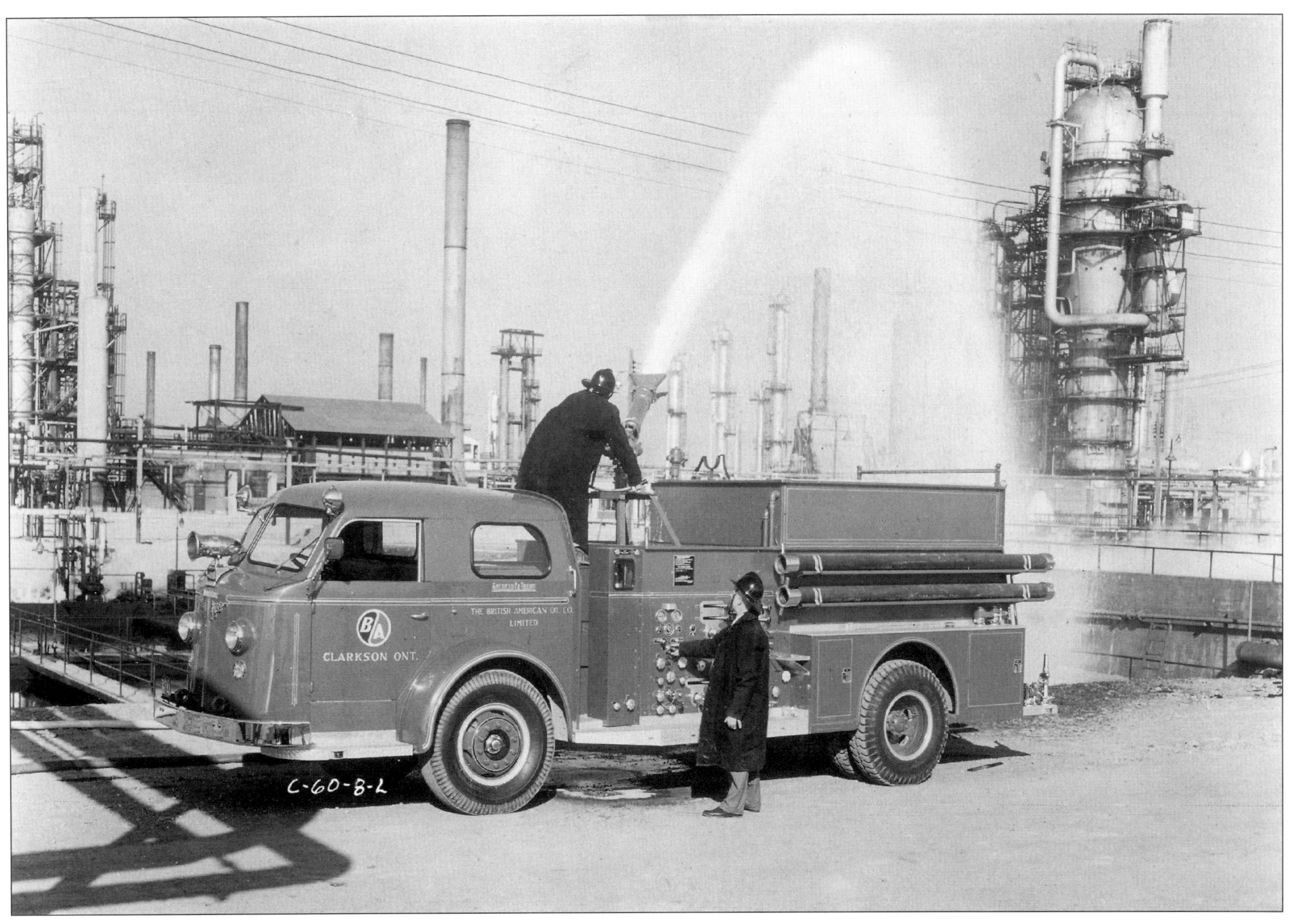

Clarkson, Ontario / British American Oil Co. Ltd. - 08/26/57; Model 810-PNC-FOAM; Serial # N-267 - American LaFrance used this training session to promote the rig's versatility and ease of operation by only two firefighters for future potential refinery customers.

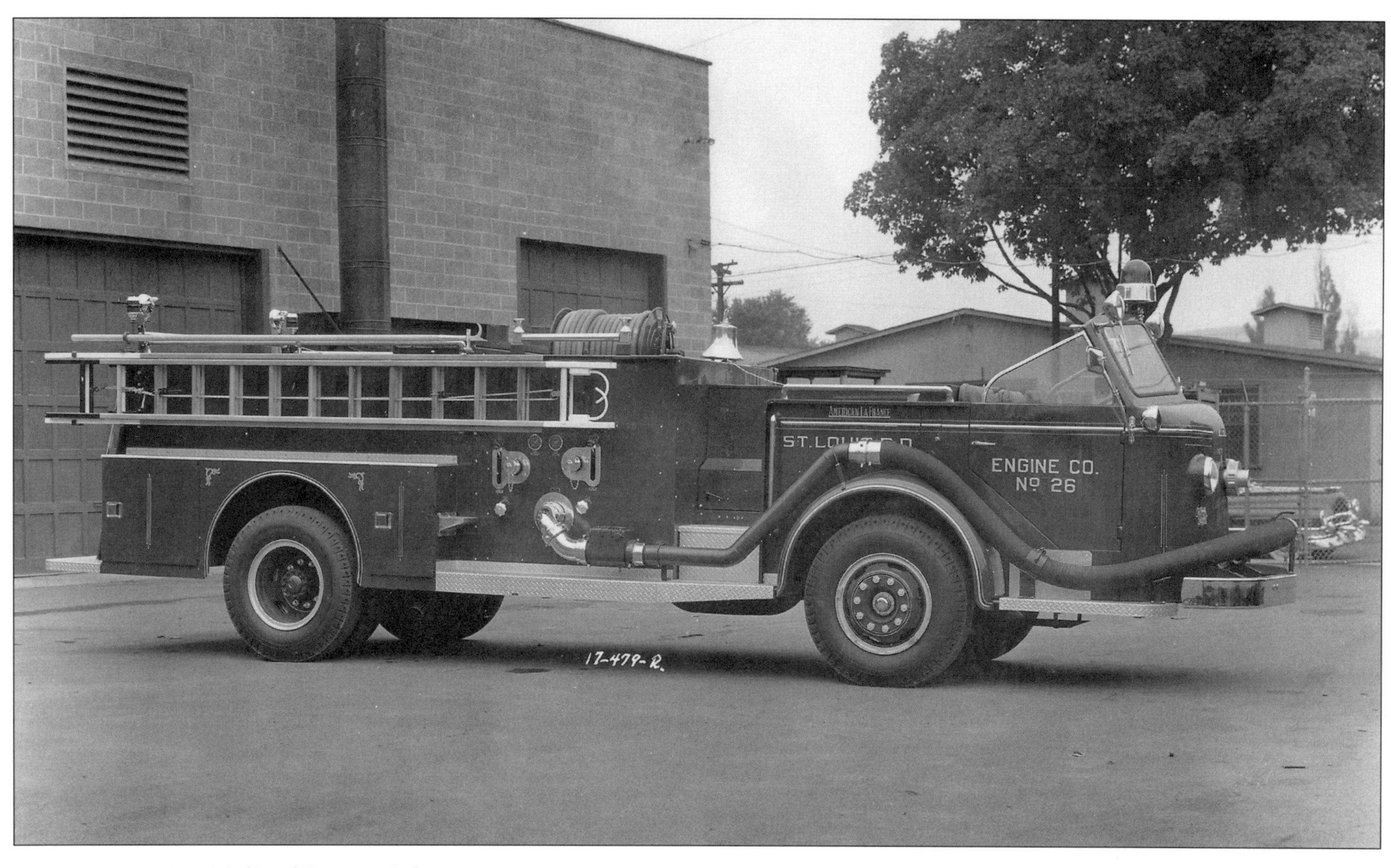

St. Louis, MO - 08/29/57; Model D-810-PKO; Serial #'s N-285 through N-287 - St. Louis went back to open cab for these three 800 Series Pumpers.

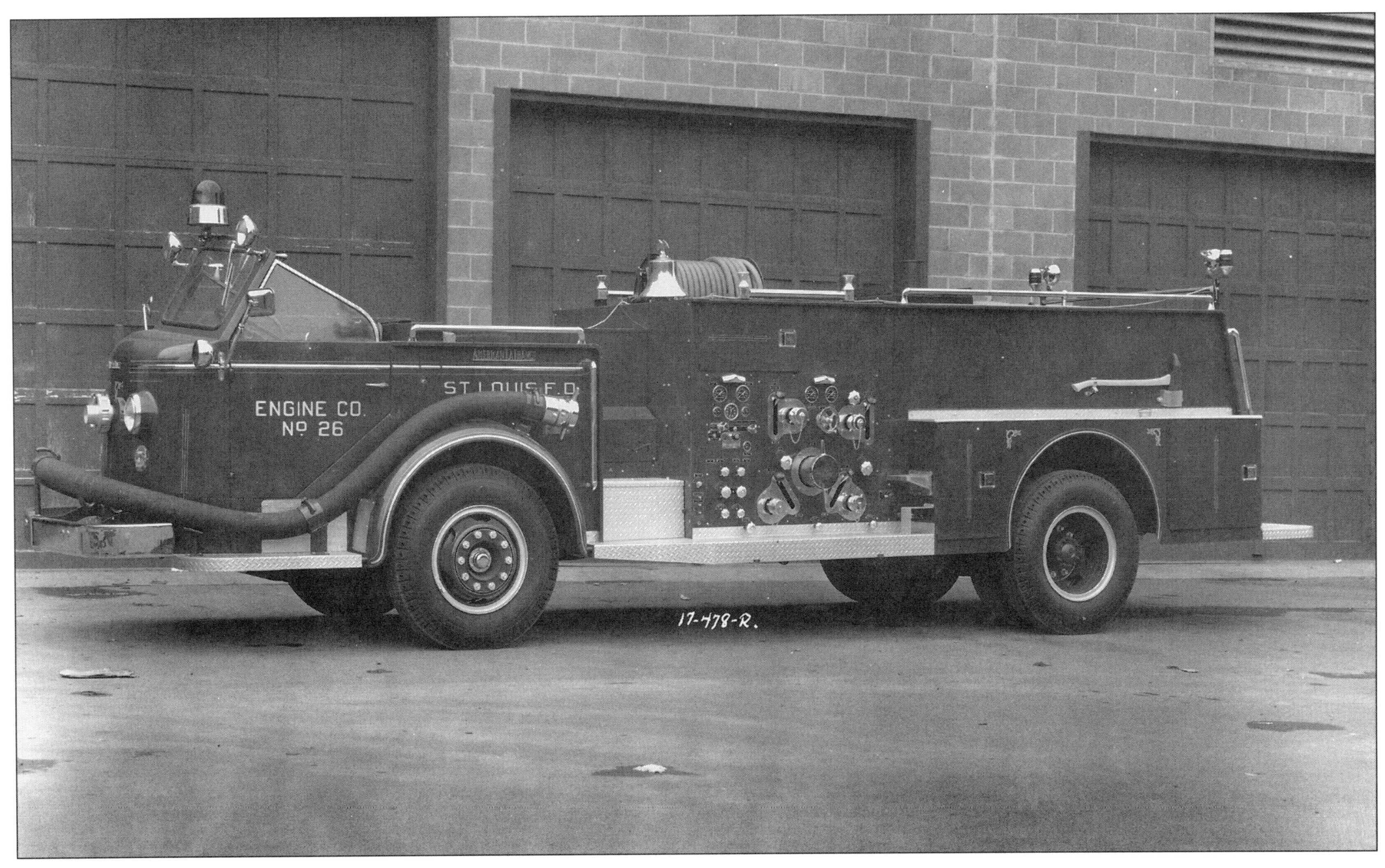

St. Louis, MO - 08/29/57; Model D-810-PKO; Serial #'s N-285 through N-287 - The absence of the hard suction trays is evident above the rear compartments, but the pre-connected, squirrel-tail hard suction, a St. Louis feature, eliminates the need for them. Note, also, the bell mounted near the top-mounted booster reel.

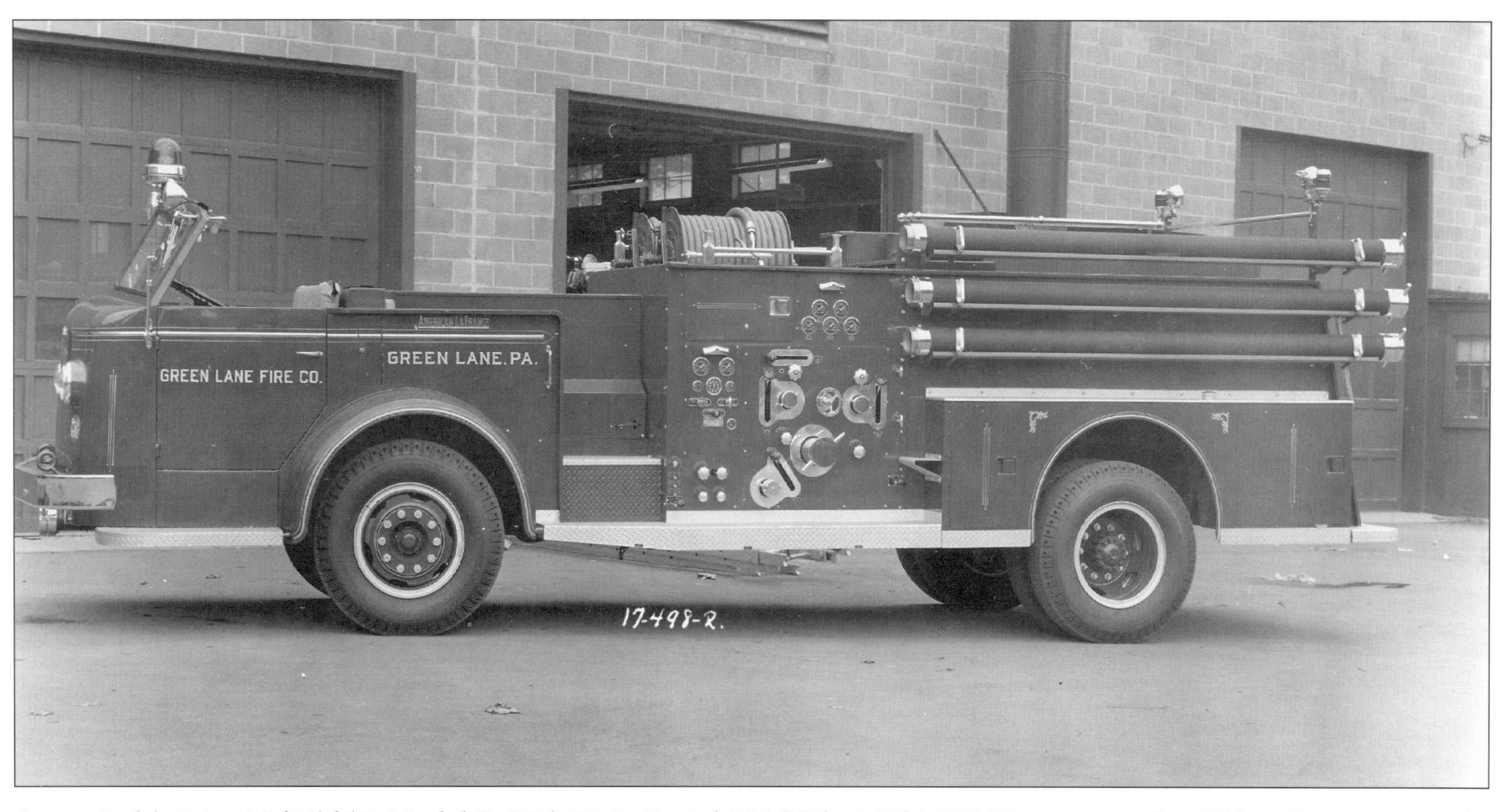

Green Lake, PA - 09/15/57; Model C-875-PDO; Serial # N-295 - A 750 GPM Pumper with a 750 gallon water tank, Green Lake's specifications called for individual pressure gauges for each 2 1/2" discharge and each booster reel as well.

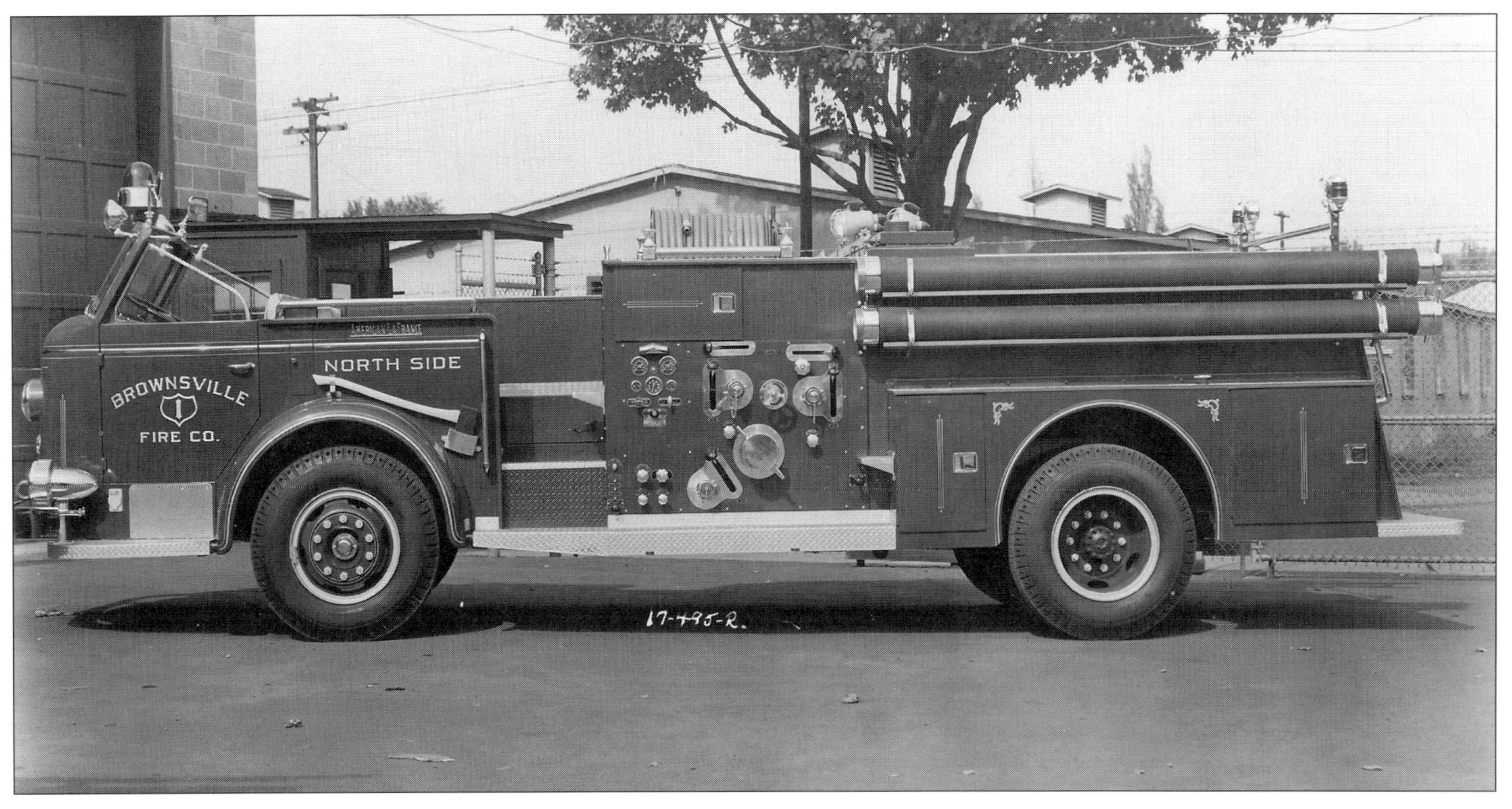

Brownsville, PA - 09/20/57; Model D-810-PEO; Serial # 9475 - A straight-on side shot by the American LaFrance photographer, this 800 Series Pumper has auxiliary Circle-D Hand Lights mounted above and just ahead of the hose bed. The smaller, chrome hand wheel just about centered on the pump panel controls the two-stage function of the pump.

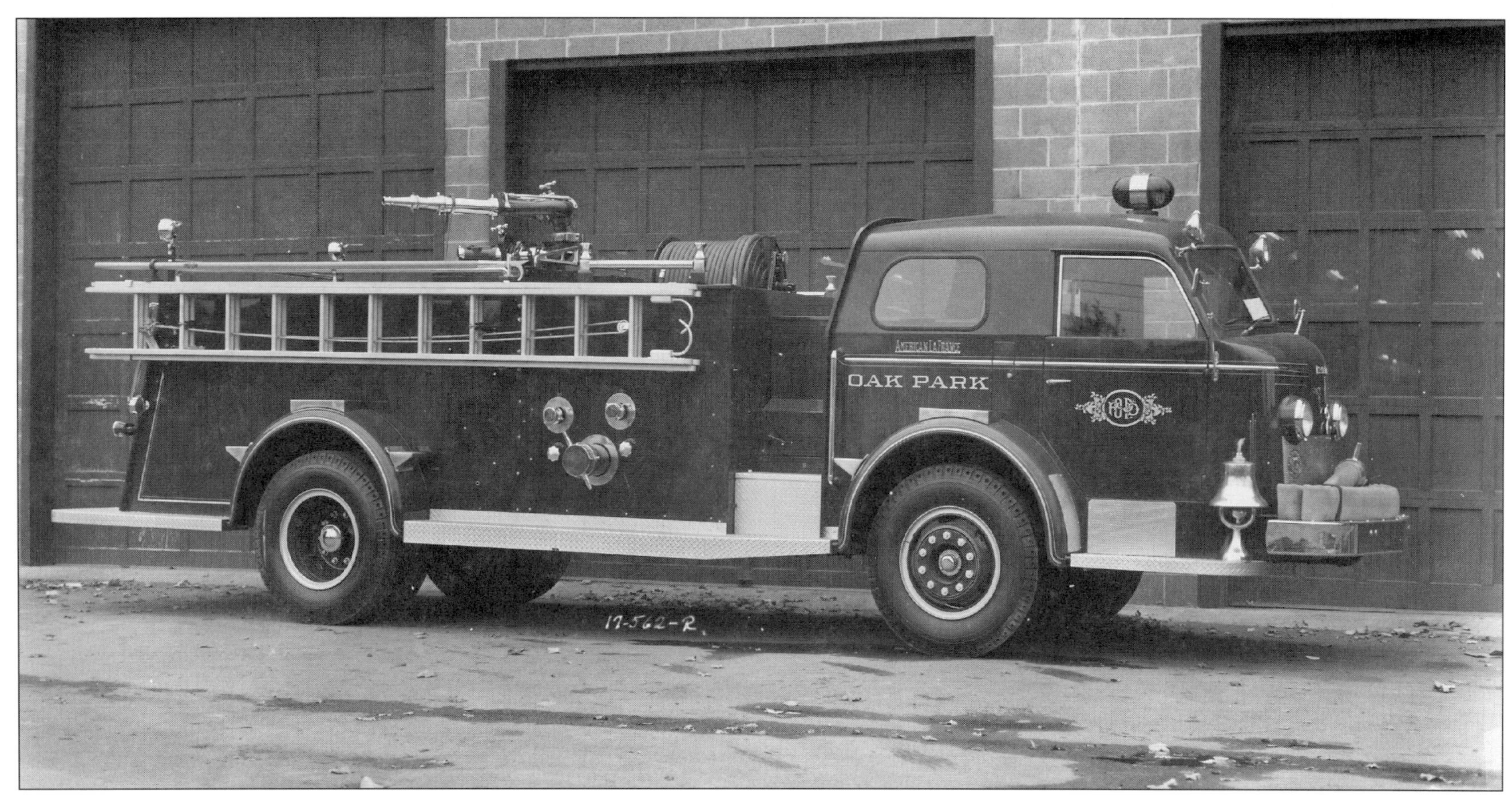

Oak Park, IL - 10/25/57; Model D-810-PJC; Serial # L-5556 - The influence of the neighboring Chicago Fire Department is evident by the Mars DX-40 'football' light on the roof.

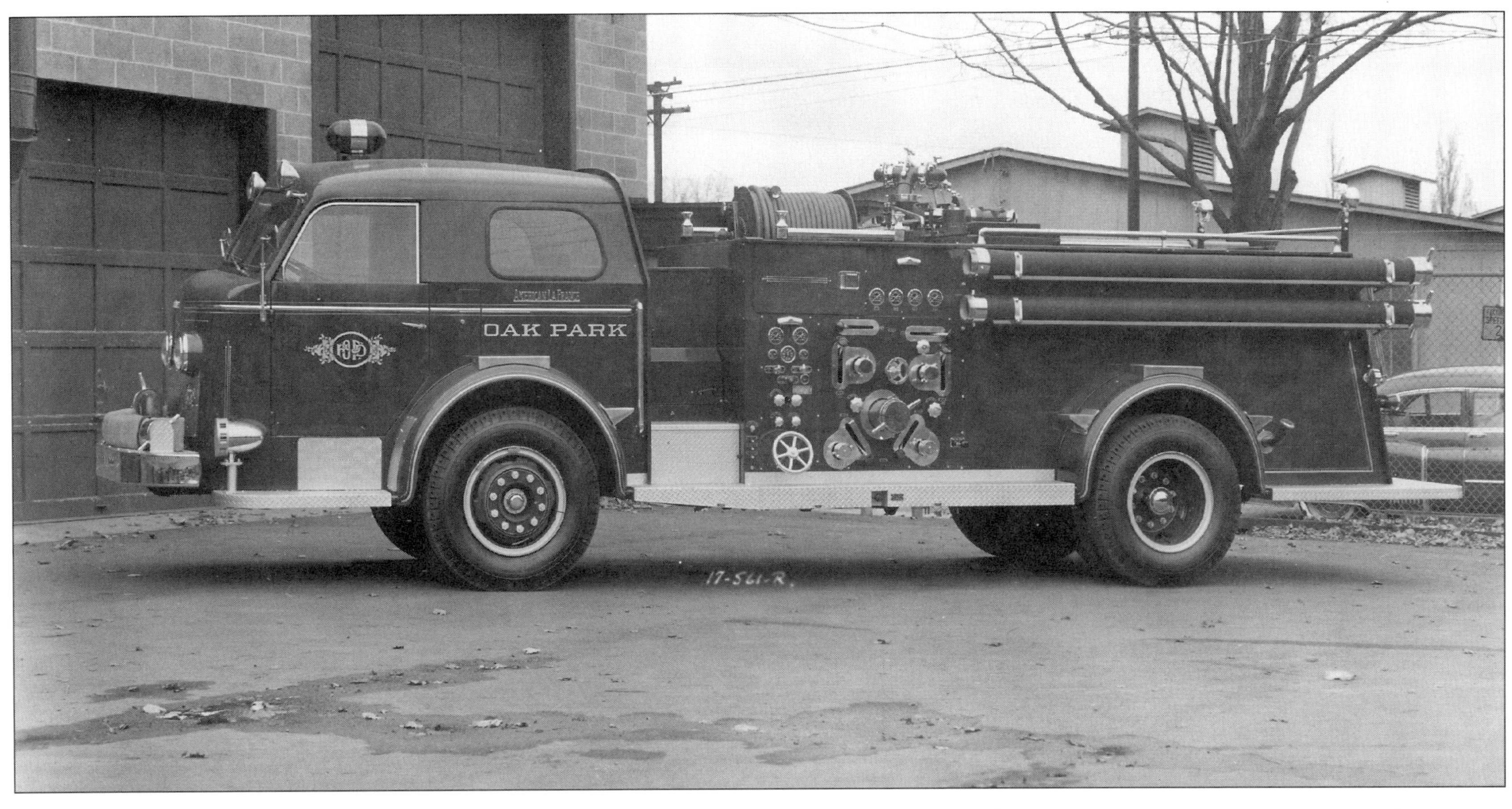

Oak Park, IL - 10/25/57; Model D-810-PJC; Serial # L-5556 - Oak Park's Pumper was equipped with a pre-connected, gated front suction, and a top-mounted portable deluge gun. Notice, also, the absence of full rear compartmentation on this 800 Series Pumper.

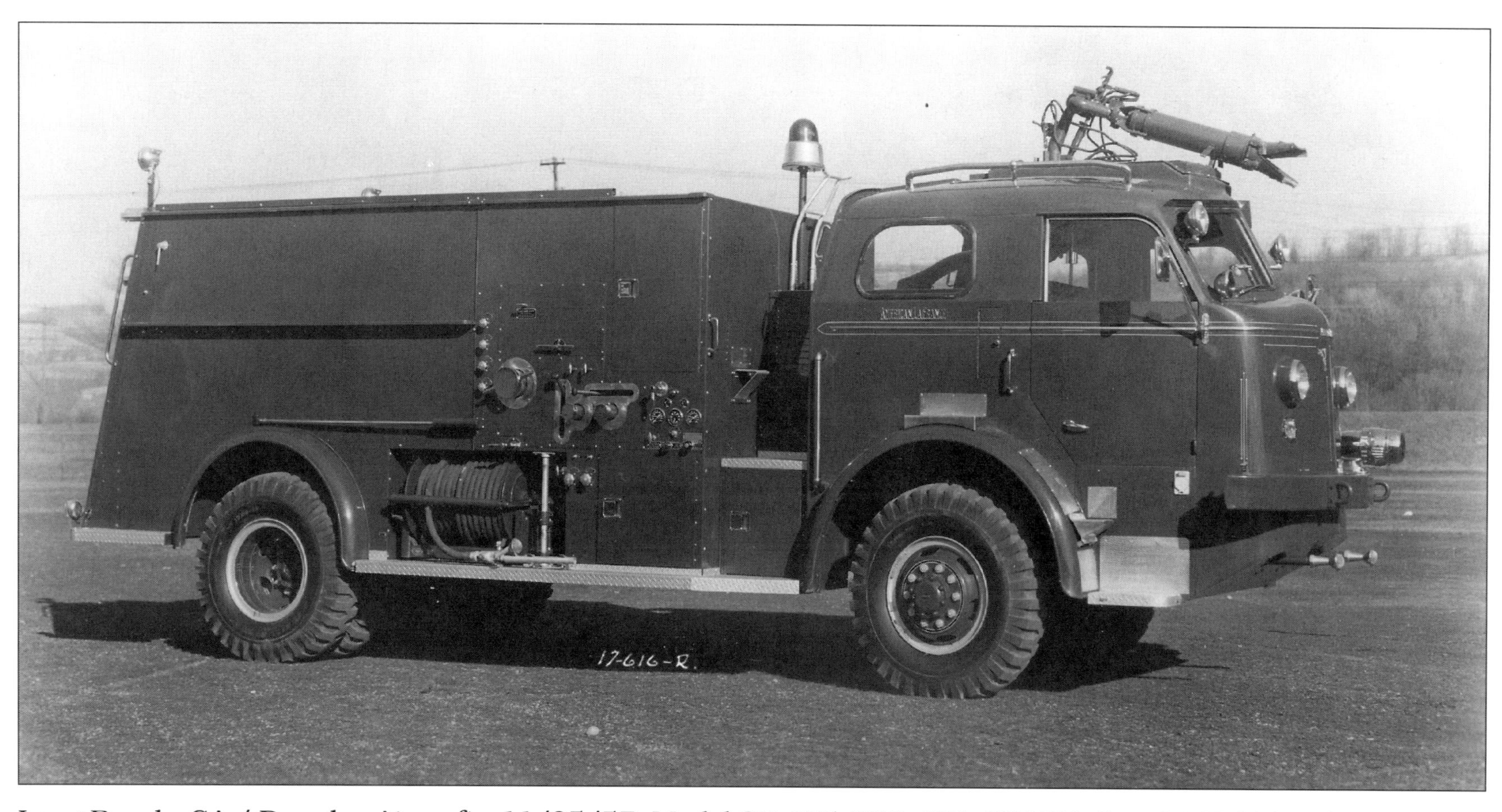

Long Beach, CA / Douglas Aircraft - 11/25/57; Model CR-875-PNC-4X4-CRASH; Serial # N-293 - This unit was made specifically for Douglas Aircraft's Lakewood Plant at Long Beach, CA. While not as big as some of the other 700 Series CFR units that ALF produced, this piece could still deliver a knockout punch if need be.

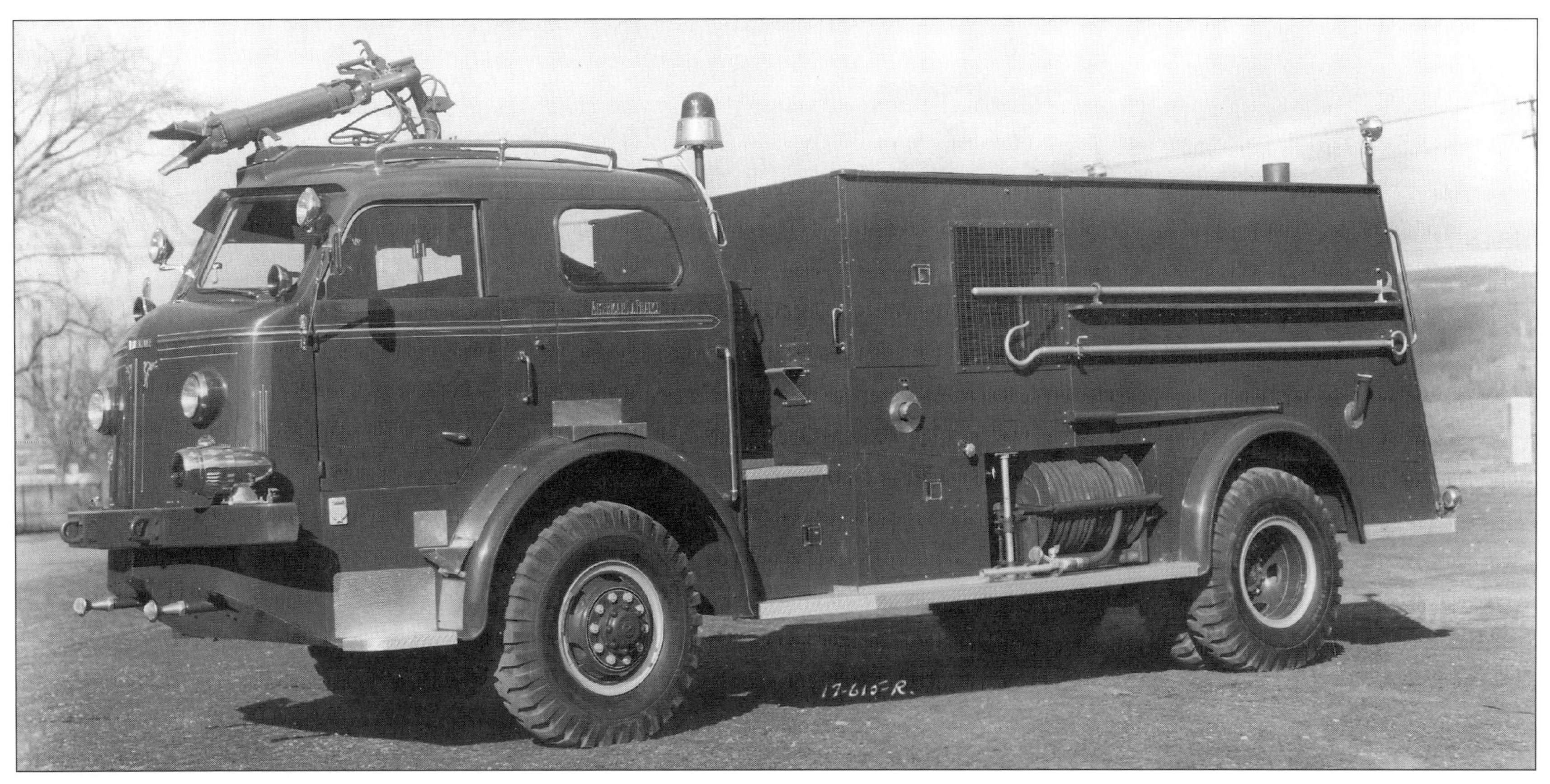

Long Beach, CA / Douglas Aircraft - 11/25/57; Model CR-875-PNC-4X4-CRASH; Serial # N-293 - The pump was rated at just 750 GPM, but that was enough to supply a good, solid master stream of water and foam mixture from the overhead, front-mounted turret.

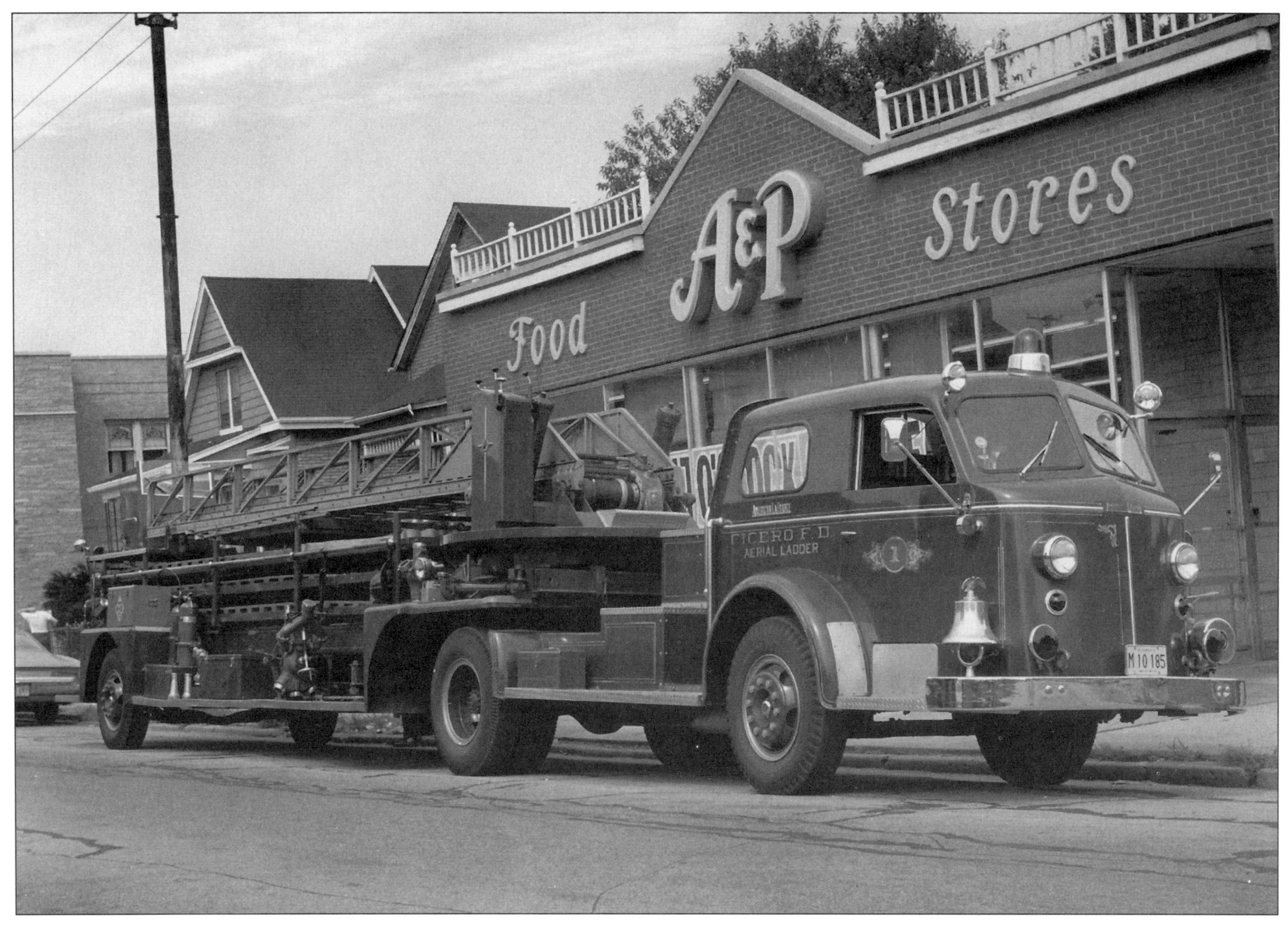

Cicero, IL - 01/22/58; Model 700-TMC; Serial # N-349 – Cicero ordered this 1958 700 Series Tractor to pull their 1954 100' Aerial Trailer. The aerial ladder was then reduced in size to a 3-section 85' size, making this photograph a 1958 tractor pulling a 1954 3-section 85' aerial trailer.

Fuller Transmissions – This sheet appears to have been a magazine page that is dated April, 1958 in the upper left-hand corner. Unfortunately, no other reference could be found as to its actual origin. It is believed that it could have been produced and promoted by the Fuller Transmission Company, a longtime supplier of components for American LaFrance Fire Apparatus. Reference is made more than once on the sheet to Fuller Transmissions (5-Speed 5-A-620 and 5-C-650) used in conjunction with American LaFrance and Continental Engines. While American LaFrance did build their own transmissions, they also used Fuller and other manufacturers as well.

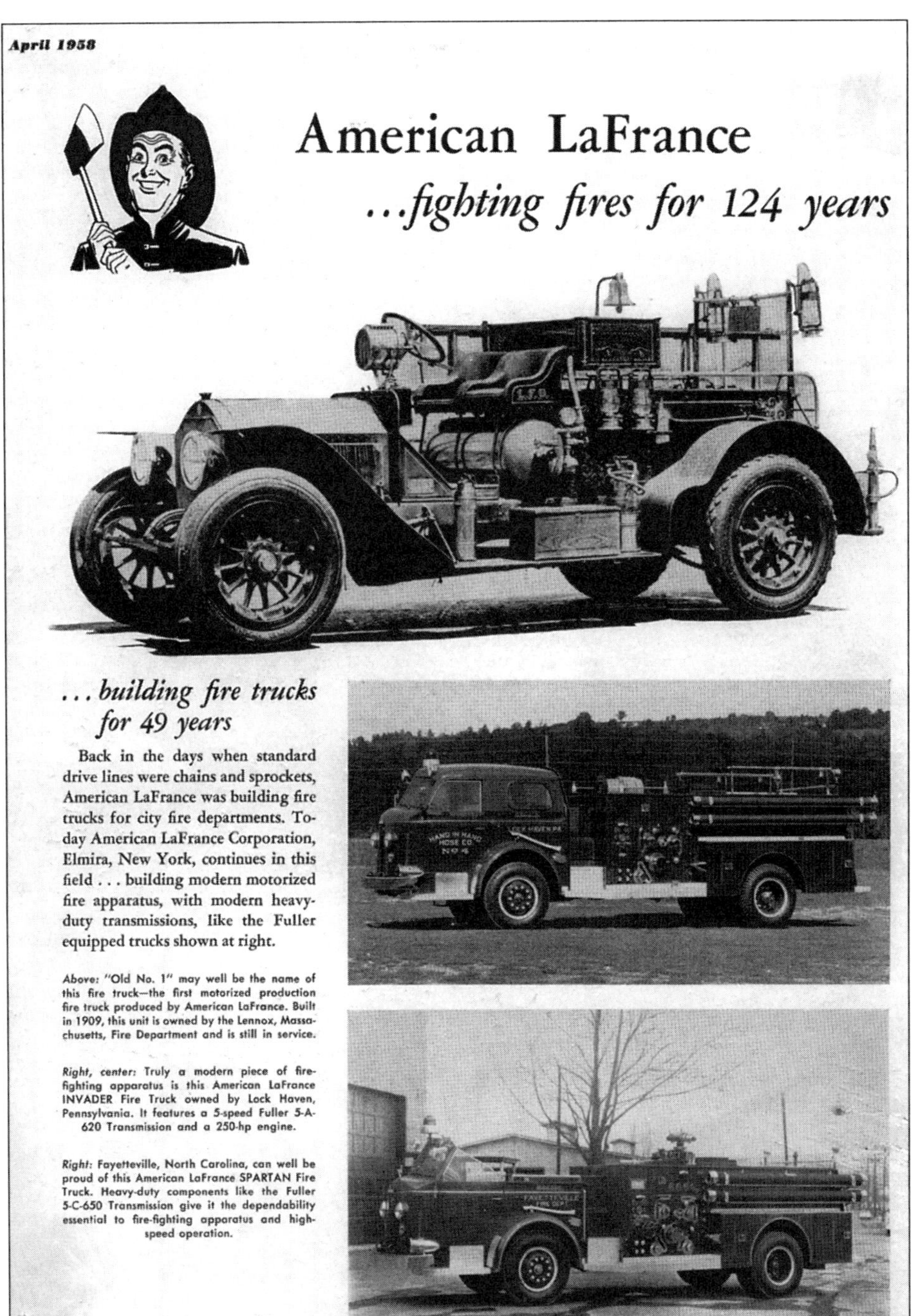

...building fire trucks for 49 years

Back in the days when standard drive lines were chains and sprockets, American LaFrance was building fire trucks for city fire departments. To-day American LaFrance Corporation, Elmira, New York, continues in this field . . . building modern motorized fire apparatus, with modern heavy-duty transmissions, like the Fuller equipped trucks shown at right.

Above: "Old No. 1" may well be the name of this fire truck—the first motorized production fire truck produced by American LaFrance. Built in 1909, this unit is owned by the Lennox, Massachusetts, Fire Department and is still in service.

Right, center: Truly a modern piece of fire-fighting apparatus is this American LaFrance INVADER Fire Truck owned by Lock Haven, Pennsylvania. It features a 5-speed Fuller 5-A-620 Transmission and a 250-hp engine.

Right: Fayetteville, North Carolina, can well be proud of this American LaFrance SPARTAN Fire Truck. Heavy-duty components like the Fuller 5-C-650 Transmission give it the dependability essential to fire-fighting apparatus and high-speed operation.

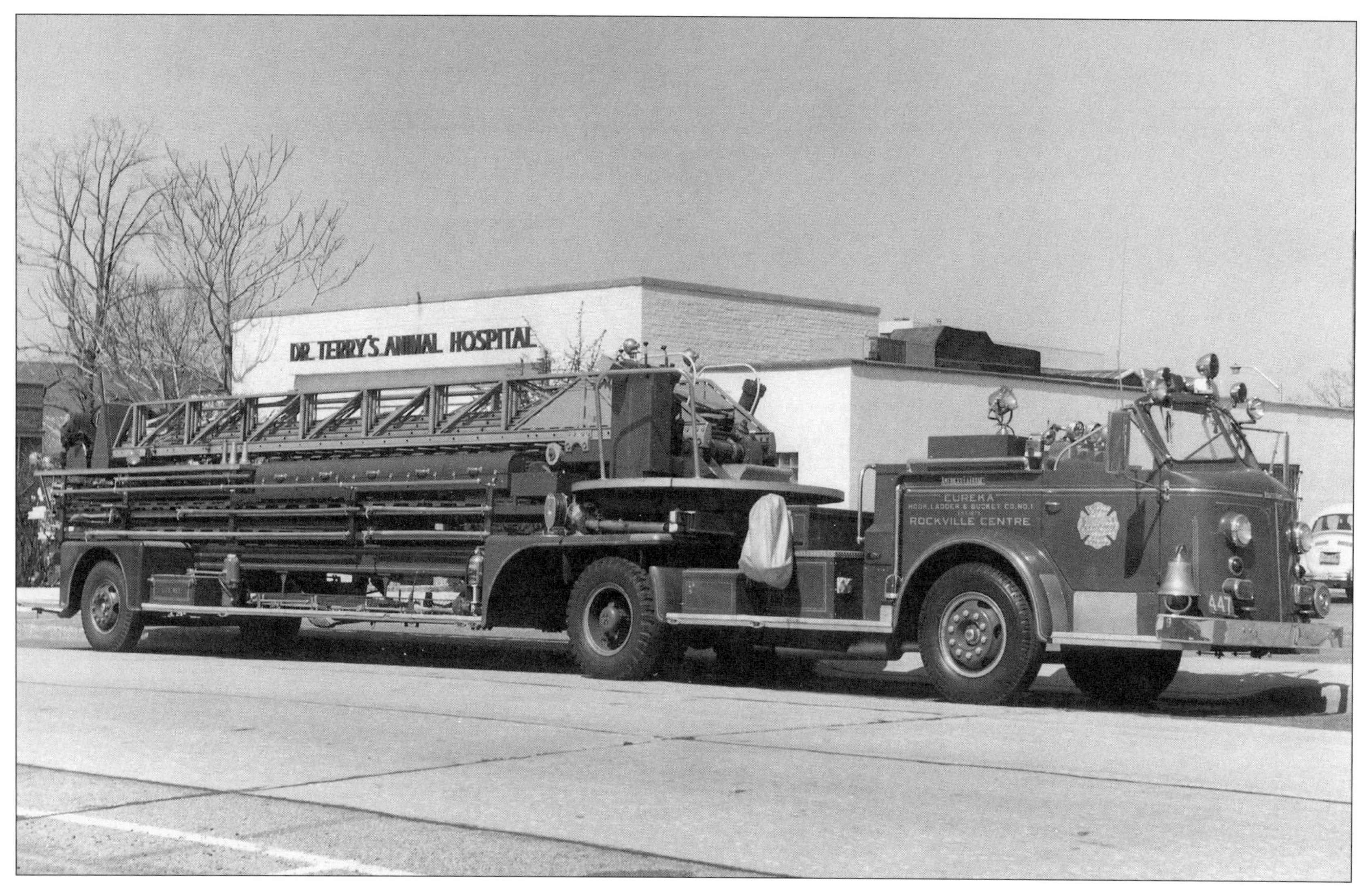

Rockville Centre, NY - 04/17/58; Model 7-100-TMO; Serial # N-361 - This TDA is far from basic. Note the fully enclosed compartments (there are five of them) directly underneath the aerial ladder. Other not-from-stock features include West Coast Mirrors and arrow-type directional signals (these would be stock on the yet-to-come Century Series).

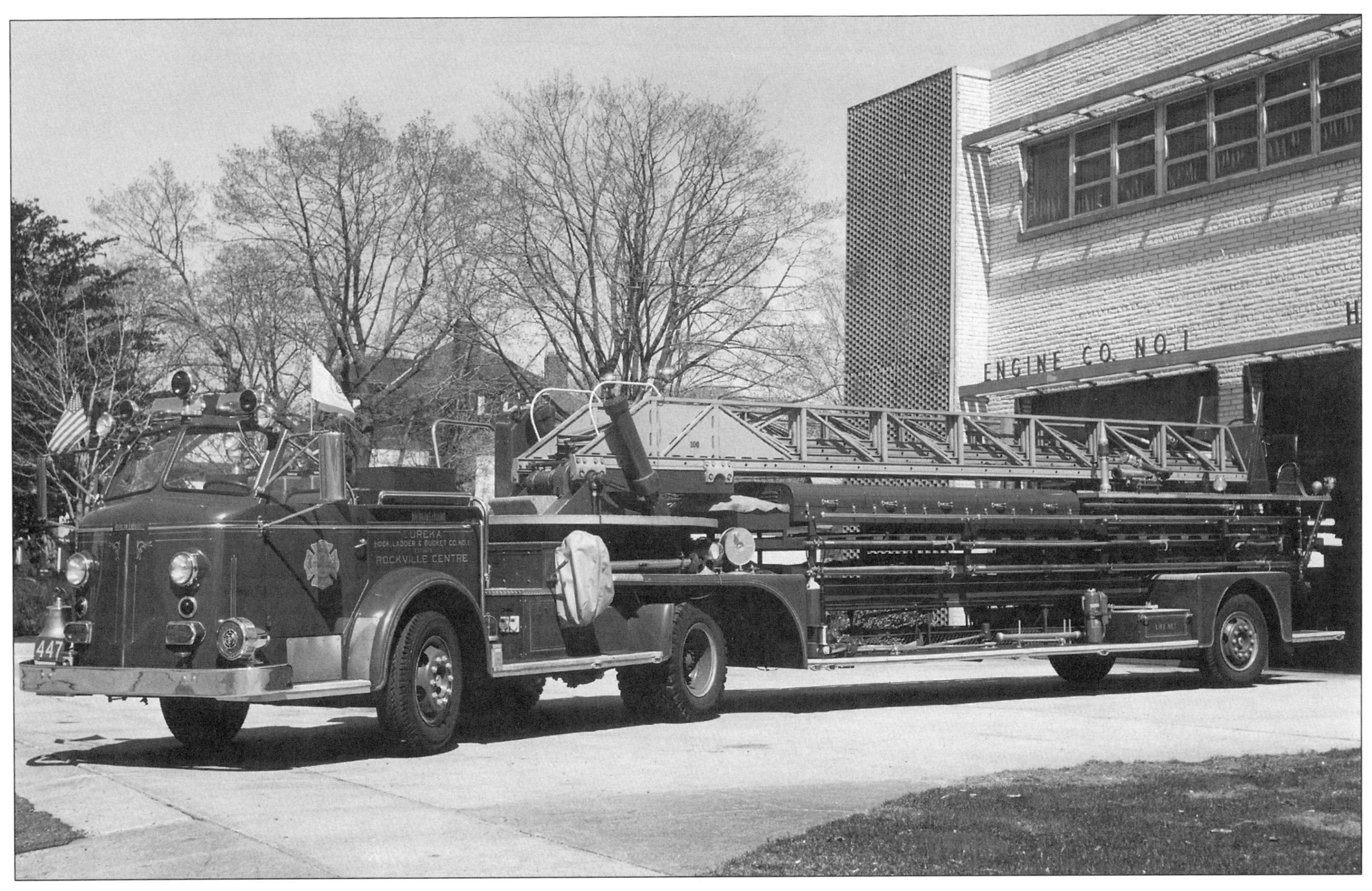

Rockville Centre, NY - 04/17/58; Model 7-100-TMO; Serial # N-361 - Running as Nassau County, NY, Ladder 447, this 100' TDA had air masks mounted on each side of the tractor.

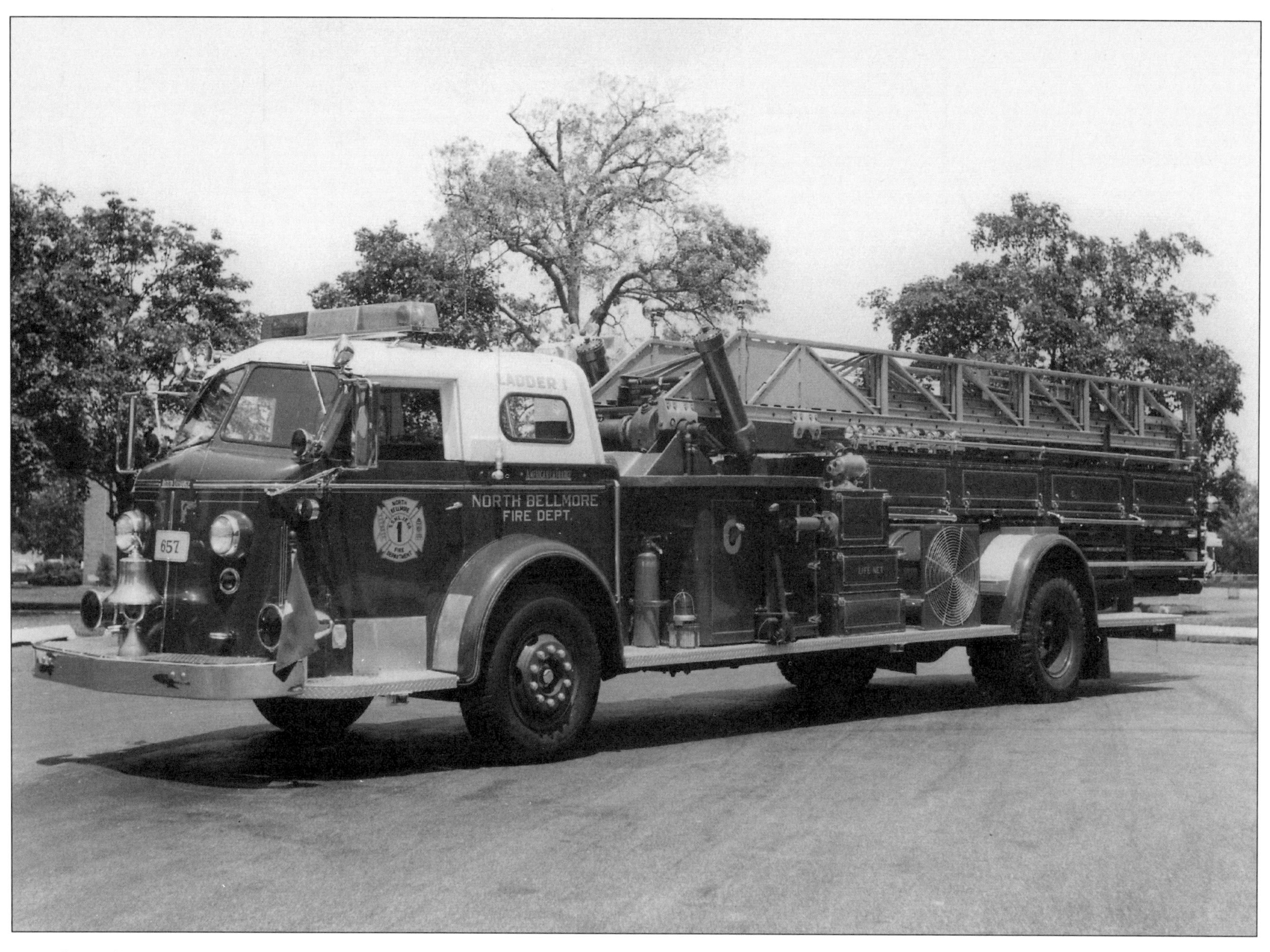

North Bellmore, NY - 04/28/58; Model 7-85-AKO; Serial # N-378 - North Bellmore took advantage of the add-on fiberglass top for their originally open-cab ladder truck.

118

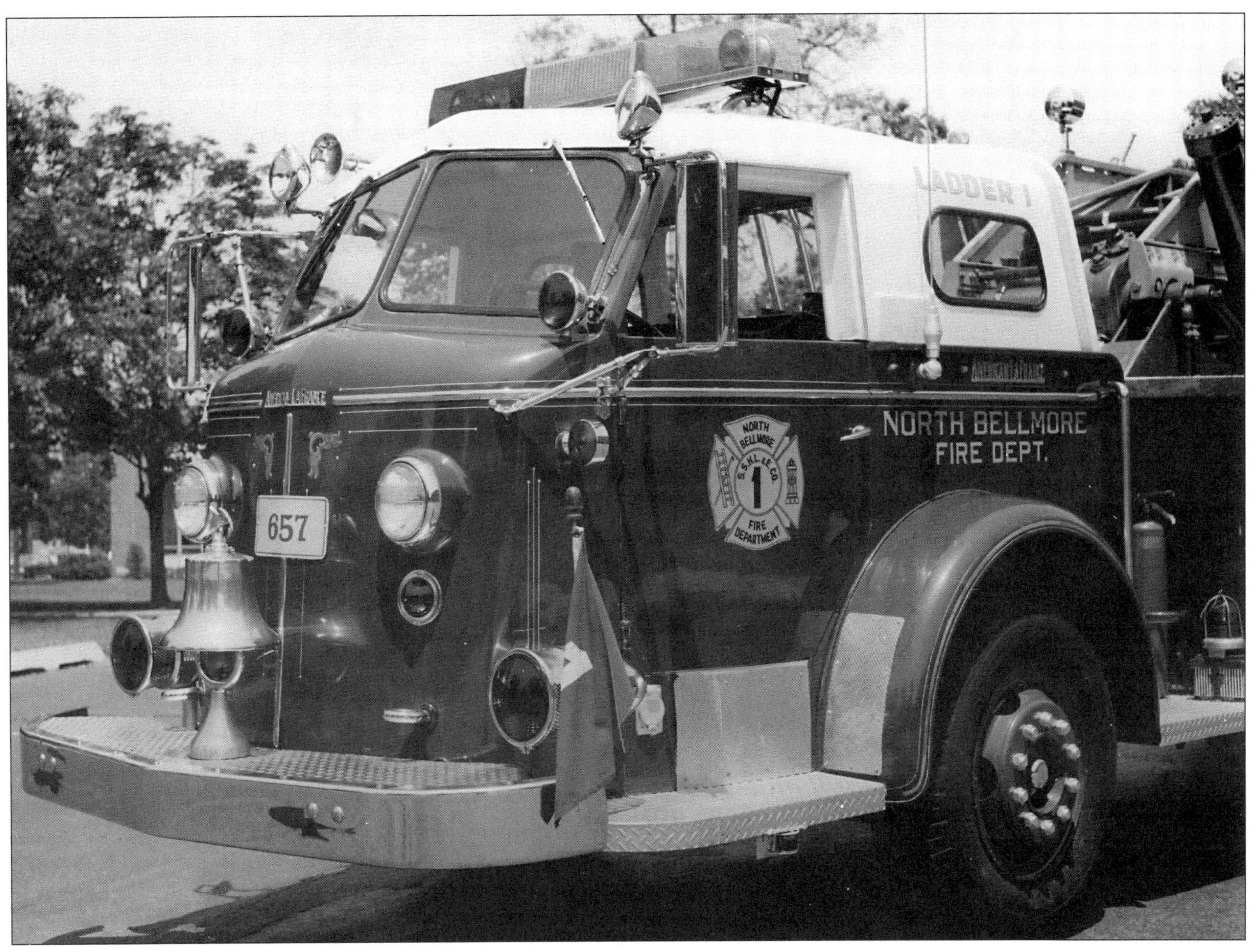

North Bellmore, NY - 04/28/58; Model 7-85-AKO; Serial # N-378 - A close-up of the front end shows twin Sterling Model 30 Sirens; the traditional bell mounted and centered on an extended front bumper; an air horn and a Federal Twin-Sonic Light Bar on the new fiberglass cab top.

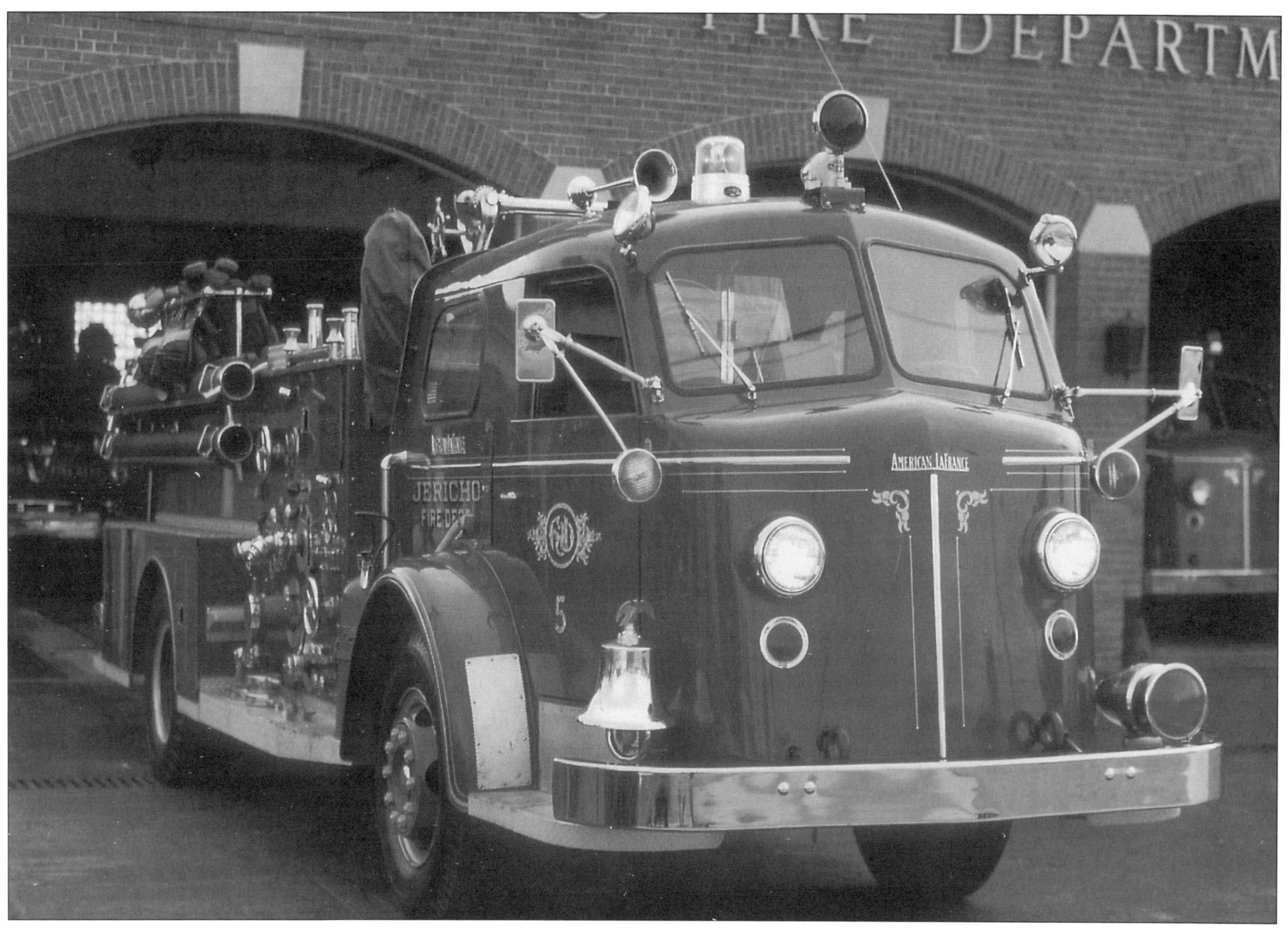

Jericho, NY - 05/08/58; Model D-875-PJC-H; Serial # L-5587 - The front end of Jericho's 800 Series Pumper was all business - a Mars Rotating Beacon with blue sealed beams; a Mars Figure 8 Light; two alternating flashers and Sterling Model 30 Sirenlight combination. An air horn on top completed the package.

120

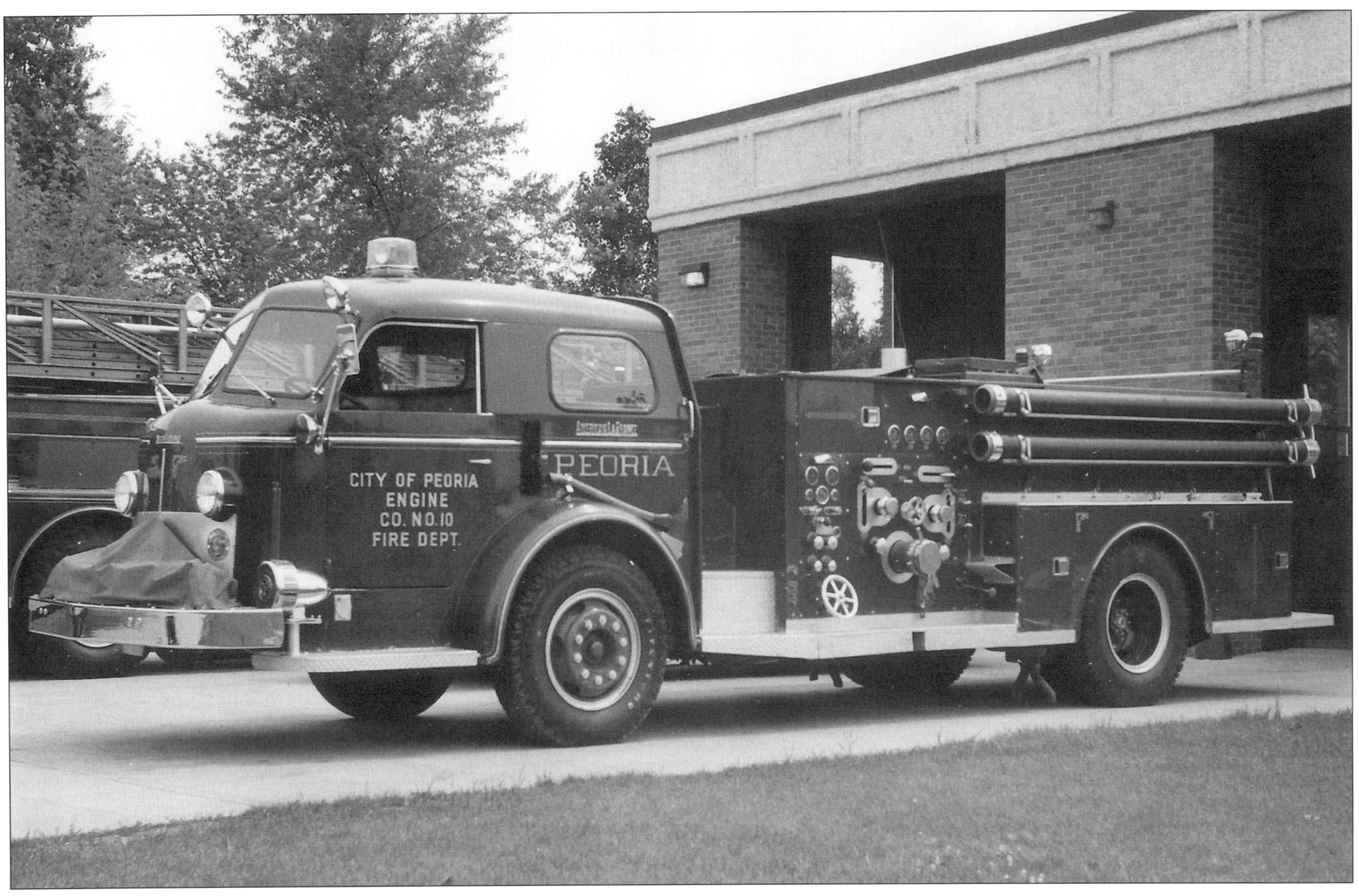

Peoria, IL - 06/18/58 - Model C-810-PKC; Serial # N-396 - Peoria's pumper was rated at 1,000 GPM and had a 300 gallon water tank. The front suction was preconnected and controlled by the Kennedy Valve hand wheel just above the running board on the pump panel.

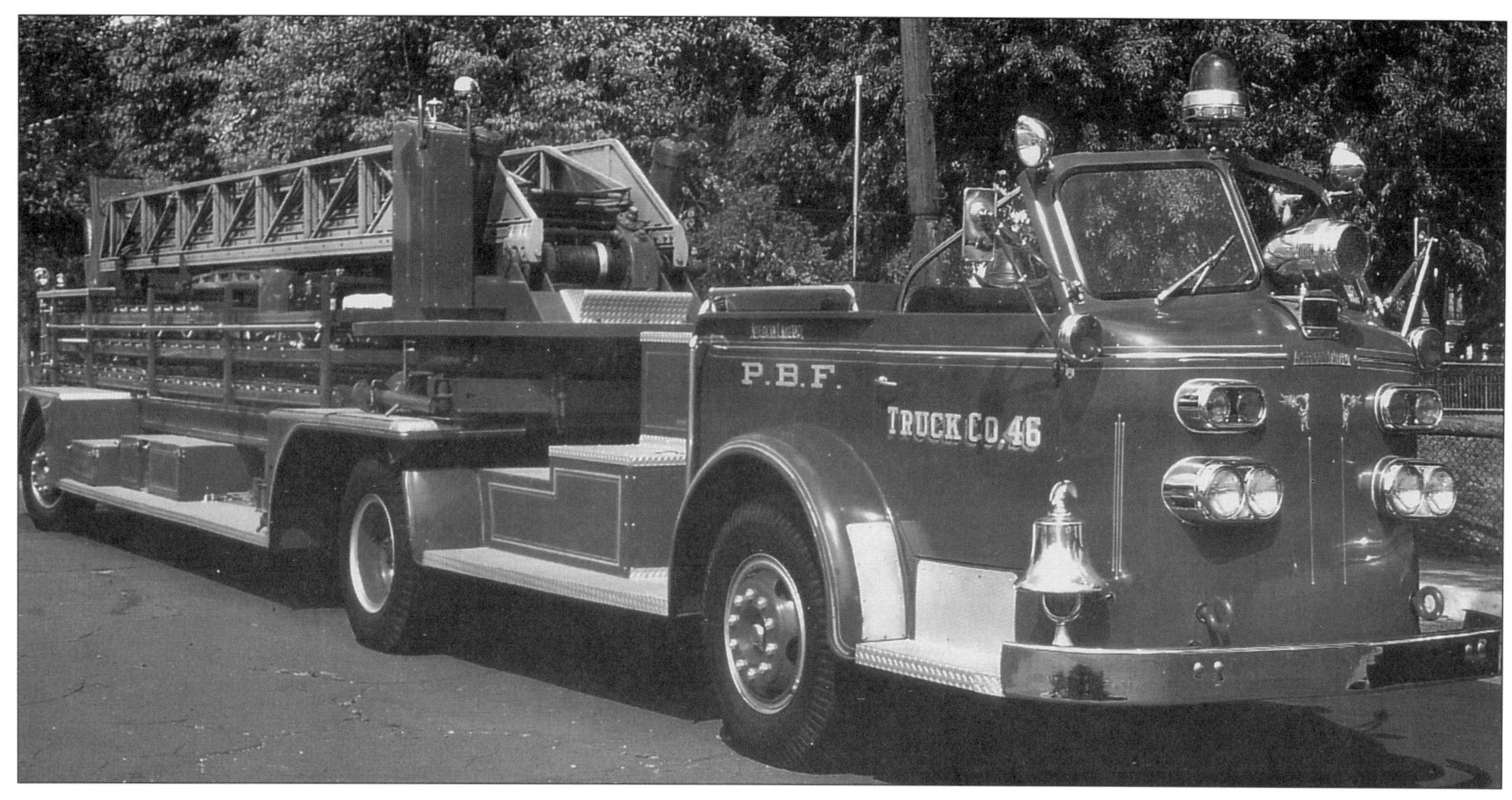

Pittsburgh, PA - 05/29/59; Model 7-100-TNO; Serial # N-434 - The 900 Series was still in the start-up production phase at this time, and some parts and accessories designed for the 900 Series showed up on late 700 Series models as well. Remember - even though decked out as you see it here, American LaFrance classified Pittsburgh's 1959 TDA as a 700 Series.

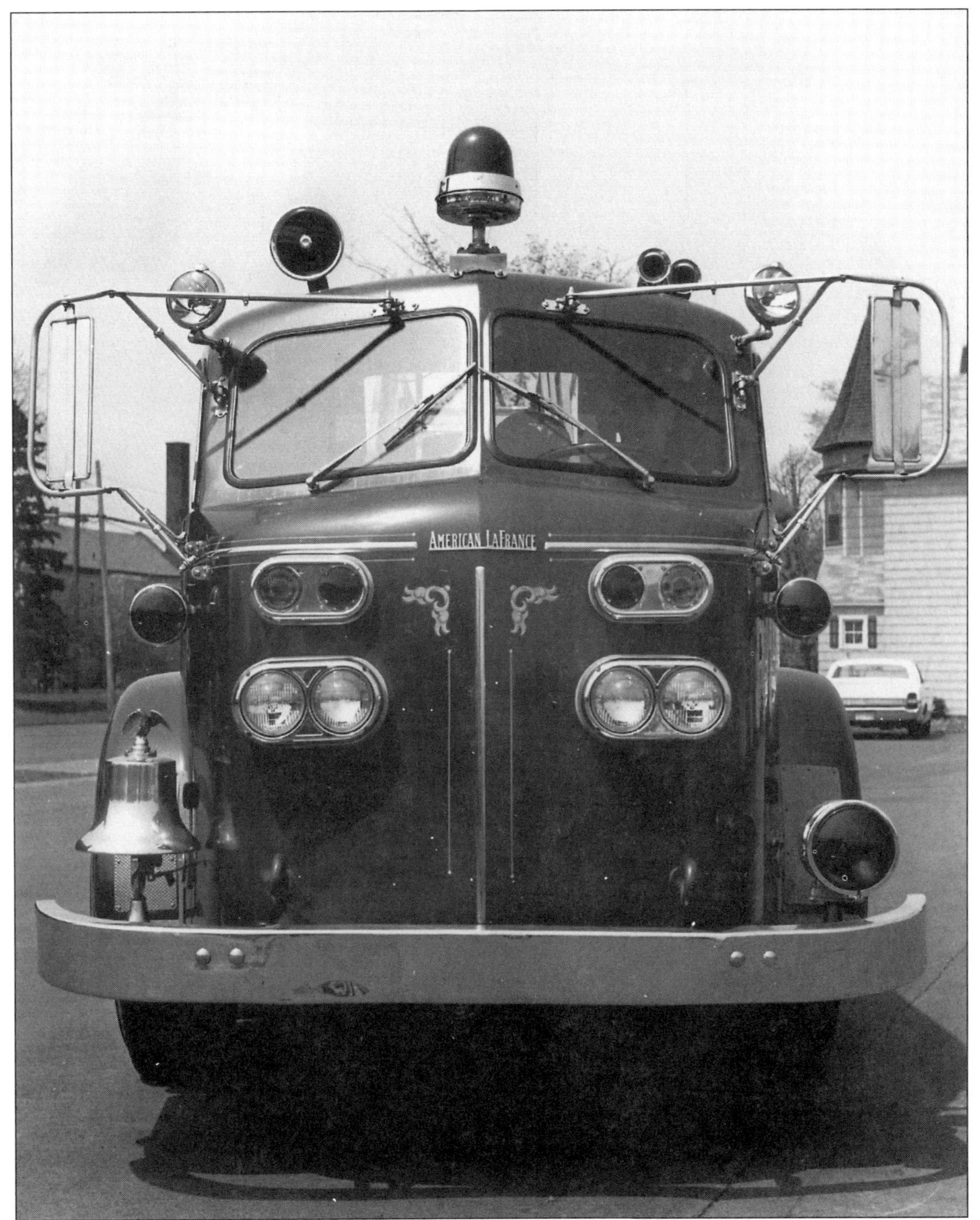

Superior, WI - 09/02/59; Model 710-QLC; Serial # N-440 - When I shot this photograph, I did so to illustrate the combined use of 700 Series and 900 Series parts and accessories on the same rig, yet coming that way from the factory. The next two photographs will show you Superior's rig in its entirety.

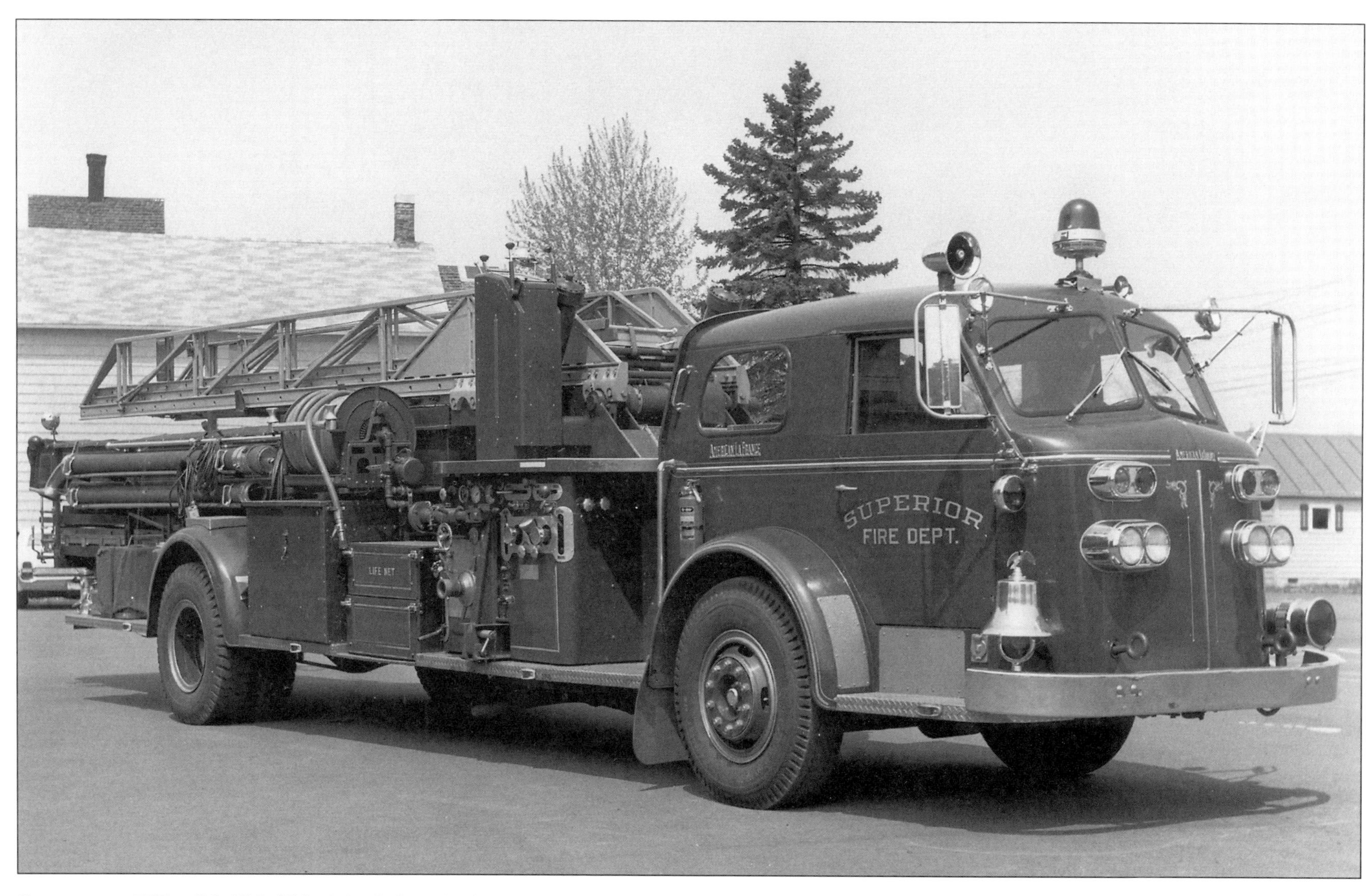

Superior, WI - 09/02/59; Model 710-QLC; Serial # N-440 - The Superior Quint components consisted of a 1,000 GPM Pump, a small water tank and a 65' aerial ladder.

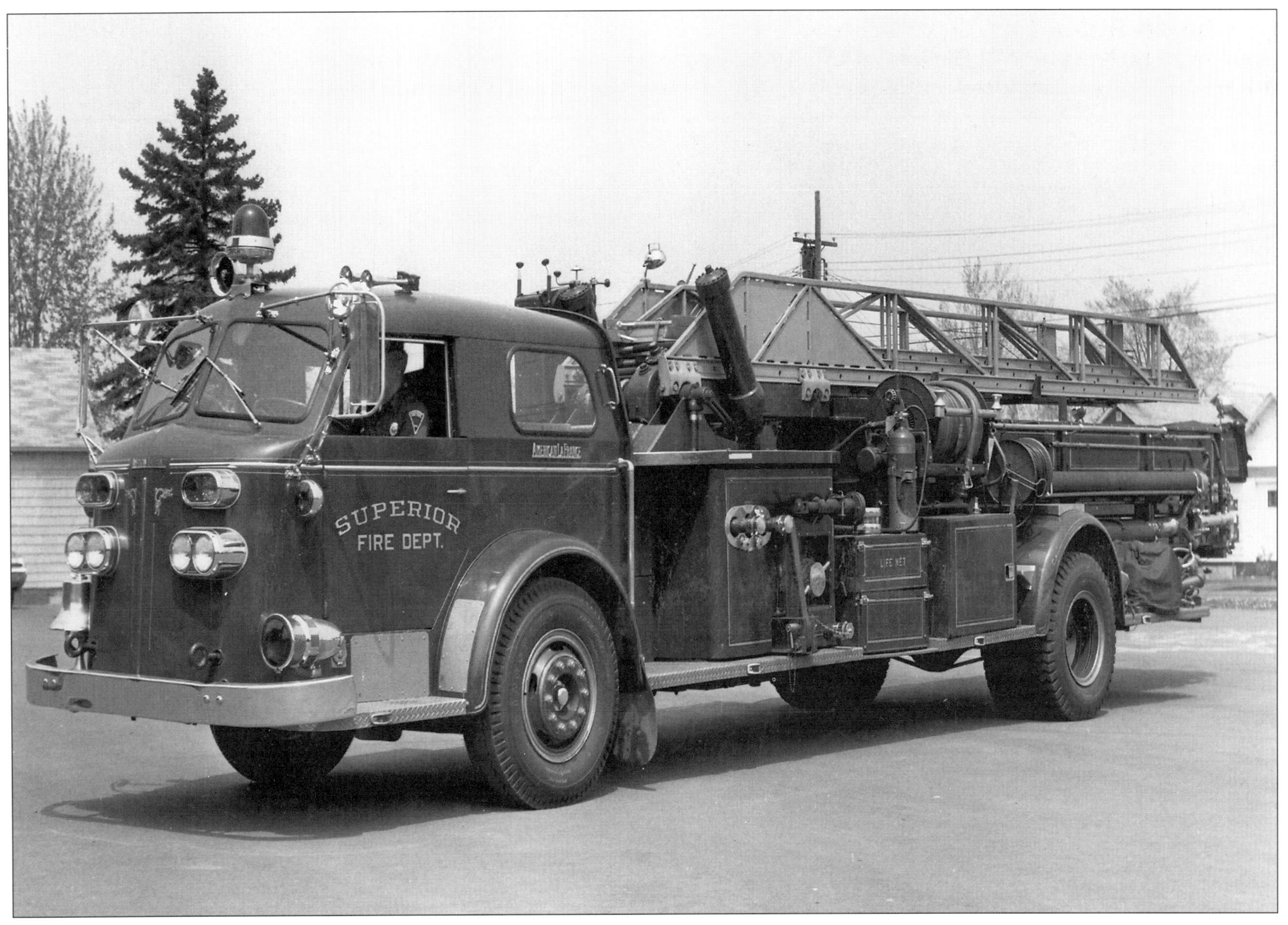

Superior, WI - 09/02/59; Model 710-QLC; Serial # N-440 - From the driver's side of the Superior Quint you can see the second electrically operated booster reel, electric power cable reel, CO 2 fire extinguisher and an extra compartment added just ahead of the rear fender.

Combined Index for:

American LaFrance 700 Series 1945 - 1952 Photo Archive (Pages indicated by a)
American LaFrance 700 & 800 Series 1953 - 1958 Photo Archive (Pages indicated by b)

More Titles from Iconografix:

AMERICAN CULTURE

AMERICAN SERVICE STATIONS 1935-1943
ISBN 1-882256-27-1
COCA-COLA: A HISTORY IN PHOTOGRAPHS 1930-1969
ISBN 1-882256-46-8
COCA-COLA: ITS VEHICLES IN PHOTOGRAPHS 1930-1969
ISBN 1-882256-47-6
PHILLIPS 66 1945-1954   ISBN 1-882256-42-5

AUTOMOTIVE

CADILLAC 1948-1964   ISBN 1-882256-83-2
CORVETTE PROTOTYPES & SHOW CARS
ISBN 1-882256-77-8
EARLY FORD V-8S 1932-1942   ISBN 1-882256-97-2
FERRARI PININFARINA 1952-1996 ISBN 1-882256-65-4
IMPERIAL 1955-1963   ISBN 1-882256-22-0
IMPERIAL 1964-1968   ISBN 1-882256-23-9
LINCOLN MOTOR CARS 1920-1942 ISBN 1-882256-57-3
LINCOLN MOTOR CARS 1946-1960 ISBN 1-882256-58-1
PACKARD MOTOR CARS 1935-1942 ISBN 1-882256-44-1
PACKARD MOTOR CARS 1946-1958 ISBN 1-882256-45-X
PONTIAC DREAM CARS, SHOW CARS & PROTOTYPES
1928-1998   ISBN 1-882256-93-X
PONTIAC FIREBIRD TRANS-AM 1969-1999
ISBN 1-882256-95-6
PORSCHE 356 1948-1965   ISBN 1-882256-85-9
STUDEBAKER 1933-1942   ISBN 1-882256-24-7
STUDEBAKER 1946-1958   ISBN 1-882256-25-5

EMERGENCY VEHICLES

AMERICAN LAFRANCE 700 SERIES 1945-1952
ISBN 1-882256-90-5
AMERICAN LAFRANCE 700&800 SERIES 1953-1958
ISBN 1-882256-91-3
CLASSIC AMERICAN AMBULANCES 1900-1998
ISBN 1-882256-94-8
FIRE CHIEF CARS 1900-1997   ISBN 1-882256-87-5
MACK MODEL B FIRE TRUCKS 1954-1966*
ISBN 1-882256-62-X
MACK MODEL CF FIRE TRUCKS 1967-1981*
ISBN 1-882256-63-8
MACK MODEL L FIRE TRUCKS 1940-1954*
ISBN 1-882256-86-7

RACING

GT40   ISBN 1-882256-64-6

LE MANS 1950: THE BRIGGS CUNNINGHAM
CAMPAIGN   ISBN 1-882256-21-2
LOLA RACE CARS 1962-1990   ISBN 1-882256-73-5
LOTUS RACE CARS 1961-1994   ISBN 1-882256-84-0
MCLAREN RACE CARS 1965-1996 ISBN 1-882256-74-3
SEBRING 12-HOUR RACE 1970   ISBN 1-882256-20-4
VANDERBILT CUP RACE 1936 & 1937
ISBN 1-882256-66-2
WILLIAMS 1969-1999 30 YEARS OF GRAND PRIX RACING
ISBN 1-58388-000-3

RAILWAYS

CHICAGO, ST. PAUL, MINNEAPOLIS & OMAHA RAILWAY
1880-1940   ISBN 1-882256-67-0
CHICAGO&NORTH WESTERN RAILWAY 1975-1995
ISBN 1-882256-76-X
GREAT NORTHERN RAILWAY 1945-1970
ISBN 1-882256-56-5
GREAT NORTHERN RAILWAY 1945-1970 VOLUME 2
ISBN 1-882256-79-4
MILWAUKEE ROAD 1850-1960   ISBN 1-882256-61-1
SOO LINE 1975-1992   ISBN 1-882256-68-9
WISCONSIN CENTRAL LIMITED 1987-1996
ISBN 1-882256-75-1
WISCONSIN CENTRAL RAILWAY 1871-1909
ISBN 1-882256-78-6

TRUCKS

BEVERAGE TRUCKS 1910-1975   ISBN 1-882256-60-3
BROCKWAY TRUCKS 1948-1961* ISBN 1-882256-55-7
DODGE PICKUPS 1939-1978   ISBN 1-882256-82-4
DODGE POWER WAGONS 1940-1980 ISBN 1-882256-89-1
DODGE TRUCKS 1929-1947   ISBN 1-882256-36-0
DODGE TRUCKS 1948-1960   ISBN 1-882256-37-9
EL CAMINO 1959-1987 INCLUDING GMC SPRINT &
CABALLERO   ISBN 1-882256-92-1
LOGGING TRUCKS 1915-1970   ISBN 1-882256-59-X
MACK® MODEL AB*   ISBN 1-882256-18-2
MACK AP SUPER-DUTY TRUCKS 1926-1938*
ISBN 1-882256-54-9
MACK MODEL B 1953-1966 VOL 1* ISBN 1-882256-19-0
MACK MODEL B 1953-1966 VOL 2* ISBN 1-882256-34-4
MACK EB-EC-ED-EE-EF-EG-DE 1936-1951*
ISBN 1-882256-29-8

MACK EH-EJ-EM-EQ-ER-ES 1936-1950*
ISBN 1-882256-39-5
MACK FC-FCSW-NW 1936-1947* ISBN 1-882256-28-X
MACK FG-FH-FJ-FK-FN-FP-FT-FW 1937-1950*
ISBN 1-882256-35-2
MACK LF-LH-LJ-LM-LT 1940-1956* ISBN 1-882256-38-7
MACK TRUCKS PHOTO GALLERY* ISBN 1-882256-88-3
NEW CAR CARRIERS 1910-1998   ISBN 1-882256-98-0
STUDEBAKER TRUCKS 1927-1940 ISBN 1-882256-40-9
STUDEBAKER TRUCKS 1941-1964 ISBN 1-882256-41-7
WHITE TRUCKS 1900-1937   ISBN 1-882256-80-8

TRACTORS & CONSTRUCTION EQUIPMENT

CASE TRACTORS 1912-1959   ISBN 1-882256-32-8
CATERPILLAR D-2 & R-2   ISBN 1-882256-99-9
CATERPILLAR D-8 1933-1974 INCLUDING DIESEL 75
ISBN 1-882256-96-4
CATERPILLAR MILITARY TRACTORS VOLUME 1
ISBN 1-882256-16-6
CATERPILLAR MILITARY TRACTORS VOLUME 2
ISBN 1-882256-17-4
CATERPILLAR SIXTY   ISBN 1-882256-05-0
CATERPILLAR PHOTO GALLERY   ISBN 1-882256-70-0
CLETRAC AND OLIVER CRAWLERS ISBN 1-882256-43-3
ERIE SHOVEL   ISBN 1-882256-69-7
FARMALL CUB   ISBN 1-882256-71-9
FARMALL F– SERIES   ISBN 1-882256-02-6
FARMALL MODEL H   ISBN 1-882256-03-4
FARMALL MODEL M   ISBN 1-882256-15-8
FARMALL REGULAR   ISBN 1-882256-14-X
FARMALL SUPER SERIES   ISBN 1-882256-49-2
FORDSON 1917-1928   ISBN 1-882256-33-6
HART-PARR   ISBN 1-882256-08-5
HOLT TRACTORS   ISBN 1-882256-10-7
INTERNATIONAL TRACTRACTOR   ISBN 1-882256-48-4
INTERNATIONAL TD CRAWLERS 1933-1962
ISBN 1-882256-72-7
JOHN DEERE MODEL A   ISBN 1-882256-12-3
JOHN DEERE MODEL B   ISBN 1-882256-01-8
JOHN DEERE MODEL D   ISBN 1-882256-00-X
JOHN DEERE 30 SERIES   ISBN 1-882256-13-1
MINNEAPOLIS-MOLINE U-SERIES ISBN 1-882256-07-7
OLIVER TRACTORS   ISBN 1-882256-09-3
RUSSELL GRADERS   ISBN 1-882256-11-5
TWIN CITY TRACTOR   ISBN 1-882256-06-9

*This product is sold under license from Mack Trucks, Inc. Mack is a registered Trademark of Mack Trucks, Inc. All rights reserved.

All Iconografix books are available from direct mail specialty book dealers and bookstores worldwide, or can be ordered from the publisher. For book trade and distribution information or to add your name to our mailing list contact

Iconografix
PO Box 446
Hudson, Wisconsin, 54016

Telephone: (715) 381-9755
(800) 289-3504 (USA)
Fax: (715) 381-9756

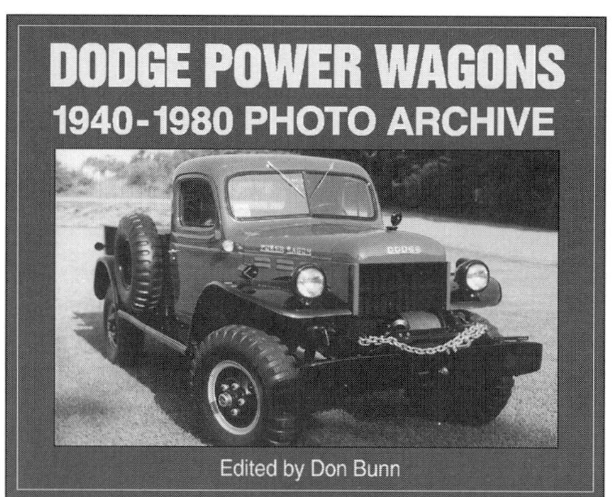

MORE GREAT BOOKS FROM ICONOGRAFIX

AMERICAN LaFRANCE 700 SERIES
Photo Archive   ISBN 1-882256-90-5

CLASSIC AMERICAN AMBULANCES
Photo Archive   ISBN 1-882256-94-8

DODGE POWER WAGONS
Photo Archive   ISBN 1-882256-89-1

FIRE CHIEF CARS 1900-1997
Photo Album   ISBN 1-882256-87-5

MACK® MODEL B FIRE TRUCKS*
Photo Archive   ISBN 1-882256-62-X

MACK MODEL CF FIRE TRUCKS*
Photo Archive   ISBN 1-882256-63-8

MACK MODEL L FIRE TRUCKS*
Photo Archive   ISBN 1-882256-86-7

*This product is sold under license from Mack Trucks, Inc. Mack is a registered Trademark of Mack Trucks, Inc. All rights reserved.

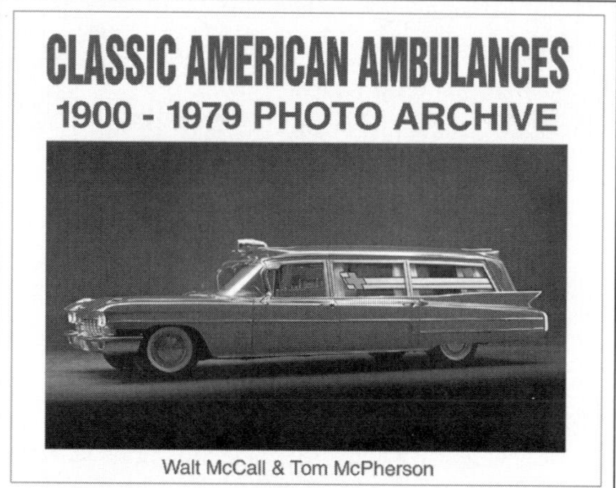

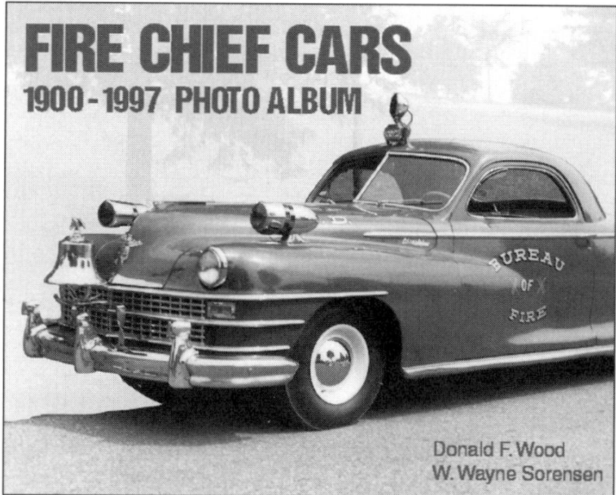

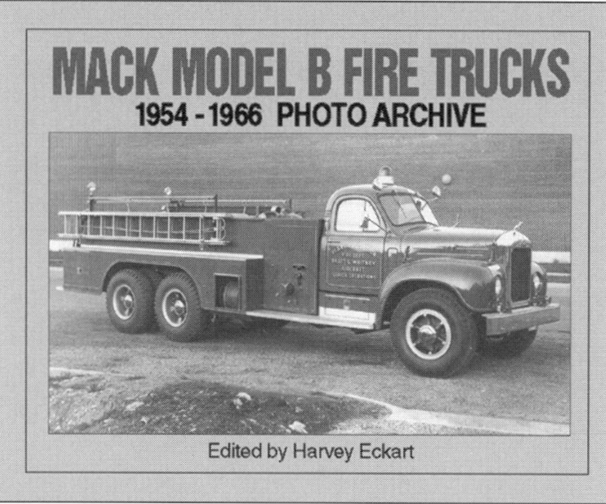

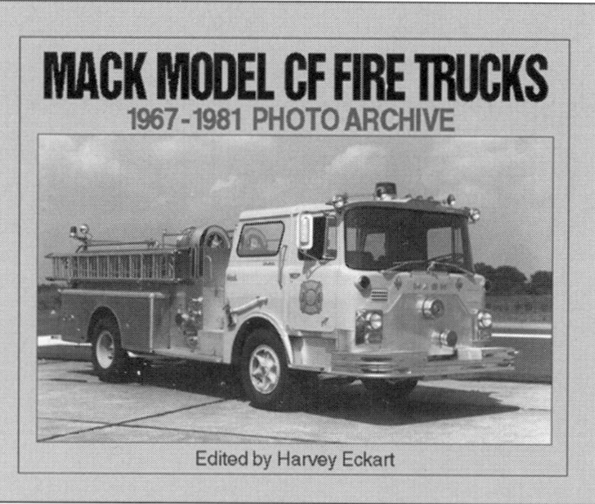

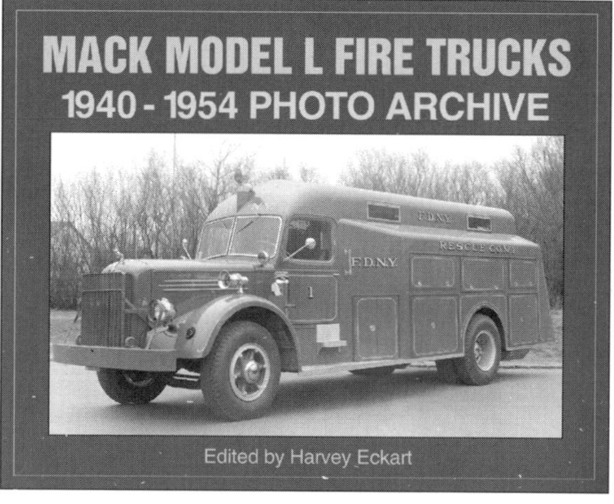